WILDLIFE
WALKS

WILDLIFE WALKS

Get back to nature at more than 475
of the UK's best wild places

Charlotte Varela

BLOOMSBURY WILDLIFE
LONDON • OXFORD • NEW YORK • NEW DELHI • SYDNEY

BLOOMSBURY WILDLIFE
Bloomsbury Publishing Plc
50 Bedford Square, London, WC1B 3DP, UK
29 Earlsfort Terrace, Dublin 2, Ireland

BLOOMSBURY, BLOOMSBURY WILDLIFE and the Diana logo are trademarks
of Bloomsbury Publishing Plc

First published in the United Kingdom 2022

A catalogue record for this book is available from the British Library.

Library of Congress Cataloguing-in-Publication data has been applied for.

ISBN: PB: 978-1-4729-8686-3; ePDF: 978-1-4729-8684-9; ePub: 978-1-4729-8685-6

2 4 6 8 10 9 7 5 3 1

Design by Rod Teasdale
Maps by John Plumer
Printed and bound in China by Toppan Leefung Printing Ltd

To find out more about our authors and books visit www.bloomsbury.com
and sign up for our newsletters.

CONTENTS

ABOUT THE WILDLIFE TRUSTS

by Craig Bennett, Chief Executive Officer

The Wildlife Trusts are on a mission to put nature into recovery across at least 30 per cent of the UK's land and sea by 2030.

We want to create more space for wildlife and restore the abundance of key species – to allow nature to work once again so that our wetlands are wet, our soils are storing carbon and our bees are pollinating. This is crucial for our efforts to tackle the nature and climate crises we currently face.

We know that with urgent action, things can be turned around.

That's why The Wildlife Trusts are leading the way in pushing for a green recovery – seeing the next decade as a time for renewal and an opportunity to rewild all of our lives. But we can't do it alone; our 870,000 members and nearly 32,500 volunteers are vital in driving this change – taking action for wildlife in their own lives and supporting us to speak up for nature.

This is possible because no matter where you live, with 46 Wildlife Trusts across the UK and on Alderney, the Isles of Scilly and the Isle of Man, there is always a Wildlife Trust taking action for nature's recovery and inspiring others to do the same. Each Wildlife Trust is an independent charity formed by people in the local community getting together to make a positive difference for wildlife, climate and future generations. Together we care for more than 2,300 nature reserves and work with land managers and other organisations to help them manage their land for nature too.

These partnerships are essential in helping us to bring wildlife back at a landscape scale: back into our countryside, but also where we live and work – in our towns and cities. This is important because people need to be at the centre of our wildlife recovery in order for it to succeed – driving it forwards by demanding for better care to be taken of our natural world that does so much for us, from locking up carbon (mitigating climate change) to storing water on our floodplains rather than in our houses. It's also important because we know that nature brings both health and well-being benefits to us all, which is why we believe that everyone, everywhere should have access to nature and benefit from the joy it brings.

We hope that by reading and enjoying this book, you become that bit closer to the beautiful wild places we have left and feel inspired to experience as many of them around the UK as you can – and then join us in calling for more!

THE WILDLIFE TRUSTS – KEY STATS

- The Wildlife Trusts manage more than 2,300 reserves covering 257,000 acres (104,000ha).

- Each year there are 12 million visits to Wildlife Trust nature reserves, and visitor and education centres.

- Volunteers give 590,000 hours per year to the Wildlife Trusts.

- 400,000 people take part in Wildlife Trust events, walks and talks each year.

- The Wildlife Trusts advise 4,500 landowners per year on wildlife-friendly land management.

- More than 150,000 people have campaigned with The Wildlife Trusts for better protection and treatment of wildlife and wild places.

- 750,000 people connected with nature through The Wildlife Trusts' annual 30 Days Wild challenge in 2021.

- The Wildlife Trusts improved 21,000 acres (8,500ha) of land for nature by working with corporations through their Biodiversity Benchmark scheme.

HOW TO USE THIS BOOK

Wildlife Walks is a companion to your discovery of the extraordinary nature that the UK has to offer. It is for free-range families and old friends; garden birdwatchers and devoted bird listers; fungi fanatics and big-sky seekers. This book is for everyone, everywhere, who loves nature in their own unique way. It has been created with help from Wildlife Trusts up and down the country, whose rangers, wardens, volunteers, supporters and members work tirelessly to protect these precious wild places for us all. We hope their enthusiasm will help fuel your own.

Wildlife Walks contains everything you need to enjoy a relaxing day out at any of these Wildlife Trust nature reserves, including handy icons listing the available facilities and access – you can see these below. You'll also find a glossary of abbreviations of site designations at the back of this book, which will explain what terms such as SSSI and LNR stand for.

Each nature reserve in *Wildlife Walks* has a map reference, which corresponds to the maps at the back of this book – you can use these to see exactly where each wild place is located and plan your trip. Postcodes have been supplied where possible, but some of these nature reserves are just too far-flung to have one, which only makes them all the more wild!

Unless otherwise stated the nature reserves are open all year during daylight hours. Most are free to enter, but there may sometimes be an entry or parking charge to support the Wildlife Trust's vital work. Check the Trust's website for fees before setting off, or perhaps go green by hopping on public transport. You could even become a Wildlife Trust member to receive discounted or free entry.

Many Wildlife Trusts run events to help you connect with the nature on their reserves – check out their websites and social media channels to see what's on. If you're not sure when you can visit a nature reserve, or need extra access information, contact the Wildlife Trust that looks after it before heading out.

Every effort has been made to ensure the information in this book is as accurate as possible, but these details may change. Nature reserves are living places with an evolving landscape and wildlife – opening hours may have changed since *Wildlife Walks* went to print, or a species of bird may be harder to spot.

Nature reserves are also fragile places. Please take your litter home, stick to footpaths and, where dogs are allowed, keep your four-legged friend on their lead to protect the plants and animals that live there. Together, we can safeguard these wildlife refuges into the future.

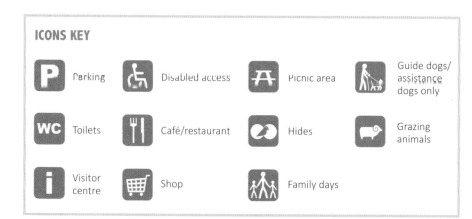

ICONS KEY

P Parking	**♿** Disabled access	**⛱** Picnic area	**🦮** Guide dogs/ assistance dogs only
WC Toilets	**🍴** Café/restaurant	**🦅** Hides	**🐑** Grazing animals
i Visitor centre	**🛒** Shop	**👪** Family days	

THE COUNTRYSIDE CODE

Respect everyone

Showing consideration for other people living, working and exploring the outdoors makes the countryside more welcoming for everyone. Park carefully so that gates and driveways aren't blocked; close any gates behind you to stop livestock escaping; and stick to footpaths, even if they're muddy, to protect crops and wildlife. Give a friendly hello to those you meet, and share the space with everyone.

Protect the environment

We all have a responsibility to protect the natural world. Take your litter home, don't have barbecues or light fires, and bag and bin all dog poo – if you can't find a bin, take it to your bin at home. Keep dogs under close control or on a lead where specified and put them on a lead around farm animals. Open access land requires you to keep your dog on a lead during the breeding season (between 1 March and 31 July) to protect vulnerable ground-nesting birds like curlews.

Enjoy the outdoors

The outdoors is great for your well-being – a place for relaxation, peace and exercise. It's even better for us when we head out on our adventures well prepared. Plan ahead by checking what facilities are available and when they might be open, look out for specific opening hours and check for notices about any restrictions. Pay attention to the weather forecast and dress for the conditions, and pack snacks and water if you'll be out for a while. The weather can change quickly in the hills, so pack all-weather gear if you're planning a day in the wilderness.

Cornish coves peppered with rockpools, tranquil Devon river valleys shaded by trees and chalky Wiltshire downs blanketed by wildflowers, the south-west corner of England is both beautiful and bursting with wildlife.

Cornwall is undoubtedly one of the best places in the UK to spot marine life. The warm current from the Gulf Stream sometimes brings exotic tourists like leatherback turtles and ocean sunfish. Basking sharks are more regular visitors, swimming off the Cornish coast from around May. These gentle giants measure more than nine metres long and use their huge, gaping mouths to capture unwitting blooms of plankton. Mount's Bay is one of their favourite feeding grounds.

Whales and dolphins are also a common sight around the south-west coast, particularly on the crossing to the Isles of Scilly. Common dolphins, harbour porpoises and even humpback whales have been spotted from the boats.

Back on dry land, the coastline is a treasure trove of rockpools harbouring all manner of weird and wonderful creatures. Beadlet anemones wave their crimson tentacles, crabs hide in the seaweed and gobies watch grumpily from submerged rocks. Further inland, cliffs and beaches give way to stunning ancient woodlands offering fairy-tale walks under gnarled trees and through magical bluebell glades. Nowhere is this truer than the Forest of Dean in Gloucestershire, which boasts a thriving population of wild boar. The species became extinct in the UK in the 13th century, but after a small number escaped from farms in the region during the 1990s, there are now thought to be around 2,600 living wild and free.

Devon can't be mentioned without also referencing Tarka the Otter. Henry Williamson's charming children's book captures the Devon countryside through the eyes of playful Tarka, who Williamson brought to life after years of tracking and observing these shy mammals. Two of the best places to catch your own fleeting glimpse of Tarka are the Rivers Dart and Torridge.

Easier to see, wherever you may be in the South West, are the birds. Open moors are patrolled by golden plovers and red grouse; estuaries fill with wading birds, ducks and geese; and hedgerows shiver with corn buntings and yellowhammers. These hedgerows often cradle precious hay meadows, where rare and beautiful insects live among a hypnotic array of wildflowers.

NOT TO BE MISSED

• **Blakehill Farm, Wiltshire**
One of the largest expanses of lowland neutral hay meadow in the UK and a slice of living history thanks to the role it played in WWII.

• **Brownsea Island, Dorset**
Among the best birdwatching spots in the South West, a breathtaking retreat for people and a haven for red squirrels.

• **The Isles of Scilly**
An enchanting archipelago, home to dizzyingly diverse plant, animal and birdlife, from seabirds and dwarf pansies on the cliffs to dolphins in the crystal-clear ocean.

• **Bovey Heathfield, Devon**
Common lizards, slow worms, adders, grass snakes, nightjars, potter wasps – Bovey Heathfield has them all.

• **Westhay Moor NNR, Somerset**
Somerset Wildlife Trust's pilot project for the Avalon Marshes, home to bitterns, otters and a winter roost for thousands of starlings.

Opposite: Penberth Cove, Cornwall

CORNWALL

About the Trust

Cornwall Wildlife Trust cares for more than 55 nature reserves – including an island – for both people and wildlife. The charity is committed to creating safe havens in which wildlife can thrive and from which it can spread. It inspires people to love and care for the natural environment and enables more people to experience, enjoy and understand it.

Cornwall Wildlife Trust
01872 273939
cornwallwildlifetrust.org.uk

Bakers Pit

Near Georgia, TR20 8LP
OS Map SW 481359;
Map Ref A7

A wonderful heathland that comes alive with the coconut scent of gorse and singing of whitethroats during summer. This is also the best time to see the heather blooming in all its glory. Majestic hen harriers and little merlins visit regularly in winter. Bakers Pit was once a china clay extraction works and you can still see the engine house and settling tanks.

Prideaux Wood

St Austell
OS Map SX 064554;
Map Ref A4

A delightful woodland surrounding historic mining operations dating back as far as the Tudor period. Only a portion of the ancient woodland remains, but Cornwall Wildlife Trust is removing many of the conifers planted during the 1960s and replacing them with thousands of native broadleaved trees to help wildlife thrive. The wood is already a refuge for a very exciting mammal: the greater horseshoe bat.

Bostraze

Pendeen, TR19 7TH
OS Map SW 394334;
Map Ref A8

Forming part of the wider Bostraze bog, this wildlife refuge is known by local farmers as 'Cuckoo Valley'. As well as cuckoos you'll find carnivorous plants like round-leaved sundew and pale butterwort. Small red damselflies thrive in the wet grassland, mossy pools and ponds, while adders bask among the vegetation.

Upton Towans SSSI

Connor Downs, TR27 5DF
OS Map SW 780514;
Map Ref A6

A collection of scenic sand dunes where silver-studded blue butterflies flutter among pyramidal orchids and petalwort. This is a great place to see solitary bees, and glow-worms light up the night with their unmistakeable lime beacons.

GREENA MOOR

Access/conditions: Footpath around the reserve except the culm grassland. Surfaces are uneven and can be wet and muddy.
How to get there: From the A39, five miles south of Bude, take the turning for Week St Mary. In Week St Mary turn right towards Week Green, then fork right. Access the reserve via a path to the left, after three-quarters of a mile. Park on the side of the road (room for two cars).
Walking time: Around 2 hours.

Greena Moor encompasses almost a fifth of the remaining area of culm grassland in Cornwall, preserved thanks to a local farming family and jointly managed with Plantlife. The summer flowering season is breathtaking, with rare species including wavy St John's wort, whorled caraway and upright vetch growing here. The purple pincushion heads of devil's-bit scabious – a favourite of the reserve's marsh fritillary butterflies – grow in the grassland; bog asphodel thrives in the heathy

areas; and bog pimpernel blooms in damp hollows. Autumn and winter rains waterlog the reserve, making it a favourite haunt for snipe.

HELMAN TOR

Access/conditions: Wilderness Trail has some narrow lanes and boardwalks. Paths can be wet and muddy with difficult terrain and some steep slopes. Breney Common entrance suitable for wheelchairs.
How to get there: 2.5 miles from Bodmin towards Lanivet.

Take the first left after passing under the A30 bridge. You can walk to Helman Tor along the Saint's Way. There are small car parks at Helman Tor and Breney Common, and limited parking at Red Moor.
Walking time: The Wilderness Trail (around five miles) takes

3–4 hours to walk.
30-minute visit: Head straight to the top of Helman Tor, where the reserve can be viewed from on-high. You can see both the north and south coasts on a clear day.

Helman Tor is Cornwall

Wildlife Trust's largest nature reserve and one of its most spectacular. It encompasses five separate sites, so the best way to explore it is to follow the Wilderness Trail. Winding through eerie willow woodlands and wildlife-rich heathland, past Neolithic settlements and ponds buzzing with nature, you'll encounter as much local history as wonderful wildlife. Helman Tor was once mined for tin, and as you walk in the footsteps of Cornwall's mining pioneers you'll spot clues to the reserve's former life in hollows caused by tin streaming – now wet pockets home to rare plants.

In spring, the willows come alive with birdsong as willow tits, reed buntings and grasshopper warblers pair up. When the warm days of summer arrive, the ponds swarm with dragonflies and damselflies while the grassland and heath brim with butterflies, including the rare marsh fritillary. The heathland is at its best in autumn, blazing with yellow gorse and the pinks and purples of heathers. Even winter is a special time of year, when the panoramic views from the top of the Tor take on a whole new quality in the crisp light.

CHÛN DOWNS

St Just, TR19 7TH; **OS Map** SW 393333; **Map Ref** A9

Access/conditions: Public footpaths around the reserve. Terrain can be difficult and muddy with some inclines.
How to get there: Small car park at Woon Gumpus, located on the B3318 one mile south of Pendeen. Chûn Castle is a one-mile ramble uphill to the east of the car park.
Walking time: 1 hour.
30-minute visit: Walk up to Chûn Castle from the car park and back.

Spectacular sea views and incredible wildlife encounters in the West Penwith Moors. Brambles, bracken and gorse offer hiding places for reptiles in spring and summer, with the gorse a particular favourite of the stunning Dartford warbler. These little birds have bewitching red eyes, rust-red breasts and slate-grey backs and are true heathland specialists. Ling, cross-leaved heath and purple-moor grass add yet more layers of colour, while you may spot rare plants including Cornish moneywort and coral necklace. Hen harriers are regular winter visitors.

Delve into the history of Chûn Downs with a short ramble uphill to Chûn Castle. This impressive Iron Age hill fort retains two extensive stone walls and the remains of several roundhouses. It's also the best vantage point for those panoramic views towards the coast.

LOOE ISLAND

East Looe, PL13 1AH; **OS Map** SX 258519; **Map Ref** A5

Opening hours: Access to the island is by authorised boat only. This runs from Easter to late summer when tide, weather and sea conditions allow. Boat fee: adults £10; children £5. Landing fee: adults £4; children £1. The visitor centre opens when the boat is running – check the Cornwall Wildlife Trust website for the latest information.

Access/conditions: Paths around the island can be wet and slippery. The boat is not specifically equipped for wheelchair access and disembarks onto a small jetty with steep steps.

How to get there: Boat leaves from floating pontoon near RNLI lifeboat station slipway in East Looe (call boatman on 07814 264514 and check Cornwall Wildlife Trust website for up-to-date information). Crossing takes around 20 minutes. There are regular trains to Looe from Liskeard and local buses from Polperro, Liskeard and outlying villages to Looe.

Walking time: Visits normally last 2 hours but can be longer depending on tides.

For such a small island, Looe hosts an incredible marriage of habitats: woodland, grassland, sand, shingle and rocky reef. Even the boat crossing is memorable – it isn't unusual to be escorted by a pod of dolphins or welcomed by a grey seal.

Looe Island is home to the largest breeding colony of great black-backed gulls in Cornwall as well as cormorants, shags and oystercatchers. Spring

sees the island bloom into life with bluebells in the woodland and dainty sea campion on the cliffs. Whimbrels drop by on the way to their northern breeding grounds and rock pipits scamper among the seaweed on the shoreline.

Summers are positively tropical – the air thick with the lime scent of hedge bedstraw and coconut fragrance of gorse. This is also the time for insect spotting. Oil beetles mate in the grassland, meadow brown butterflies drink from bramble flowers and burnet moths fill the air with flashes of crimson. The thrift-strewn cliffs are a great vantage point for sea-watching and you may be lucky enough to catch a glimpse of a basking shark feeding close to the coast.

WILDLIFE FACT: GREY SEAL

With adult males weighing more than 200kg, grey seals are Britain's largest mammal. Their Latin name, *Halichoerus grypus*, might mean 'hooked nosed sea pig', but these characterful creatures charm all who lay eyes on them. They're common around the Cornish coast, basking on rocks and hunting in the surf. Their numbers dropped to just 500 in the early 20th century but there are now more than 120,000 in Britain – 40 per cent of the world's population!

CABILLA AND REDRICE WOODS

Bodmin, PL30 4BE; **OS Map** SW 129652; **Map Ref** A2

Access/conditions: Public footpaths are good underfoot but can be wet and slippery. Some steep inclines.

How to get there: Take the train to Bodmin Parkway, then a 10-minute walk. By car, from A38 east of Bodmin, take the turning towards Cardinham. Cross the bridge over the River Fowey and take the first track on the right.

Walking time: 1.5 hours.

30-minute visit: From the entrance follow the main track for 500m, then left over the stile. Follow this track until it rejoins the main track and head right to return to the entrance.

Among the largest ancient woodlands in Cornwall, Cabilla and Redrice Woods is a peaceful refuge for all who visit. No two visits are the same and there is always something to make you stop, investigate and smile. Spring is by far the most spectacular season as wood anemones, bluebells and wild garlic enter full bloom, lifting your spirit after the grey winter. As the days lengthen, migratory pied flycatchers, chiffchaffs and willow warblers arrive from Africa, joining busy nuthatches, treecreepers and woodpeckers for the breeding season. In summer the woodland rides teem with butterflies and on calm, dusky evenings up to five species of bat emerge to hunt, including the greater horseshoe. Dormice live here too, but they hide away during daylight hours. You may be lucky enough to spot another rarity, the blue ground beetle, which lives only here, at one site in Wales and at just a handful of other sites in Devon and Cornwall. Late autumn brings a fungal bonanza and is also a great time to spot an otter or kingfisher along the river.

WINDMILL FARM

Helston, TR12 7LH; **OS Map** SW 693152; **Map Ref** A10

CORNWALL

Access/conditions:
Challenging terrain – disabled access is limited and the reserve isn't suitable for pushchairs. In winter the ground is waterlogged and gates can be impassable.
How to get there: The reserve is one mile north of Lizard village. There is a regular bus service from Helston to Lizard. By car, take A3083 from Helston to Lizard and turn right at the 'Wild Camping' sign. Follow the lane until you see the windmill.
Walking time: 1–2 hours.
30-minute visit: From the yard, head south towards the arable fields and see how many birds you can spot. Or from the windmill, walk west onto the main heath for butterflies.

Nestled near Lizard village, on the Lizard Peninsula, Windmill Farm can be a scenic stop on a longer exploration of this Area of Outstanding Natural Beauty or a destination itself. Dragonflies dart over the ponds, arable crops attract house sparrows and reed buntings, and breeding grasshoppers and willow warblers sing from the scrub and hedgerows. Swallows and meadow pipits hunt over the hay stubbles while skylarks soar into the sky on a magic carpet of song. The late spring and early summer months offer a riot of floral colour, with the distinctive lilac of Cornish heath and bright

yellow gorse brightening up the heathland. This is also when marsh fritillary butterflies are on the wing. Not that the pace of life slows in autumn, when migrating wheatears and whinchats rest on hay bales before departing for Africa. In winter, snipe and woodcock hide in the boggy areas of the reserve. You may even hear the pig-like squeal of a water rail.

If you're a bit of a local history buff you'll want to seek out the 17th century windmill, Bronze Age barrows and WWII pillboxes here. The windmill was once the hideout of one of Cornwall's most notorious gangs!

DEVON

About the Trust

Formed in 1962, Devon Wildlife Trust believes that wildlife conservation isn't simply about protecting what hasn't yet been destroyed. It is also about embracing large-scale, ambitious work to create new wild areas, reversing the decline in our wild plants and animals, and helping people to engage with the natural world in their daily lives. The Trust's vision is to create bigger, better and more-connected wild places that will help nature thrive and bring joy to all.

Devon Wildlife Trust
01392 279244
devonwildlifetrust.org

Andrew's Wood

Near Kingsbridge, TQ7 4EA
OS Map SX 714519;
Map Ref B12

A perfect slice of the beautiful South Hams where the views from the top stretch over undulating hills as far as the eye can see. Once dominated by farms and open fields, the reserve is now a haven for nature with vibrant woodland glades, meadows and ponds. Exmoor ponies graze the land to ensure that beautiful flowers like heath lobelia blossom. You could spot common lizards, grass snakes and tawny owls.

Halwill Junction

Okehampton, EX21 5XY
OS Map SS 443003;
Map Ref B6

An ex-railway junction where the bustle of steam engines has been replaced by the buzz of wildlife. Goat willows, ferns and broad-leaved helleborines line the former railway edges. Green woodpeckers and summer warblers are birding highlights, while wood white butterflies flutter along the edges of the cycleway. The easy path is accessible for wheelchairs.

Lady's Wood

South Brent,
TQ10 9JE
OS Map SX 688951;
Map Ref B7

Lady's Wood was Devon Wildlife Trust's first nature reserve and is a gateway to the wild Dartmoor landscape. Bluebells and hazel dormice are the stars, but you can also find wood anemones, yellow archangel and great spotted woodpeckers. A walk takes around 40 minutes but being so close to Dartmoor means the possibilities for longer adventures are endless.

Marsland

Hartland, EX23 9PQ
OS Map SS 303077;
Map Ref B2

A magical mix of woodland, coastline and butterfly-filled meadows – all in a single stream valley. Few people forget their first visit. Pearl-bordered and small pearl-bordered fritillaries fill the woodland glades in spring and early summer, while dormice thrive in the canopy of oak, ash, holly, hazel and sycamore trees. Where the woodland gives way to coastal heath you'll find bright purple heather, coconut-scented gorse and bracken-covered slopes rolling away towards the sea. Marsland lies on the South West Coast Path, so why not extend your walk to breathe in deep lungfuls of ocean air?

Rackenford and Knowstone Moors

Near Tiverton
OS Map SS 851211;
Map Ref B1

Step out onto the largest surviving area of culm grassland in Devon and lose yourself in unbroken views as far as Dartmoor and Exmoor. The reserve is best enjoyed at a slower pace, where you can comb the heath and bog for devil's-bit scabious, meadowsweet and carnivorous sundews. The insect life is dazzlingly diverse: marbled whites, marsh fritillaries and dingy skippers; keeled skimmer dragonflies and narrow-bordered bee hawk-moths. Birds include barn owls, curlews and willow tits.

Warleigh Point

Tamerton Foliot, PL5 2SL
OS Map SX 450608;
Map Ref B11

Woodland walks give way to stunning estuary views at this oasis of calm on the edge of Plymouth. Nuthatches, treecreepers and great spotted woodpeckers live among the trees, while redshanks, little egrets and shelducks feed on nutritious mud-dwelling invertebrates in the estuary. Warleigh's plant life is just as impressive, with butcher's broom and rare wild service trees growing in the wood. Look out for silver-washed fritillary butterflies in the sun-soaked glades.

Dunsdon

Near Holsworthy, EX22 7JW
OS Map SS 295078;
Map Ref B5

A wild walk through Dunsdon's open fields and across its boardwalks will introduce you to a wonderful community of plants and animals. Traditional grazing helps 189 species of flowering plant and 26 species of butterfly to thrive, including lesser butterfly-orchids, petty whin and whorled caraway and marsh fritillary butterflies. In 2012, Dunsdon was named Devon's 'Coronation Meadow' and the reserve is a seed-donor site for new wildflower meadows nearby.

Halsdon

Near Great Torrington, EX19 8ND
OS Map SS 553131;
Map Ref B3

Exceptional walks through woodland and alongside a classic Devon river. If you're lucky you may spot an otter, but not all of Halsdon's wildlife is quite so elusive. Keep your eyes peeled for kingfishers and sand martins in summer and goosanders in winter. Autumn is the perfect time for a fungi hunt while long-tailed tits chatter away overhead. As spring arrives, the drumming of great spotted woodpeckers echoes through the trees.

BYSTOCK POOLS

Near Exmouth, EX8 5EE; **OS Map** SY 034843; **Map Ref** B9

Access/conditions: A short 'Access for All' path leads around the reservoir. The rest of the reserve has boardwalks and rough paths.
How to get there: Take A376 from Exeter to Exmouth, then B3179 through Woodbury. Take first right-hand turn as you leave the village, signed for Exmouth. At the end of the road turn right onto B3180. Once you pass the turning for Exmouth (to the right) take the left turn a few hundred metres down the road. Reserve entrance is on the left by the reservoir.
Walking time: 1 hour.
30-minute visit: A short walk takes in the picturesque reservoir and surrounding heath.

Bystock Pools is one of Devon Wildlife Trust's most popular nature reserves, and it's easy to see why. One minute you'll be looking out across a lily pad-filled lake or strolling across heathland boardwalks, and the next you'll be climbing the gentle slopes of a wildflower meadow as butterflies erupt from the grass. This reserve is best known for its dragonflies: the black and yellow golden-ringed dragonfly, metallic downy emerald dragonfly, and magnificent blue and green emperor dragonfly fill the summer air with dancing colour as they buzz over the open water and heathland. When night falls, glow-worms fill the grassy meadow with pinpricks of light and nightjars *churr* mechanically on the open heath. When the sun rises once more, willow warblers, blackcaps and stonechats chime into the dawn chorus.

DUNSFORD

Near Exeter, EX6 7EG; **OS Map** SX 805883; **Map Ref** B8

Access/conditions: Wide, level paths lead through the reserve. Muddy in parts with a steep climb to the top.
How to get there: Two reserve entrances: one at Steps Bridge and the other not far from Clifford Bridge. Regular buses run between Moretonhampstead and Exeter past the Steps Bridge entrance. If coming by car, park in the Dartmoor National Park car park 200m past Steps Bridge.
Walking time: 1.5 hours.
30-minute visit: Choose any path for a linear walk or simply wander down to the picturesque river.

Beautiful at any time of year, Dunsford is famous for its spring displays of wild daffodils and sits in prime position on the edge of Dartmoor. Walk alongside the River Teign as it winds through a steep-sided valley of oak, ash and birch. You could spot kingfishers, goosanders and dippers on the river – maybe even an otter – or a herd of fallow deer passing stealthily through the wooded valley.

Spring brings crowds of visitors eager to see the daffodil show – one of Devon's natural wonders.

Step into the reserve from the Clifford Bridge side to climb to the top of Dunsford, where great views over the Teign Valley await. This is also the place to watch fritillary butterflies skimming over the tops of the bracken-covered slopes. If you want a longer walk, the reserve joins lanes and footpaths leading along the Teign Valley to Fingle Bridge and Castle Drogo.

BOVEY HEATHFIELD

Bovey Tracey, TQ12 6TU; **OS Map** SX 824765; **Map Ref** B10

Access/conditions: Several routes around the reserve, unfortunately not suitable for wheelchairs.
How to get there: From A38 take A382 towards Bovey Tracey. Turn right at traffic lights then take second left into Cavalier Road. Turn left into Dragoon Close. Gravel track on the right leads to the reserve. Park along the roadside in Dragoon Close.
Walking time: 1.5 hours.
30-minute visit: Stroll to the viewpoint overlooking Hay Tor on Dartmoor.

One of the best remaining examples of the heathland that once dominated this part of Devon, Bovey Heathfield is a fantastic place to spot reptiles, with common lizards, slow worms, adders and grass snakes all hiding, scuttling and slithering through the heather. Your best chance of seeing them is to visit on a warm, still morning in spring when they bask in the sunshine.

Early summer brings nightjars all the way from Africa. They lie expertly camouflaged on the reserve floor during the day, but as night falls, their otherworldly calls and

WILDLIFE FACT: ADDER

Heathlands like Bovey Heathfield are strongholds for adders. These beautiful snakes have piercing ruby eyes and a distinctive zigzag stripe down their back. They generally hibernate underground from November–February but have been recorded out and about in all months of the year. Adders are the UK's only venomous animal and are seriously under threat from persecution, habitat loss and disturbance. They are very misunderstood, preferring to slither silently away from danger than be caught in an altercation. They only bite when they're taken by surprise or feel seriously threatened.

wing-clapping fill the air. Late summer offers a show of colour as the heather blooms bright pink and contrasts with the butter-yellow gorse.

Can you spot small collections of clay clinging to plants alongside the paths? These are the 'pots' made by heath potter wasps. Inside lie the insects' larvae along with a store of food – usually a live, paralysed caterpillar!

MEETH QUARRY

Hatherleigh, EX20 3ER; **OS Map** SS 546077; **Map Ref** B4

Access/conditions: A series of colour-coded trails allows access on foot, bike, horseback or mobility scooter. The red trail is suitable for wheelchairs and mobility scooters.

How to get there: Accessible by foot or bike from the Tarka Trail. By car, use A386 Hatherleigh to Great Torrington Road. On entering Meeth village look for signage to the Tarka Trail and Meeth Quarry nature reserve. Enter a service road here and drive just under one mile before reaching the reserve.

Walking time: A three-mile Meeth Quarry Wild Walk is a great introduction to the area and takes around 90 minutes.

30-minute visit: From the car park, take the red 'Easy Access Trail' to the lakeside viewpoint.

Meeth Quarry's industrial past has dramatically shaped its present. Settling ponds that once helped to purify clay-contaminated water are now home to 14 types of dragonfly and damselfly. Huge amounts of waste material known as 'spoil' was dug from the quarries and discarded in piles, creating sparse, open areas perfect for brown hares. Since production stopped in 2004 the quarries have been allowed to flood, much to the delight of the waders and wildfowl that flock to the lakes. The peaceful hide on the banks of Stockleigh Lake is a great place to sit and watch little grebes, water rails, goosanders and tufted ducks all feeding, bickering and breeding. Ospreys have been known to stop off for a fish supper on migration. But there is much to see before you even reach the hide. Grazing Exmoor ponies keep orchids, lady's smock and bird's-foot trefoil blooming in the grassland. These four-legged conservationists, along with the Trust's two-legged conservation team, are helping foxes, newts, grass snakes and wood white butterflies to return here too.

SOMERSET

About the Trust

Somerset Wildlife Trust is dedicated to protecting the wildlife that makes living, working and visiting the county so special. With over 21,000 members and a landholding of more than 4,200 acres (1,700ha), the Trust is a powerful force for conservation that safeguards wetlands, woodlands and meadows; provides homes for wildlife such as dormice, otters and hedgehogs;

and transforms landscapes, bringing nature back into people's lives.

**Somerset Wildlife Trust
01823 652400
somersetwildlife.org**

Bubwith Acres

Cheddar
OS Map ST 474538;
Map Ref C10

Limestone grassland and heath high up on the Mendip Hills. Botanical highlights include small scabious, harebells, heath bedstraw and heath milkwort. Peregrines occasionally fly overhead, ravens are common visitors and reptiles bask on the dry-stone walls. Butterflies include grizzled skippers, dingy skippers and dark green fritillaries.

Great Breach Wood

Compton Dundon
OS Map ST 505325;
Map Ref C14

An oak and ash woodland home to rare beetles, moths and flies. Knapweed, selfheal and cowslips grow in the glades and silver-washed fritillaries feed from brambles along the rides. Sharp-eyed visitors may spot a purple hairstreak fluttering

high in the oak canopy, and the keen-eared may hear lesser spotted woodpeckers tapping away.

Huish Moor

Wiveliscombe
OS Map ST 034287;
Map Ref C15

A brilliant bog that blooms with ragged robin, marsh violets, bilberry, meadowsweet and heath spotted orchids. Dragonflies include golden-ringed, southern hawker and black-tailed skimmer. Butterflies include green hairstreak, small pearl-bordered fritillary and small heath. Paths can be slippery in wet weather.

Quants

Lowton
OS Map ST 188175;
Map Ref C18

A wildlife-rich mosaic of woodland, grassland and heathland where the

exposed Greensand Springline wets some parts of the reserve, encouraging sphagnum mosses, giant horsetail and bog pimpernel to grow. On drier ground, bluebells, early dog-violets and sweet woodruff grow in the woodland. To date, more than 30 species of butterfly have bred here, including the silver-washed fritillary.

Sutton's Pond

Chilton Trinity
OS Map ST 296396;
Map Ref C13

A worked-out clay pit now thriving with open water and reedbeds. Dragonflies and damselflies perch on water lilies while diving beetles and water stick insects live beneath. Spot great crested grebes, kingfishers, reed buntings and, in spring and summer, sedge, reed and Cetti's warblers. Some paths and the bird hide near the car park are suitable for wheelchairs.

Thurlbear Wood

Thurlbear
OS Map ST 274213;
Map Ref C17

Lose yourself among ancient trees, bird's-nest orchids and dancing butterflies. Blue tits, nuthatches and green woodpeckers nest in the old trees while woodcock shelter on the forest floor in winter. The night belongs to Bechstein's bats, badgers and dormice, while sun-soaked spring days are the best time to see adders and slow worms basking in the rides. More than 200 species of fungi have been recorded, including the butter waxcap.

DRAYCOTT SLEIGHTS

Draycott; **OS Map** ST 485505; **Map Ref** C11

Access/conditions: Some stony tracks and steep climbs.
How to get there: By car, take the new road from Draycott on the A371. Park considerately on the roadside, respecting the needs of farm vehicles.
Walking time: Around 1 hour, but allow longer to take in the spectacular view across the Quantocks, Bristol Channel and Somerset levels.
30-minute visit: Stroll through the main gate and along the track lined with beech trees to the dew pond.

High on the southern slopes of the Mendip Hills, this special reserve rewards walkers with breathtaking views. But don't rush to the top – there is so much to see on lower ground.
    Of the 200 species of plant recorded here, 40 are

rare, such as pale flax, spring cinquefoil, autumn gentian and pyramidal orchids – all brightening up this windswept, rocky landscape. The rainbow intensifies in June and July with the emergence of common blue, marbled white and, in most years, small blue butterflies. Skylarks and meadow pipits breed in the grassland in summer, while linnets and goldfinches forage in the scrub during autumn and winter. Peregrines and sparrowhawks hunt the skies above while little owls glare grumpily from tree branches. If you're lucky you may spot a hare in the grassland, or an adder basking on the south-facing slopes.

NETHERCLAY COMMUNITY WOODLAND

Roughmoor; **OS Map** ST 207252; **Map Ref** C16

Access/conditions: Mostly level ground with paths cut between newly planted trees. Can be very muddy in wet weather.
How to get there: North of Bishop's Hull in Taunton. Parking on the lane is limited but the Silk Mills Park and Ride, Bishop's Hull village and the edge of Taunton are within easy walking distance.
Walking time: 1 hour.
30-minute visit: A brisk walk around the whole reserve should take 30 minutes.

It may be young, but Netherclay Community Woodland, nestled on the bank of the River Tone, is full of life. Volunteers helped to plant this patch of improved pasture with native broadleaved trees to create a home for wildlife and a sanctuary for the local community. The northern and western boundaries are lined with beautiful hedgerows made up of English elm, hawthorn, blackthorn, field maple, elder, common dogwood, pedunculate oak and ash. This fantastically diverse tangle of trees is the perfect habitat for butterflies and moths, with good numbers of brown hairstreaks seen fluttering along their length in late summer. In spring, holly blues dance their merry way along the hedgerow blossoms, with orange-tailed clearwing moths appearing soon after.

The river is a great place to spot kingfishers and dippers as well as shyer species like otters and water shrews. Salmon and brown trout spawn upstream, and a pair of small ponds along the line of the northern boundary are home to amphibians.

WESTHAY MOOR

Westhay, BA6 9TX; **OS Map** ST 456437; **Map Ref** C12

Access/conditions: Some all-weather paths but others can be very wet and muddy in winter. Some hides have wheelchair ramps.
How to get there: Reserve car park reached via a minor road between Westhay village and Godney.
Walking time: 45–60 minutes.
30-minute visit: Head up Dagg's Lane Drove from the car park to the North Drain bridge for a view over the reserve. Listen out for Cetti's warblers!

Get ready to step back in time – Westhay Moor is part of the mystical Avalon Marshes on the Somerset Levels and offers a unique insight into thousands of years of shifting landscape. Reclaimed from the remnants of industrial-scale peat extraction and home to the largest surviving remnant of lowland acid mire in the South West, the reserve is a mecca for wildlife all year round. That said, you'd be mad to miss a walk here in spring, when bitterns boom from their hiding places in the reeds and bearded tits, Cetti's warblers and reed warblers raise their young.

Summers are a riot of shimmering colour as beguiling dragonflies take to the skies. Along with crowds of swallows, swifts and martins, they provide an irresistible buffet for hungry hobbies, which hunt alongside other raptors like marsh harriers, peregrine falcons and the odd hen harrier.

In winter, tens of thousands of overwintering birds like teal make Westhay Moor their home, eking out a living alongside the resident wading birds, wildfowl and otters. Linger until dusk to watch hypnotic starling murmurations swirling above the reeds.

AVON

About the Trust

Avon Wildlife Trust is a charity on a mission. It wants to restore nature on a grand scale across the Avon region – managing 30 special nature reserves, championing landscape-scale conservation, influencing local and national decision-makers, and inspiring people of all ages to connect with nature in their daily lives.

Avon Wildlife Trust
01179 177270
avonwildlifetrust.org.uk

Dolebury Warren

Bristol, BS40 5DL
OS Map ST 455590;
Map Ref C7

Once home to an Iron Age hill fort – now a haven for wildflowers and butterflies. Small scabious, early purple orchids and eyebright flower in the limestone grassland. Small blue and marbled white butterflies fill the air. There are spectacular views across North Somerset, but the terrain is very steep, strenuous, and sadly not suitable for wheelchairs or pushchairs.

Hellenge Hill

Bleadon, BS24 0NQ
OS Map ST 344570;
Map Ref C9

Spectacular views across the Somerset Levels greet you at this wildlife-rich grassland. Look out for rare plants like honewort and Somerset hair-grass alongside green-winged orchids, carline thistle and autumn lady's-tresses. Birds shelter in the gorse bushes and you may see adders basking on the slopes.

Walton Common

Off B3124, Clevedon, BS21 7AP
OS Map ST 423736;
Map Ref C2

Both people and butterflies lose themselves among the flowers at Walton Common. Brown argus, common blues, grizzled and dingy skippers, green and purple hairstreaks and dark green fritillaries flutter among thyme, marjoram, St John's wort and violets. Glow-worms are found on the common and whitethroats nest in the woodland.

Weston Big Wood

Portishead, BS20 8PW
OS Map ST 456750;
Map Ref C1

One of the most wildlife-rich woodlands in Avon.

In springtime the ground is covered with wood anemones, violets and masses of bluebells while woodpeckers, nuthatches and tawny owls can be seen year-round. The steep paths can get muddy, so watch your feet after rain.

Willsbridge Valley

Willsbridge, BS30 6EX
OS Map ST 665708;
Map Ref C3

Once the site of milling and quarrying, Willsbridge Valley now supports bountiful wildlife. The woodlands are at their best in spring: full of bluebells, red campion and birdsong. Frogs, toads and dragonflies thrive in the ponds and kingfishers and dippers hunt along the stream. Foxes and badgers live in the valley, where noctule and greater horseshoe bats feed on the many insects found here as darkness falls.

GOBLIN COMBE

Bristol, BS48 3DF; **OS Map** ST 459653; **Map Ref** C5

Access/conditions: Very steep access. Steps, paths and the footpaths along the floor of Goblin Combe can be very muddy and slippery.
How to get there: Bus from Bristol city centre to Cleeve, then a 10-minute walk. By car, take J19 from M5, then B3128 and A370 to Cleeve Hill Road. Limited parking on Cleeve Hill Road.
Walking time: 2–3 hours.
30-minute visit: Walk up the steps to a viewpoint at the top of the valley.

What could be better than a wildlife walk paired with magical views across Mendip? Goblin Combe holds a wonderful mix of airy grassland above a damp wooded gorge cut into the limestone by melting ice-age snows. The grasslands are the best place for butterfly spotting, with an impressive 30 species recorded so far. Grizzled skippers, dingy skippers, brown argus and green hairstreaks all busy themselves around the flowers, whose ranks are just as impressive. Autumn gentian, autumn lady's-tresses and yellow-wort bring splashes of pink, cream and yellow to the grassland in late summer.

The woodland conceals rarities like moonwort and hazel dormice, and throngs with fungi in autumn. Look out for common inkcaps, oily waxcaps, white saddle and lilac bonnet.

BROWNE'S FOLLY

Bathford, BA1 7TW; **OS Map** ST 794660; **Map Ref** C4

Access/conditions: Some paths are muddy in winter and feature steep slopes. Take extreme caution when approaching rock faces.
How to get there: Buses run from Bath bus station to Dover's Park. By car, take the minor road from Bathford to Kingsdown, taking a steep right-hand turn to Monkton Farleigh. The nearest car park is near the brow of the hill on Prospect Place.
Walking time: 1.5–2 hours.
30-minute visit: Head towards

the folly building for views over the valley.

Standing high above the river Avon with commanding views towards Bath, Browne's Folly boasts flower-rich grasslands and ancient woodland on the remains of old Bath stone quarries. Delightful downland flora now covers the spoil heaps and wild thyme, harebells and nine species of orchid are regular sights. The rare fly orchid, with its rich malbec lip, is a particular highlight, with its flowerheads said to resemble 'wingless bluebottles impaled on the stalk'. The old mines offer a safe sanctuary for the threatened greater horseshoe bat while damp cliff-faces support a fascinating variety of ferns, fungi and spiders. Pockets of ancient woodland on the lower slopes are home to woodpeckers and unusual plants like Bath asparagus. This rarity is a pretty relation of star of Bethlehem and was once abundant in the woods around Bath.

FOLLY FARM

Bishop Sutton, BS39 4DW; **OS Map** ST 665708; **Map Ref** C6

Access/conditions: 'Access for All' trails suitable for wheelchairs and pushchairs. Some hillside paths can be slippery and muddy.
How to get there: Buses run from Bristol to nearby Bishop Sutton or Clutton. By car, take A368 towards Weston-super-Mare; just after the right turn to Chew Magna, Folly Farm is signposted on the left. Parking for disabled visitors is next to the farmhouse.
Walking time: The full circuit walk takes around 2 hours. The woodland walk takes 1.5 hours.
30-minute visit: Take the 'Access for All' trail through the woods.

Wildflower meadows, woodland and spectacular views over Chew Valley and the Mendips; Folly Farm is a special nature reserve. Unspoilt by pesticides and fertilisers, the meadows brim with flowers such as betony, ox-eye daisies and heath spotted-orchids in summer. Later in the season they become coated with drifts of black knapweed and devil's-bit scabious, which attract ringlet, small

tortoiseshell, gatekeeper and marbled white butterflies. Dowling's Wood is another wildflower wonderland, coated with primroses, bluebells and early purple orchids in spring. Buzzards, great spotted woodpeckers and nuthatches can be seen in the woods all through the year, as well as secretive tawny owls, which use the tree holes to raise their families.

Folly Farm is home to the Folly Farm Centre, which sits in 18th century farm buildings restored by Avon Wildlife Trust. School trips, meetings and weddings are now held here, with all profits going to the Trust.

WALBOROUGH

Weston-super-Mare, BS23 4XR; **OS Map** ST 316579; **Map Ref** C8

Access/conditions: Public footpaths cross the site, including a surfaced path for visitors who are less mobile. Open access to the grassland areas but keep off the saltmarsh to avoid disturbing the birds.
How to get there: From M5, take J21 onto A370 and drive towards Bleadon via A370 and The Runway. Park along Uphill Way, where you can.
Walking time: Around 2 hours.
30-minute visit: The loop walk takes in the tidal inlet. From here, walk up onto the limestone grassland for stunning views and wildflowers.

Stunning limestone grassland stretches down to a wildlife-rich saltmarsh at this rejuvenating coastal nature reserve. Walborough is exceptional for plants, both in the grassland and on the saltmarsh. The grassland flora includes nationally rare species like Somerset hair-grass, with its wheat-like heads, and honewort,

a delicate relative of parsley with tiny white flowers, as well as more common but no less beautiful blooms. Green-winged orchids, early purple orchids, autumn lady's-tresses and cowslips add splashes of violet and yellow. On the saltmarsh, sea barley, slender hare's-ear, sea clover and patches of sea-lavender flourish in the brackish ground.

Prime position on the coast means Walborough is a great place to watch birds,

especially during autumn and winter. This is when wildfowl and waders from across the pond migrate to the estuary, with some of the star visitors being redshanks, dunlin, shelducks and black-tailed godwits. Smaller birds like skylarks, rock and meadow pipits, linnets and, occasionally, twite, winter on the saltmarsh. Summer is the best time to spot other winged visitors: butterflies including brown argus, grizzled skippers, dingy skippers and graylings.

GLOUCESTERSHIRE

About the Trust

Gloucestershire Wildlife Trust works closely with local communities, landowners and partners to deliver much-needed conservation work across more than 2,400 acres (1,000ha) of nature reserves and within the wider landscape of Gloucestershire. It delivers a vast range of engagement activities and projects, and provides free public access to its nature reserves, enabling people of all backgrounds to get closer to nature.

Gloucestershire Wildlife Trust
01452 383333
gloucestershirewildlifetrust.co.uk

Frith Wood

Near Stroud, GL6 7QS
OS Map SO 877087;
Map Ref D4

A magnificent ancient woodland dating back more than 1,000 years. Rare plants including wood barley, white helleborine and yellow bird's-nest grow alongside bluebells and wild garlic. Although small and seldom seen, a very rare snail called *Ena montana* has been recorded here.

Dimmel's Dale

Chalford, GL6 8DU
OS Map SO 902026;
Map Ref D5

Dimmel's Dale lies in the Golden Valley. Yellow meadow anthills draw hungry green woodpeckers down onto a grassland brimming with betony, common spotted-orchids and dyer's greenweed.

Marbled white, gatekeeper and common blue butterflies thrive. Dippers forage along the brook.

Siccaridge Wood

Chalford, GL7 6LN
OS Map SO 935035;
Map Ref D7

Part of the Golden Valley Wildlife Way. Bluebells carpet the woodland floor in spring and lily-of-the-valley grows in a glade. Angular Solomon's-seal, herb-paris and bird's-nest orchids can also be found. Silver-washed fritillary and comma butterflies love the open rides.

Three Groves Wood

Chalford, GL6 7NS
OS Map SO 911030;
Map Ref D6

Scour the trees for nuthatches, spotted flycatchers and green

woodpeckers, and search carefully on the woodland floor for two rare snails restricted to ancient woods: *Ena montana* and *Zenobiella subrufescens*. Silver-washed fritillary and gatekeeper butterflies are summer highlights.

Midger Wood

Lower Kilcott, GL12 7EH
OS Map ST 794892;
Map Ref D11

A haven of ancient woodland flowers in spring: bluebells, wild garlic, wood anemones, herb-paris and primroses. Buzzards and ravens often call overhead while willow warblers fill the air with song during summer. Hazel dormice scamper through the ash, oak and maple canopy by night.

LANCAUT

Chepstow, NP16 7JB; **OS Map** ST 539966; **Map Ref** D8

Access/conditions: Steep gradients over rocky and slippery ground. There is a large boulder scree halfway through the reserve. Accessible viewpoint just off Offa's Dyke Path, which overlooks Wintour's Leap.
How to get there: Train to Chepstow then a bus. Small area for parking 200m from the entrance.
Walking time: 2 hours.

Lancaut lies in one of the four most important woodland areas in Britain. With 60 acres (24ha) of cliffs, disused quarries, woodland, saltmarsh and the spectacular limestone Wye Gorge to explore, you'll leave feeling completely renewed. There is an incredible amount of wildlife to see, including 350 plant species and some very special trees. Small-leaved lime, wild service trees and rare whitebeams grow alongside old oak, field maple and yew trees. The open rock faces are decorated by hairy violets, lesser calamint, red valerian and shining crane's-bill, and are perfect nesting sites for peregrine falcons and ravens. Hunting kestrels, sparrowhawks and goshawks use the cliff-edges as lofty vantage points. Down in the woods, spring arrives in a riot of colour with blooming bluebells, dog-violets and wood anemones. Spring tides have been known to bring the occasional seal to the river.

COOMBE HILL CANAL AND MEADOWS

Near Tewkesbury, GL19 4BA; **OS Map** SO 887272; **Map Ref** D1

Access/conditions: 1km walk from the car park along the canal towpath to the entrance. Towpath is level but can be muddy after wet weather. Reserve is inaccessible during natural winter flooding as it is part of a floodplain.
How to get there: Bus from Gloucester, Cheltenham and Tewkesbury to Coombe Hill. Follow the lane off the A38 that runs alongside the Swan Inn. Small area for parking at the wharf end of the canal.
Walking time: 3 hours.
30-minute visit: Follow the canal until the entrance to the meadows. Return via the opposite side of the canal.

An ancient landscape of endless skies, floods and farming, which fringes the River Severn. Just as beautiful on a frost-bitten winter morning as a balmy summer's day, the reserve is a peaceful retreat for birdwatchers, walkers, families and everyone in-between. Pintails, teal and wigeon descend on the wetland in impressive

numbers during winter, then as the water recedes in spring, snipe, redshanks, oystercatchers, lapwings and curlews move in to forage around the shallow pools and nest on the scrapes.

Coombe Hill is also a great place to spot birds of prey, with magnificent raptors including hen harriers, peregrine falcons and goshawks dropping by. But birds aren't the only draw –

this reserve is one of the best places in Gloucestershire for dragonflies and damselflies. Seventeen species have been recorded, including the hairy dragonfly, scarce chaser and emperor dragonfly.

GREYSTONES FARM

Bourton-on-the-Water, GL54 2EN; **OS Map** SP 172209; **Map Ref** D2

Opening hours: Nature reserve open year-round, seven days a week. Shop and Discovery Barn open Thursday–Sunday, 10am–4pm, between spring and autumn. Café open daily, 9am–4pm. The meadow walk closes in winter to protect snipe and the meadow.

Access/conditions: The area around the visitor centre and the path to the replica Iron Age roundhouse are wheelchair and pushchair friendly. Walking trails are on level paths or grassy tracks.

How to get there: Buses to Bourton-on-the-Water from Cheltenham, Cirencester and Stow-on-the-Wold. By car, take Station Road from the A429 Fosse Way, into Bourton-on-the-Water. Park in the main village car park next to Co-op petrol station and walk five minutes to the reserve. Two parking spaces available at the farm for wheelchair users and people with limited mobility (contact the Trust to book in advance).

Walking time: 1.5 hours.

30-minute visit: Head along the Oxfordshire Way to the river.

Greystones Farm is a magical place that can be visited time and again and still surprise you. As well as wonderfully

diverse ancient meadows brimming with wildflowers, the reserve is home to Iron Age burial pits, a wildlife-friendly farm, sparkling rivers

and a Discovery Barn where pipistrelle, Natterer's, long-eared and lesser horseshoe bats roost. The meadows are full of colour in spring

and summer, with great burnet, marsh orchids, ragged robin, devil's-bit scabious, meadowsweet and knapweed all vying for your attention, and that of the many butterflies. Orange-tips, meadow browns, brimstones, small coppers and ringlets all delight in the nectar buffet. Listen for water voles rustling through the vegetation alongside the River Eye, followed by a distinctive 'plop' as they enter the water. Otters use the river as a highway and kingfishers brighten up the waterway when they zip by on hunting trips. Beautiful and banded demoiselles add yet more colour when they emerge in early summer. You may be lucky enough to see barn owls hunting in the meadows in the evening before heading to the office building to roost.

LOWER WOODS

Wickwar, GL9 1BY; **OS Map** ST 746881; **Map Ref** D12

Access/conditions: Narrow paths and steps can be muddy and slippery after wet weather. Flatter paths close to the car park are accessible for all-terrain wheelchairs and pushchairs in the drier months.

How to get there: One mile from Wickwar and 1.5 miles from Hawkesbury Upton along narrow lanes. Train to Yate (Bristol to Gloucester line). Buses run from Yate to Wotton via Wickwar and Hawkesbury Upton (not Sunday). Walk to Lower Woods via footpaths. Park at Lower Woods Lodge.

Walking time: 1.5–2.5 hours.

30-minute visit: Enjoy the red waymarked route or walk through East Stanley Wood. Enter the gate directly opposite the sheds and keep turning first right to return to the car park.

Delve deep into nature at one of the largest ancient woodlands in south-west England. Twenty-three separate woods come together – their boundaries unchanged for centuries – to form 700 acres (300ha) of unforgettable wild space. Some areas even hark back to medieval times, with the individual woodlands and coppices separated by fingers of grazed common land and old grassy roads called 'trenches'. There is no shortage of plants to admire – 72 species, in fact (the highest number recorded in the South West). Bluebells carpet the woodland floor in early spring alongside early purple orchids, greater butterfly-orchids and herb-paris. This latter bloom is an indicator of ancient woodland and a strange-looking plant, whose symmetry attracted medieval herbalists to use it in marriage rituals. In summer, the old meadow is adorned with ragged robin, common spotted-orchids, betony and devil's-bit scabious. Stroll the woodland rides to see white admiral and silver-washed fritillary butterflies. The best places for birds are around the edges of the woods, in scrub or the coppiced areas around the car park. Woodcock hide, camouflaged, on the woodland floor and summer walks are brightened by the striking black and white plumage of pied flycatchers. Lower Woods is just as memorable in autumn and winter, when the field maples turn brilliant yellow and the wild service trees pink and gold. Blackthorns become festooned with fat, blue-black sloes and mysterious fungi peek out from the leaf litter.

CRICKLEY HILL

Gloucester, GL4 8JY; **OS Map** SO 934160; **Map Ref** D3

Opening hours: Entrance gate open 6am–6pm, November–February; 6am–7pm, March and October; 6am–9pm, April–September. Café is open 9am–4pm, seven days a week. Parking charges apply.

Access/conditions: The Crickley Hill Circular Walk is accessible by all-terrain pushchairs, wheelchairs and the available-for-hire tramper/mobility scooter. Contact the Trust to book the tramper (info@ gloucestershirewildlifetrust. co.uk or 01452 383333).

How to get there: Take A417 to Air Balloon roundabout. Take first exit onto A436 then immediate left onto Leckhampton Hill. Reserve entrance is on the left.

Walking time: With different walking trails, a café and connection to the Cotswold Way, you could spend anything from a few hours to a full day exploring.

30-minute visit: Take an easy stroll along the portion of the red Crickley Hill Walk that encircles the café and toilets. Gloucestershire Wildlife Trust joint-owns Crickley Hill with the National Trust – a powerful partnership that safeguards the wildlife and human history of this much-loved wild place. Perched high above the city of Gloucester and the Severn Vale, the views are tremendous.

From the deep shade of wild garlic-scented beech woodland to the steep slopes of wildflower-rich grassland, there is plenty of natural magic to see, smell and hear. More than 1,300 species of plant and animal have been recorded here, from rare birds, butterflies and wildflowers to reptiles and toadstools. Chiffchaffs and cuckoos announce the arrival of spring, when common spotted-orchids start to bloom in the grassland. As the days grow ever warmer, the wildlife wonders grow more abundant. Green woodpeckers feed from anthills, bee orchids appear as pink pinpricks hiding in the grass, and large skipper and chalkhill blue butterflies emerge to drink from the flowers. Huge Dryad's saddle mushrooms can be found growing on beech trees in The Scrubs, exuding a watermelon scent when young.

Crickley Hill also offers a taste of Iron Age local history, with the remains of a hill fort and evidence of settlements dating back 5,000 years.

WILTSHIRE

About the Trust

Wiltshire Wildlife Trust is restoring, reconnecting and recreating wild places across Wiltshire, forming a Living Landscape for both people and wildlife. Everyone is welcome to visit the Trust's nature reserves, on any day of the year, and they are all free of charge.

Wiltshire Wildlife Trust
01380 725670
wiltshirewildlife.org

Blackmoor Copse

Salisbury, SP5 1AG
OS Map SU 234288;
Map Ref D18

A haven for rare butterflies including pearl-bordered fritillaries, purple emperors, silver-washed fritillaries and Duke of Burgundy. Dormice scamper through the trees and sunny glades are sprinkled with violets, bluebells and common spotted-orchids.

High Clear Down

Marlborough, SN8 2LE
OS Map SU 237762;
Map Ref D15

Sloping chalk downland blanketed by a kaleidoscope of flowers. Visit in May to see blue chalk milkwort and early gentian in bloom. Fragrant, pyramidal and common spotted-orchids add splashes of bright pink. Duke of Burgundy, brown argus and Adonis blue butterflies thrive on the abundant nectar and skylarks fill the sky with song. No formal paths, so tread carefully to avoid trampling the flowers.

Jones's Mill the Vera Jeans Nature Reserve

Pewsey, SN9 5JN
OS Map SU 169611;
Map Ref D16

Fen, wet woodland, ponds and wet grassland seated on peaty soils. Common lizards, water shrews and countless dragonflies thrive alongside red kites, kingfishers and herons. Rare plants like bogbean and bog pimpernel grow alongside yellow flag irises, marsh orchids and water avens.

Landford Bog

Near Salisbury, SP5 2AR
OS Map SU 258184;
Map Ref D21

A floating carpet of feathery moss with expanses of heather and purple moor-grass nestled on the edge of the New Forest. Carnivorous sundews and pale butterwort wait to ensnare insects. Yellow-striped raft spiders lurk at the edge of puddles.

Middleton Down

Wilton, SP5 5DT
OS Map SU 047238;
Map Ref D20

Traditional chalk downland with stunning views. Admire autumn lady's-tresses, common spotted, fragrant, bee and frog orchids. Adonis blue, common blue and marbled white butterflies feed from trefoils and vetches. Glow-worms sparkle on the slopes on late summer evenings. Look out for oil beetles and narrow-bordered bee hawk-moths in spring.

Ravensroost Wood

Malmesbury, SN5 0AG
OS Map SU 024876;
Map Ref D13

Ancient woodland with rare wild service trees. Blackcaps, wrens, willow warblers and whitethroats perform an incredible dawn chorus in spring. Redwings spend the winter, tawny owls hoot noisily in December and lesser spotted woodpeckers start drumming in January. More than 450 species of fungi emerge in autumn.

Why not extend your walk to the adjoining Avis Meadows and Distillery and Warbler Meadows?

Clouts Wood
Wroughton, SN4 9DG
OS Map SU 143802;
Map Ref D14

Starting at Kings Farm Wood, enjoy a stroll through Diocese Meadows, Church Hill Pastures

and up through the valley of Markham Banks en route to Clouts Wood. Bath asparagus appears in late June – green hellebore, wood vetch and herb-paris grow too. Beetles, bats and woodpeckers thrive on the dead wood.

COOMBE BISSETT DOWN

Salisbury, SP5 4NA; **OS Map** SU 111248; **Map Ref** D19

Access/conditions: Not suitable for wheelchairs/pushchairs. Mobility scooter access via RADAR key on kissing gates.
How to get there: Bus runs from Salisbury to the Fox and Goose pub at Coombe Bissett, then a 10-minute walk. By car, from Salisbury to Blandford Road (A354) at Coombe Bissett, take turning to Homington. After 0.5 miles turn right into Pennings Drove.
Walking time: 3 hours.
30-minute visit: Take the 'Short Loop' trail.

If you like to combine your wildlife walks with local history then you'll love Coombe Bissett Down. The coombe's steep slopes feature medieval terraces called strip lynchets and, in summer, they blaze with floral colour and scent.

The Wiltshire Wildlife Trust's carefully planned grazing system means that by late May and early June the grassland brims with pyramidal orchids, harebells, bee orchids, devil's-bit scabious and Wiltshire's county flower: the incredibly rare and impossibly beautiful burnt-tip orchid. Yellowhammers, goldfinches and skylarks fill the air with song

and butterflies dance here, there and everywhere. Adonis blue, chalkhill blue, dingy skipper and marbled white are just a few of the different types you could spot. Wiltshire's first record of a wasp spider was made here, so keep your eyes peeled for these large black and yellow arachnids sitting on webs strung between the vegetation.

BLAKEHILL FARM

Cricklade, SN6 6RA; **OS Map** SU 073923; **Map Ref** D10

Access/conditions: At Blakehill Farm, level paths suitable for wheelchairs and pushchairs with gates and stiles on some routes. Sloping ground at Stoke Common Meadows, which is very wet in winter.
How to get there: Bus

runs from Cricklade to Cirencester via Leigh and Ashton Keynes. Another bus runs from Swindon to Royal Wootton Bassett via Minety. By car, reserve is signposted off B4040, Malmesbury Road, between Minety and

Cricklade, adjacent to village of Leigh.
Walking time: 3 hours.
30-minute visit: The network of access routes provides flexibility for visitors who want to explore the reserve at their own pace.

Wiltshire Wildlife Trust has turned this former military airfield into a wildlife-rich hay meadow and pasture. Old WWII runways still leave traces in the changes in vegetation, but they thrive with life. Brown hares, roe deer, skylarks and kestrels all use the grassland to feed, breed and shelter. Through the summer, adder's-tongue ferns, great burnet, ox-eye daisies and bird's-foot trefoil grow alongside rare spiny restharrow and dyer's greenweed. Above the flowers fly small copper, brown hairstreak, common blue and marbled white butterflies. Wheatears, whinchats and barn owls are just some of the avian highlights; 14 species of dragonfly flit above the ponds; and you may spot a grass snake on the hunt.

Why not extend your walk down the footpath to Stoke Common Meadows? In May, bluebells bloom beneath a copse of 50- to 150-year-old oak trees, while in winter, snipe and teal seek shelter in the gently sloping meadows.

LANGFORD LAKES

Steeple Langford, SP3 4NH; **OS Map** SU 037370; **Map Ref** D17

🅿 ⓦⓒ ♿ ⓘ 🍴 📷 👟

Opening hours: Visitor centre and Kingfisher Café open 10am–4pm, Wednesday–Sunday.
Access/conditions: Visitor centre, hides and walking trails all suitable for wheelchairs and pushchairs.
How to get there: 250m from National Cycle Route 24. There is a bus between Salisbury and Bath – nearest stop is 500m away in Steeple Langford. By car, just off A36 Salisbury to Westminster road, follow sign for The Langfords. In Steeple Langford turn into Duck Street – reserve entrance is on left after crossing the river.
Walking time: You could easily spend half a day watching the wildlife. A simple stroll around the paths takes 1–1.5 hours.
30-minute visit: Sit in one of the hides and look out onto the lakes to see an ever-

changing variety of birds, dragonflies and butterflies.

Nestled in the Wylye Valley between Salisbury and Warminster, Langford Lakes is a birder's paradise, a family favourite, and welcomes absolutely everyone. The four lakes and wet scrape offer a vital stopping-off point and resident habitat for about 150 different bird species, from dabbling ducks to jewel-blue kingfishers. The five hides are the perfect place to take in the peaceful atmosphere and watch the birds – you may even see a passing osprey!

In spring, watch for great crested grebes shaking their heads in courtship. Reed warblers, waders and terns drop in on their summer migration, with redshanks and sandpipers probing the mud. As winter advances, shovelers and wigeon join year-round residents including gadwall, water rails and, occasionally, the rare and secretive bittern.

As well as creating islands, ponds and wader scrapes, when it bought the lakes in 2001, Wiltshire Wildlife Trust has breathed new life back into an 800m stretch of the Wylye River and transformed a neighbouring field into the Great Meadow wetland.

LOWER MOOR

Cricklade, SN16 9TW; **OS Map** SU 007939; **Map Ref** D9

Opening hours: Visitor centre and Dragonfly Café open 10am–4pm, Wednesday–Sunday.
Access/conditions: Wheelchair access to one hide and across the boardwalk to Mallard Lake. From here, footpath can be muddy. No toilets.
How to get there: Bus from Malmesbury to Cirencester (via Crudwell, Chelworth and Oaksey) stops in Somerford Keynes, then a 20-minute walk. By car, leave Oaksey towards Somerford Keynes, cross the railway line and follow an S-bend. Entrance is on the right immediately after S-bend.
Walking time: Circular walk from the visitor centre past ponds, lakes and woodland takes 1 hour, but you could spend a whole day extending your walk to adjoining Clattinger Farm, Lower Moor Farm, Sandpool and Oaksey Moor Farm Meadow.
30-minute visit: Visit the bird hide on Cottage Lake and see what you can spot.

Lower Moor is a wonderful waterscape of three lakes, two brooks, ponds and wetland scrapes linked by boardwalks, ancient hedges, woodland and meadows.

It's a brilliant example of sustainable tourism, with a visitor centre, bird hides, paths and an otter holt all built using sustainably sourced timber and recycled waste materials. Lower Moor is the gateway to four neighbouring reserves: Clattinger Farm, Lower Moor Farm, Sandpool and Oaksey Moor Farm Meadow. The lakes sustain a fantastic range of waterbirds including great crested grebes, teal, shovelers and goosanders; water voles and otters use Flagham Brook; and sunny days bring emperor, southern hawker and downy emerald dragonflies.

Wander onto Clattinger Farm in April to see the thousands of delicately patterned snake's-head fritillaries in flower. In June they're succeeded by meadow saffron, tubular water-dropwort, orchids and downy-fruited sedge.

Sandpool is grazed by belted Galloway cattle, with a path leading into a wet woodland that will enchant you with bees, butterflies and birds. Come at dusk to spot barn owls or visit in late winter/early spring to sit in the bird hide and watch herons raising their chicks.

Oaksey Moor Farm Meadow is another link in this chain of incredibly special grasslands. In summer you can see devil's-bit scabious, green-winged orchids, pignut and pepper saxifrage. Look out for ruddy darter and four-spotted chaser dragonflies hovering above the pond.

DORSET

About the Trust

Dorset Wildlife Trust was founded in 1961. Supported by 26,000 members, a committed group of volunteers and passionate local wildlife lovers, the Trust is Dorset's largest nature conservation charity, protecting and championing wildlife on its 42 nature reserves and preserving even more wild space through partnerships with others.

Dorset Wildlife Trust
01305 264620
dorsetwildlifetrust.org.uk

Bracketts Coppice

Yeovil, BA22 9QX
OS Map ST 513073;
Map Ref E10

A hidden gem in west Dorset. Otters use the stream, roe deer reside in the pastures and dormice nest in woodland where several species of bat, including the very rare Bechstein's bat, roost. Summer brings green-winged orchids and butterflies including marsh fritillaries and purple hairstreaks.

Higher Hyde Heath

Wareham, BH20 7NY
OS Map SY 854899;
Map Ref E15

A reptile refuge where all six of the UK's native reptiles bask and slither. Dragon and damselflies dart over the peaty pools and secretive nightjars are camouflaged among the ground vegetation. Look out for Dartford warblers, grayling butterflies and sticky sundews.

Sopley Common

Christchurch, BH23 6BJ
OS Map SZ 129971;
Map Ref E17

Heathland, bog pools and woodland teeming with rare wildlife. Look out for sand lizards, smooth snakes, heath tiger beetles and black darter dragonflies. Dartford warblers and stonechats call from the gorse and fluffy cotton-grass heads bob in the wetter areas.

Powerstock Common

Maiden Newton, DT2 0EJ
OS Map SY 546973;
Map Ref E12

An unmissable reserve at any time of year. Bluebells, herb-paris and early purple orchids bloom in spring; marsh fritillaries take to the wing over the damp grassland in summer; rutting deer roar in autumn; and hares scamper through the frosty undergrowth in winter. Newts breed in the network of ponds and lesser horseshoe bats hunt along the 'edge' habitats.

Tadnoll and Winfrith Heath

East Knighton, DT2 8LQ
OS Map SY 804863;
Map Ref E14

An iconic piece of the Dorset landscape where nightjars *churr* after dark and the dry heath blooms purple with heather. Silver-studded blue butterflies flit around the open heath and marsh cinquefoil thrives in the wet meadows. Keeled skimmer and golden-ringed dragonflies stalk their boggy kingdom.

FONTMELL DOWN

Shaftesbury, SP7 0DT; **OS Map** ST 887184; **Map Ref** E7

Access/conditions: Uneven ground, steep slopes and narrow paths with gates and stiles. Can be slippery in winter.

How to get there: Bus from Shaftesbury stops at Compton Abbas and Fontmell Magna. By car, from Shaftesbury, head south on B3081 and follow signs to Melbury Abbas. Park in National Trust car park at Spread Eagle Hill or small quarry car park at Brandis Down.

Walking time: The 3km circular trail starting from Spread Eagle Hill car park takes 2 hours.

30-minute visit: Walk the most northerly part of the reserve, known as 'The Curlews and Burys'.

Stunning chalk downland flowers, beautiful butterflies and spectacular views over the Blackmore Vale – what more could you want from a wildlife walk?

Ancient chalk grassland is now very rare (around 80 per cent has been lost in the last 70 years), but this precious remnant is thriving. Look for bee orchids, greater butterfly-orchids and the rare early gentian as skylarks sing above your head. The patchwork of grassland and scrub is home to 35 species of butterfly together with rare birds, mammals, moths, mosses and lichens. Silver-spotted skippers, hazel dormice, yellowhammers and barred tooth-striped moths are just a handful of the wild wonders you could encounter during your visit.

UPTON HEATH

Broadstone, BH21 3RX; **OS Map** SY 991941; **Map Ref** E16

Access/conditions: Sand and gravel tracks with slopes. Flat section along central bridleway and on easy access trail. Ground is boggy and uneven away from paths.

How to get there: By car, best accessed from Springdale Road car park (reached from Wareham Road running through Corfe Mullen). Alternatively, park at the end of Longmeadow Lane (just off A35).

Walking time: 2–3 hours.

30-minute visit: From Springdale Road car park, take the public bridleway

into the reserve and stroll around the easy access trail.

A heathland oasis right on the doorstep of Poole. Whether you're potty about plants, smitten with snakes or dotty for dragonflies, it won't take long for you to fall under Upton Heath's spell. Common lizards, sand lizards, slow worms, smooth snakes, adders and grass snakes all live here, basking among the bracken or between patches of heather. An astonishing 16 species of dragonfly have been recorded darting around the reserve, from dazzling golden-ringed dragonflies to bright red common darters.

If you can tear your eyes away from the wildlife, don't forget to simply stand on the open heath and take in the big skies, colourful plants and riot of birdsong. The views across Poole Harbour, Corfe Castle and the Isle of Purbeck are breathtaking.

LORTON MEADOWS

Weymouth, DT3 5QH; **OS Map** SY 674826; **Map Ref** E13

Access/conditions: Gates at most entrances. Unsurfaced paths.
How to get there: From B3159 (Dorchester Road), turn into Lorton Lane and continue to the end of the lane, where you will reach the car park.
Walking time: Allow a whole morning or afternoon to explore.
30-minute visit: Take the Legacy Trail through East Bottom and the Coffin Plantation to the first viewpoint at the edge of Littlemoor Meadows.

A green haven of peaceful meadows, hedgerows and woodland with some fabulous wildlife, right in the middle of town. Multiple trails and pathways offer so much opportunity to explore – take a short stroll through the shady woodland or follow one of the longer trails across the top of the meadows.

As the first morning light filters through the woodland and mist blankets the ponds, days here begin with the vibrant chirping of song thrushes and often end with the emergence of ghostly barn owls. On bright summer days the meadows and hedgerows are busy with insect life; from marbled white and grizzled skipper butterflies dancing over wildflowers and grasshoppers 'singing' their scratchy tunes, to burnet moths, soldier beetles and emperor dragonflies. A summer amble along the pathways will also reward you with the sight of colourful bee orchids and corky-fruited water-dropwort. The scrub and hedgerows burst with the songs of lesser whitethroats and garden warblers, and on warm evenings noctule bats sweep up and down the reserve's flight lines.

BROWNSEA ISLAND

Poole, BH13 7EE; **OS Map** SZ 031877; **Map Ref** E21

Opening hours: Check Dorset Wildlife Trust website for most up-to-date ferry and entrance fares, booking information and opening hours.

Access/conditions: Main track, boardwalk, Villa Wildlife Centre and two hides are easily accessible.

How to get there: Travel to the island via ferry from Poole Quay. Buses run to Poole Quay from Rockley Park, Hamworthy, Turlin Moor, Upton and Creekmoor. By train, Poole station is 0.5 miles from Poole Quay. By car, follow signs to Poole Quay and park in visitor car park.

Walking time: The Wildlife Trust shares management of Brownsea with the National Trust. A walk along the Dorset Wildlife Trust Nature Trail will take around 1 hour – exploring the whole island

and relaxing in the visitor centre can take up to a day.

30-minute visit: Head along the boardwalk to the first hide to watch the birds on the lagoon.

Brownsea Island is a very special place – a breathtaking retreat for people, a haven for wading birds, and one of the few places left in the UK where you can catch a glimpse of a red squirrel. Currently 250 of these iconic creatures live on the island and are often seen scampering up and down the trees, gathering and devouring nuts.

Red squirrels aren't the only stars here. The lagoon is a vital safe haven for overwintering birds including avocets, black-tailed godwits and huge groups of spoonbills. Settle into a bird hide and watch these elegant

birds swishing their spoon-shaped bills through the water as they feed, filtering through the silt. In summer, a new wave of migratory birds arrive on the lagoons. Common terns, Sandwich terns and numerous different gulls fill the air with raucous chatter as they raise their families, often joined by avocets. The reedbeds and alder carr offer sheltered foraging spots to water voles, sika deer, kingfishers and water rails.

If you can tear yourself away from the wildlife, take a walk through the woods and follow the footpath to meet glorious views across Poole Harbour. Or head to the Villa Wildlife Centre in the middle of the reserve, enjoy a picnic on a bench in the sunshine and watch squirrels nibbling seeds on nearby feeders.

KINGCOMBE MEADOWS

Toller Porcorum, DT2 0EQ; **OS Map** SY 554990; **Map Ref** E11

Opening hours: Visitor centre open 10am–4pm, Monday–Friday.

Access/conditions: Access to the meadows is via field, bridle or kissing gates. Ground may be rough and uneven in places and can be very wet.

How to get there: By car, take A37 to Yeovil. From Dorchester, turn left on A356 just after Grimstone. Continue past Maiden Newton and turn left at the top of the hill to Toller Porcorum. Take the right turn signposted Lower Kingcombe and drive for a mile until you see the Kingcombe Visitors Centre sign on the right.

Walking time: While away a day here.

30-minute visit: Take the nature trail signposted with green arrows.

Step back in time at this traditional working farm where a patchwork of flower-rich meadows is broken up by thick hedges, streams, ponds, ancient green lanes and wooded areas. Rather than misting the land with pesticides, Dorset Wildlife Trust enlists the help of grazing animals to manage the reserve and, as a result, it positively overflows with wildlife – some common and easy to see, others rare elsewhere in the UK.

The luxuriously thick hedgerows offer shelter to dormice and provide highways for other mammals. Birds love the hedges too, with yellowhammers and linnets – whose calls are rarer in the intensively managed land beyond – making their homes among the tangle of branches. The ancient trees drip with lichens, mosses and ferns while the River Hooke, which winds its way through the centre of the reserve, teems with beautiful demoiselles and brown trout.

If you must linger somewhere, make it the grasslands. Chalk slopes burst with spring cowslips, harebells and bee orchids while the valley bottom is blanketed by southern marsh orchids, sneezewort and devil's-bit scabious. These stunning wildflower displays bring clouds of dancing marbled white, meadow brown and ringlet butterflies. In autumn, the waning flowers are replaced by an incredible 27 different species of waxcap.

ALDERNEY

About the Trust

Alderney Wildlife Trust is dedicated to protecting the island's wildlife and environment for the future, working alongside the small island community to achieve more for nature. From woodland to wetland, grassland to heathland, sand dunes to rocky shores, Alderney is small but extremely rich in wildlife, both on land and at sea.

Alderney Wildlife Trust
01481 822935
alderneywildlife.org

ALDERNEY COMMUNITY WOODLAND

Les Rochers

Access/conditions: Some paths at the top of the woodland are wheelchair-friendly but steep slopes and narrow paths make lower trails inaccessible.
How to get there: Approaching from St Anne, take Longis Road then turn left onto Val Longis. Take the first right onto Les Rochers to park at the bunker off this road. Approaching from Braye Harbour turn left off Braye Hill by St Anne's School, continue for around 300m and park by Blanchards builders' merchants. From both locations you can reach the reserve in 20 minutes.
Walking time: 1.5 hours.
30-minute visit: Park off Le Rochers and take the Meadow Trail through the grassland and around the wooden bunker.

Alderney Community Woodland is a nature reserve with a difference: a refuge for the local community and wildlife alike. By planting this woodland (11,000 trees and counting!), the Trust has doubled Alderney's native broadleaf tree cover, and with more planting to come, the reserve will eventually form a wooded backbone across the island. Dotted with WWII bunkers, remnants of Victorian quarries and trails, there is so much to explore in terms of both history and wildlife.

The Woodland is a fantastic place to get away from it all. Listen out for a high-

pitched call in the coniferous woodland – you may have found a firecrest! These tiny songbirds measure in at just 9cm in length but are easily recognised by their white eye-stripe and bright orange crest

feathers. Bats hunt along the woodland edges, with eight species now recorded on Alderney.

Take the Meadow Trail by the golf course at the bottom of the reserve and

you could be in with a chance of seeing an Alderney blonde hedgehog. This is one of their favourite places to grab a snack and they're often seen foraging around the scrub in the woodland.

LONGIS RESERVE

Longis Bay

Access/conditions: Some areas, including access paths to both bird hides, are suitable for wheelchairs, but most paths aren't suitable for wheelchair users or those with limited mobility.
How to get there: From St Anne, take Longis Road all the way to The Nunnery Heritage Site. If driving, park at the Nunnery, by Raz Causeway or in the bays near Mannez Lighthouse. On foot, you can reach the reserve in 30 minutes.
Walking time: 1.5 hours.
30-minute visit: From the Nunnery Heritage Site car park walk down to the sandy beach or visit the hide at Longis Pond.

Longis Reserve is Alderney's largest and most diverse nature reserve. As you stroll along the coastal trails you might glimpse rare plants such as small hare's-ear, sand crocuses, bastard toadflax and orange bird's-foot. You can find Alderney sea lavender on the rocky shore around Houmet Herbe and, during late May and June, enjoy sightings of the beautiful Glanville fritillary. This special butterfly is virtually restricted to coastal landslips on the southern half of the Isle of Wight and the Channel Islands, along with

a few coastal locations on the mainland, but is common across this reserve.

Longis Reserve has two ponds, which you can watch from the comfort of bird hides and soak up the peaceful atmosphere. Alderney lies along the flyway of countless migratory birds, so there is no end to what you might spot. In summer, Mannez Pond attracts water rails, Cetti's warblers and hungry sparrowhawks as well as plenty of dragonflies. Longis Pond is surrounded by dune grassland grazed by a small

herd of cattle and is home to a resident population of little grebes. Snipe and water rails are seasonal visitors, foraging along the reed-line.

Don't miss a walk along the coast path where, if you are lucky, you can watch seals basking in the lee of Houmet Herbe or spot dolphins swimming offshore. In winter, the intertidal zone fills with oystercatchers, turnstones, ringed plovers, dunlin and curlews all busy rooting out tasty morsels to see them through the tough months ahead.

ISLES OF SCILLY

About the Trust

More than 50 per cent of Scilly is looked after by the Isles of Scilly Wildlife Trust, which is dedicated to protecting, restoring and creating sustainable, nature-rich habitats on land and at sea. As well as actively managing 1,675 acres (678ha) of land for the benefit of nature and people, among other activities, the Trust engages more than 3,000 people and protects 53 nationally important Scheduled Ancient Monuments annually.

Isles of Scilly Wildlife Trust
01720 422153
ios-wildlifetrust.org.uk

THE ISLES OF SCILLY

St Mary's, TR21 0NS; **OS Map** SV 900114; **Map Ref** A11

Opening hours: Open all year. Restricted access in some areas either all or some of the year to give wildlife space to thrive. Please keep to paths and watch the wildlife from a respectful distance so it doesn't feel the need to fly, swim or run away. If in doubt, visit the Trust's website or call the office for advice about leaving the wildlife undisturbed.
Access/conditions: Network of permissive paths around the inhabited islands – can be uneven, single-track and muddy.
How to get there: Planes fly from south-west mainland airports to St Mary's and the *Scillonian III* passenger ferry sails from Penzance to St Mary's (March–November;

foot passengers only; 01736 334220). Helicopters fly from Penzance to St Mary's or Tresco (01736 780828).
Walking time: Walks of varying lengths in the 4,562 acres (1,846ha) of open access land

and beaches leased by the Isles of Scilly Wildlife Trust from the Duchy of Cornwall, spread over some 100 islands and islets, including the inhabited islands of St Mary's, St Agnes and Gugh, Bryher and St Martin's.

Walks can take anything from 1 hour to a whole day. For inspiration, pick up a map detailing paths, routes and restrictions from the Tourist Information Centre.
30-minute visit: Take one of the pleasant walks around the Garrison, or from Porth Cressa around Peninnis to Old Town through the Lower Moors nature trail and back to Hugh Town.

Scilly is like nowhere else, complete with its own species of shrew and ant: the Scilly shrew and St Martin's ant. Your adventure starts before you even arrive – ferry crossings often yield common dolphins, Manx shearwaters, ocean sunfish and tuna.

When you do set foot on the islands, you'll never forget them. Spring is heralded in March by a Scilly speciality: the dwarf pansy. This tiny flower stands no higher than 1cm tall in dune grasslands like those found at Rushy Bay on Bryher. Another rarity, found only in Scilly and the Channel Islands, is orange birds-foot, which blooms in heathlands that beam pink with ling and bell heather during summer. This is also seabird breeding time and you'll find fulmars, guillemots and razorbills nesting at Daymark on St Martin's. Puffins can be seen between April and the end of July as they breed on some of the uninhabited islands. Scilly's underwater world is dizzyingly diverse, with grey seals, dolphins and intriguing rockpool creatures thriving in the crystal-clear waters. Autumn is the best time to look for rare migrant birds, while in winter life slows down for everyone but the farmers, who fill the air with the heady scent of their narcissus harvest.

SOUTH EAST

When you set eyes on the iconic white cliffs and breathtaking downs of Kent and Sussex, or the hidden glades and mystical woodland of the New Forest, it's hard to believe that the South East region sits right on the doorstep of London.

Nestled in the Thames basin, Surrey and Berkshire entice visitors with glorious heathland, home to Dartford warblers, woodlarks and all six of Britain's native reptiles: adder, grass snake, smooth snake, common lizard, sand lizard and slow worm. Sleek hobbies hunt dragonflies by day and then, as the summer sun sets, nightjars fill the air with their otherworldy *churring*.

Journey further south and the landscape transforms into rolling chalk hills rich in wildflowers: the unforgettable backdrop of the North and South Downs. An orchid hunt is essential, with early purple, pyramidal and fragrant orchids blooming alongside weird and wonderful rarities including military, man and monkey orchids. These sun-warmed, flower-rich grasslands are in turn rich in butterflies, with chalkhill and Adonis blue, Duke of Burgundy and silver-spotted skipper the specialities of the region.

But it isn't all about rolling hills – the South East is the most wooded region in England. In spring, many of these enchanting woodlands are carpeted with bluebells, wood anemones and wild garlic. Later, the trees sing with summer migrants which, in Kent and Sussex, include the melodious nightingale.

The wonderful thing about the South East is that you don't even need to venture into the countryside to see something memorable. Right in the centre of London, where stag beetles duel and ring-necked parakeets fly noisily overhead, you may catch sight of a peregrine falcon hunting across the city skyline. Even here, in Britain's most densely populated region, the opportunities for watching spectacular wildlife really are everywhere.

NOT TO BE MISSED

Bowdown Woods, Berkshire
Mysterious woodland, butterfly-filled glades and open heathland forming a crucial part of the West Berkshire Living Landscape.

Chobham Common, Surrey
A sprawling heathland known for fantastic populations of dragonflies, butterflies and birds, plus more than 300 species of flower!

Ebernoe Common, Sussex
A historic woodland home to rare barbastelle and Bechstein's bats and turtle doves. Don't miss an autumn fungi hunt.

Sydenham Hill Wood, London
The largest remaining tract of the Great North Wood. Look out for stag beetles among rotten logs.

Sandwich and Pegwell Bay, Kent
One of the best places in the UK to see migrating birds such as nightingales, cuckoos, sanderlings and waxwings.

Opposite: New Forest National Park, Hampshire

HAMPSHIRE AND ISLE OF WIGHT

About the Trust

Hampshire & Isle of Wight Wildlife Trust is the leading local conservation charity in Hampshire and the Isle of Wight. It looks after more than 50 nature reserves and works with other organisations to protect wildlife and connect wild places across the two counties.

Hampshire & Isle of Wight Wildlife Trust
01489 774400
hiwwt.org.uk

Emer Bog and Baddesley Nature Reserve

North Baddesley, SO51 9BN
OS Map SU 388219;
Map Ref E6

Explore footpaths and boardwalks winding their way through woodland, grassland, bog and heath. Stonechats, hobbies, adders, grass snakes, beautiful demoiselles and golden-ringed dragonflies are some of the top spots.

Flexford Nature Reserve

Chandler's Ford, SO53 1SZ
OS Map SU 424215;
Map Ref E5

A green haven amid urban development. Wild garlic flourishes in the ancient woodland, sneezewort blooms in the wet meadows and woodpeckers, redpolls and siskins flit through the trees. Visit in summer for white admiral butterflies.

Eaglehead and Bloodstone Copses Nature Reserve

Brading, PO36 0NT
OS Map SZ 582877;
Map Ref E23

Spring brings a stunning display of bluebells, wood anemones and primroses. Visit in summer to see woodland butterflies such as silver-washed fritillaries and white admirals, and watch red squirrels foraging in autumn.

Noar Hill Nature Reserve

Alton, GU34 3LW
OS Map SU 742319;
Map Ref E3

A former medieval chalk workings now brimming with beautiful flowers and butterflies that create an unforgettable oasis of colour. Juniper and pyramidal orchids, and dingy skipper, chalkhill blue and brown hairstreak butterflies can all be seen.

Roydon Woods Nature Reserve

Brockenhurst, SO42 7UF
OS Map SU 315009;
Map Ref E18

Follow the network of paths through the home of badgers, nightjars and tawny owls. Blankets of wildflowers attract a host of beautiful butterflies and moths, including small pearl-bordered fritillaries.

Winnall Moors Nature Reserve

Winchester, SO23 8DX
OS Map SU 490306;
Map Ref E2

Reed warblers, sedge warblers, kingfishers, yellow irises and snipe thrive at this lush oasis just a stone's throw from the city. Spring is a riot of colour and birdsong.

Blashford Lakes Nature Reserve

Ringwood, BH24 3PJ
OS Map SU 151083;
Map Ref E9

Visitor centre open daily, 9am–4.30pm.

A refuge for overwintering birds such as pochards, gadwall, bramblings and bitterns. In spring, bluebells carpet the woodland floor, and in summer, clouds of dragonflies and damselflies sparkle like jewels in the sun.

ARRETON DOWNS NATURE RESERVE

Newport, PO30 3AA; **OS Map** SZ 533875; **Map Ref** E22

Access/conditions: Unsurfaced paths with sloping and uneven ground.
How to get there: Bus passes through Arreton from Newport and Sandown. By car, from Newport take A3056 towards Arreton; before entering the village turn left towards Arreton Manor (on the right bend).
Walking time: 1 hour.
30-minute visit: Tour the Down.

Arreton Down is famed for its flowers. The season begins with a blaze of yellow – primroses and cowslips giving way to horseshoe and kidney vetches. Scabious, harebells, musk thistles and the rare bastard toadflax follow, painting the Down with swatches of pink, purple and cream. A member of the orchid family, autumn lady's-tresses, appears in early autumn, then as winter approaches, the flowers set seed and migratory birds take advantage of the food and shelter.

This abundance of plant life means the reserve is a fabulous place to spot wildlife year-round. Chalkhill blue butterflies live alongside Adonis blues, brown argus and dingy skippers. The air rings with the songs of yellowhammers, goldfinches and linnets, while summer visitors include whinchats, redstarts and spotted flycatchers.

ST CATHERINE'S HILL NATURE RESERVE

Winchester, SO23 9PA; **OS Map** SU 484276; **Map Ref** E4

Access/conditions: Paths are unsurfaced and uneven in places and there are steps up the hill. A bridleway runs through the south of the site, connecting to Twyford and St Cross Road footpaths.
How to get there: Leave M3 at J9 (from the north) or J10 (from the south) following signs for Alton (A31). At the next roundabout keep straight on towards Southampton (A33) and then Winchester.
Walking time: 2–3 hours.
30-minute visit: Park off Morestead Road and walk onto the Dongas for the large chalkhill blue population and stunning downland flowers.

Summer strolls at St Catherine's Hill are unforgettable. A dramatic climb up wooden stairs reveals show-stopping views over Winchester city and the Itchen Valley floodplains. At the summit you'll discover the earthworks of an Iron Age fort, the buried ruins of a Norman chapel, and a copse of beech trees where green woodpeckers cackle. Kestrels hunt in the valley below and skylarks fill the air with chatter.

The walk to the summit of the hill is just as exhilerating as the view from the top. The grassland is dotted with rock-roses, kidney vetch and bee, butterfly, fragrant and musk orchids. The flowering season ends in style, with masses of devil's-bit scabious and delicate autumn lady's-tresses. Huge numbers of chalkhill blue butterflies drink from the flowers in summer, along with brown argus, marbled whites and regular influxes of clouded yellows. Even winter walks bring wildlife wonders: flocks of redwings and fieldfares and tinkling goldfinches.

LYMINGTON AND KEYHAVEN MARSHES NATURE RESERVE

Lymington, SO41 8AJ; **OS Map** SZ 318927; **Map Ref** E20

Access/conditions: No direct access onto the marsh to protect the seabirds. The marsh can be viewed from the sea wall running around Hampshire County Council's Lymington and Pennington Marshes reserve.

How to get there: By bus to Milford-on-Sea, then a five-minute walk. By car, head south from Lyndhurst on A337 through Lymington and Pennington, turn left onto B3058 and on through Milford-on-Sea to Keyhaven. Park in the public car park at Keyhaven.

Walking time: Three routes: the three-mile circuit takes 1.5 hours, the five-mile circuit takes 2.5 hours, and the seven-mile circuit takes 3.5 hours.

30-minute visit: Walk along the sea wall, returning along the same route.

In summer, the saltmarsh and mudflats play a vital role in the lives of breeding and migrant birds, offering them a safe refuge to feed and raise a family. Several thousand pairs of black-headed gulls nest here every year alongside Sandwich and little terns and oystercatchers. Even fish breed here, using the creeks within the mudflats as nurseries for their fry.

Spring also brings an influx of insects, which fill the bellies of hungry swallows and wheatears fresh from their flight from Africa. In autumn, wading birds and wildfowl flee the freezing temperatures of their Arctic breeding grounds to find refuge on the marsh for winter. You could see dunlin, black-tailed godwits, wigeon and brent geese from your vantage point by the sea wall. If you're lucky you may spot a marauding marsh harrier, peregrine falcon or merlin too.

WILDLIFE FACT: AN EPIC MIGRATION

Our shores are essential to the survival of the birds that migrate here every spring and autumn: either much warmer or cooler than their home grounds, with less competition for food, safer breeding grounds and fewer predators. Some migrations are truly epic – Arctic terns fly up to 35,000km from Antarctica to join us for summer.

FARLINGTON MARSHES NATURE RESERVE

Portsmouth, PO6 1UN; **OS Map** SU 685045; **Map Ref** E19

Access/conditions: A rough path runs for 2.5 miles around the outer sea wall. It is exposed to wind and sea spray and a RADAR key is required for disabled access.

How to get there: Bus runs from Portsmouth Harbour to Havant, stopping at Farlington Sainsbury's, then a 15-minute walk. Nearest train station is Hilsea. By car, the reserve is off the A27/A2030 roundabout.

Walking time: 2.5-mile circular walk from western entrance takes 2.5 hours. Walk from Broadmarsh is 4.5 miles.

30-minute visit: Walk to the lake viewpoint. It's especially good from July–October around high tide, when thousands of waders roost on the lake.

Farlington Marshes offers wonderful walks all year round, but it really comes alive during winter when a staggering number of migratory birds arrive to seek refuge. Dark-bellied brent geese, wigeon, teal, avocets, redshanks and dunlin flock to the area, creating unrivalled birdwatching opportunities as they feed, chatter and, when a bird of prey drops by, wheel spectacularly above the marsh at high tide. Short-eared owls hunt over the Point Field and southern end of the main marsh.

Spring and autumn bring a whole new cast of migratory characters: redstarts, spotted flycatchers, wrynecks, wheatears and whinchats flitting around the Point Field and bushes. In summer, lapwings, redshanks, meadow pipits and skylarks settle down on the marsh to breed, while the grassland fills with butterflies as well as scarcer insects that thrive in the brackish landscape. Salty as Farlington Marshes may be, plants flourish here. They certainly aren't everyday species – look out for sea barley, bulbous foxtail, slender hare's-ear, grass vetchling and corky-fruited water-dropwort.

LOWER TEST NATURE RESERVE

Totton, SO40 3BR; **OS Map** SU 365145; **Map Ref** E8

Access/conditions: Test Way public footpath crosses the reserve with sections of boardwalk. A permissive path leads to two bird viewing screens and a hide towards the south of the reserve.

How to get there: By train or bus from Totton and Southampton; by car from M27/M271. There is on-road parking in Testwood Lane.

Walking time: A four-mile figure-of-eight trail runs around the site and takes at least 90 minutes to walk. There is a trail guide on the Wildlife Trust's website.

30-minute visit: Follow the boardwalk connecting the hide and viewing screens at the southern end of the reserve.

This patchwork of floodplain meadows, marshes and reedbeds is just a stone's throw from the busy Southampton Waters and docks, but it seems in another world entirely. The meeting of salt and fresh water encourages a wonderful variety of plants and animals to thrive. The staccato, scratchy songs of reed, sedge and Cetti's warblers fill the air during spring and summer, while colourful dragonflies like black-tailed skimmers and broad-bodied chasers dart overhead. There are plenty of plants to see too, including green-winged orchids and water avens. Autumn sees gatherings of sand martins and swallows preparing to return home to Africa, and sometimes exciting rare birds such as ospreys and marsh harriers. Winter is the time to settle in to the hide and enjoy wonderful views of great flocks of wigeon, teal and other overwintering ducks and waders.

PAMBER FOREST AND UPPER INHAMS COPSE NATURE RESERVE

Tadley, RG26 3EQ; **OS Map** SU 617621; **Map Ref** E1

Access/conditions: Many tracks and paths. Some can get muddy in spring and winter.

How to get there: Bus from Basingstoke, and get off just before Tadley at Skates Lane. By car, from Tadley, take Silchester Road and turn right into Impstone Road.

Walking time: Allow at least 2 hours for a reasonable circuit and longer to cover the whole 479-acre (194ha) site.

30-minute visit: From Impstone Road, walk across the pasture to Bowmonts Brook, follow the brook downstream and walk back up the public bridleway.

This spectacular woodland can feel a little intimidating on your first visit, but only because there is such a wealth of footpaths and trails to explore. The two-mile waymarked trail is a great introduction and takes in the forest's best viewpoints.

There is so much to see along the way. In spring you'll hear the melodious songs of blackcaps and garden warblers in the trees overhead, while a flush of spring flowers blooms beautifully by your feet. Primroses and wood anemones come first, joined by wild daffodils, violets, St John's wort, Solomon's-seal and star of Bethlehem in the stream valleys. As the season warms, the sunlit rides and clearings grow busy with

white admiral, silver-washed fritillary and purple emperor butterflies drinking thirstily from the flowering plants. But butterflies aren't the only must-see insects. The pools of Pamber Forest come alive with dragonflies during summer, including the striking golden-ringed dragonfly.

This reserve is wonderful for family days out. Find your way to the 'Donkey Tree' – one of Pamber's oldest trees at more than 300 years old – and see how many members of your family it takes to wrap your arms around its trunk.

NEWCHURCH MOORS NATURE RESERVE
Newchurch, PO36 0NL; **OS Map** SZ 565856; **Map Ref** E24

Access/conditions: Unsurfaced paths. Lower lying sections can be wet and muddy through winter.
How to get there: Take A3054, Newnham Road and Rowlands Lane to School Lane. You can park in Newchurch car park in School Lane.
Walking time: 3 hours.
30-minute visit: Explore part of the circular route around Martin's Wood.

This rich tapestry of habitats – floodplain meadow, grazed pasture, marshland, fen, river and woodland – creates a home for barn owls, buzzards and dormice. The reserve was created in 2019 thanks to generous donations from the Trust's supporters and a gift in the will of Gwendolen Bunce. Two new pieces of land, combined with the existing Martin's Wood nature reserve, created the Trust's largest Isle of Wight reserve at an incredible 124 acres (50ha).

Spring is the perfect time to visit as wood anemones, primroses, bluebells and wood avens come into full bloom on the woodland floor. Brimstone, small white and green-veined white butterflies emerge in time with the flowers, feeding in fluttering clouds on sun-drenched days. Among the growing melody of songbirds you can pick out bullfinches, treecreepers, long-tailed tits and blackcaps, as well as the distinctive drumming of great spotted woodpeckers. Keep an eye on the trees to catch red squirrels leaping from branch to branch.

The low-lying wetlands, visible from the rights of way, are home to important creatures like water voles, kingfishers, snipe and woodcock, while elsewhere on the reserve, burrowing bees make their homes in the sandy soil. Can you catch them emerging from their tiny bee-holes?

BERKS, BUCKS AND OXON

About the Trust

Berks, Bucks and Oxon Wildlife Trust (BBOWT) has a vision of more nature everywhere. Working with 1,700 volunteers, it is restoring nature across three beautiful counties, empowering people to connect with their local wildlife and campaigning to make nature's recovery a reality.

BBOWT
01865 775476
bbowt.org.uk

Bernwood Meadows

Near Horton-cum-Studley, OX33 1BJ
OS Map SP 606111;
Map Ref F13

More than 100 plant species have been recorded and it's worth just standing for a moment to take in the hum of insects and spectrum of colour during spring and summer. Green-winged orchids flourish, meadowsweet perfumes the wet furrows, and rare black and brown hairstreak butterflies breed in the ancient hedgerows. Car park open March–August.

Dry Sandford Pit

Near Abingdon, OX13 6JW
OS Map SU 467997;
Map Ref F18

An extraordinary mosaic of fossil-rich cliffs, limey fenland, ponds, streams, chalk grassland, scrub and woodlands bursting with plants and animals. Solitary bees and wasps – including the rare five-banded tailed digger wasp – burrow into the sandy cliff faces. In summer, the fenland bursts into life with thousands of orchids including marsh helleborines.

Wildmoor Heath

Crowthorne, RG45 7PW
OS Map SU 838630;
Map Ref F24

Wildmoor Heath is a precious survival of rare heathland habitat home to a rich but fragile community of fungi, insects, reptiles, birds, mosses and flowering plants. The open heath is prime habitat for Dartford warblers; keeled skimmer and golden-ringed dragonflies zip across the bog; and summer evenings whirr with the *churring* of nightjars nestled cryptically among the heather.

Iffley Meadows

Oxford, OX4 4BL
OS Map SP 525039;
Map Ref F16

In spring, the sight of thousands of purple and white-chequered snake's-head fritillaries at these ancient wet meadows will take your breath away. Their beauty is only enhanced by the adder's-tongue ferns, great burnet and ragged robin, as well as orange-tip butterflies and banded demoiselles. Listen out for Cetti's warblers singing from their hiding places by the ditches.

Inkpen Common

Near Newbury, RG17 9QT
OS Map SU 382643;
Map Ref F21

A flower-filled ancient heathland fringed by a woodland ringing with birdsong. The scarce pale dog-violet, lousewort and heath milkwort grow alongside three types of heather and the unusual parasitic plant common dodder, which has no leaves, only pink thread-like stems and dense heads of white and pink flowers. In late spring and summer, warblers serenade you from the woodland edge and you may spot a common lizard, slow worm or grass snake.

Finemere Wood
Near Aylesbury, HP22 4DE
OS Map SP 721215;
Map Ref F1

Finemere Wood has the thrilling atmosphere of a very old wild place. Spring is particularly special, when the rides are edged with primroses and bluebells carpet the woodland floor. A good variety of bees buzz around the meadows throughout the summer and butterflies abound. In fact, this nature reserve is one of the best places to spot the magnificent purple emperor.

Moor Copse
Near Reading, RG8 8EY
OS Map SU 634738;
Map Ref F20

A diverse wildlife treasure trove astride the River Pang, Moor Copse is a haven of peace and beauty so memorable it inspired E. H. Shepard to illustrate *The Wind in the Willows*. The woodland is still home to badger and friends today, and there are wildflower meadows, fascinating fungi and intriguing insects to discover. Beautiful demoiselles and brown hawker dragonflies spend summer hunting along the river, autumn brings dead man's fingers and green elfcup fungi to the woods, and in winter, you may see a fox or stoat.

Rushbeds Wood
Near Bicester, HP18 0RU
OS Map SP 673154;
Map Ref F2

A wonderful ancient woodland of ash, field maple, aspen, hazel and oak trees along with blackthorn, hawthorns, spindles and a few old hornbeams. In April and May, look out for the moschatel plant, otherwise known as

'town hall clock' because of the unusual arrangement of the flower heads. The wood is also excellent for butterflies including purple hairstreaks, purple emperors and black hairstreaks. If you're lucky, you may catch a glimpse of the handsome silver-washed fritillary settling on bramble flowers.

Sydlings Copse
Oxford, OX3 9TY
OS Map SP 559096;
Map Ref F14

Embark on a sensory journey through this secluded wildlife gem, once described as one of the richest habitats in middle England. Boasting ancient

broadleaved woodland, limestone grassland, reedbed, fen, a stream and rare Oxfordshire heathland, the reserve supports more than 400 plant species. This is all on top of linnets, grass snakes, slow worms, solitary wasps, purple hairstreak butterflies and many more wildlife wonders.

CHIMNEY MEADOWS

Near Abingdon, OX18 2EH; **OS Map** SP 354013; **Map Ref** F17

Access/conditions: Flat terrain but bumpy underfoot and boggy in winter. There is a bridge and some gates. Some paths and two hides are suitable for those with limited mobility. Public access to certain areas, including Duxford Old River and the National Nature Reserve, is limited to guided walks only, to protect wildlife.

How to get there: From A420, heading south-west from Oxford, take a right turn signposted Tadpole Bridge and Bampton. Turn right just after Tadpole Bridge. Take the right at the T-junction towards Chimney. Park in designated car park.

Walking time: At least 3 hours.

30-minute visit: Many wildflower-rich meadows are within easy reach of the car park.

Chimney Meadows is a brilliant example of arable restoration. Fields once planted with wheat and barley are now colourful, species-rich wildflower meadows that support as much bird and insect life as they do floral and fungal. Threatened wading birds like curlews breed here, and skylarks and whitethroats fill the air with a unique soundtrack.

Spring and summer see the wildflower meadows at their best. Cowslips spark this burst of new life in spring, and as time progresses, the meadows pass through new colour phases with yellow rattle, common knapweed, ox-eye daisies and pepper-saxifrage adding multi-faceted pigments. In winter, the River Thames floods the meadows and brings an influx of wetland birds, including lapwings, golden plovers and snipe to the marshy grassland.

DANCERSEND WITH PAVIS WOODS

Near Wendover, HP23 6LB; **OS Map** SP 905089; **Map Ref** F15

Access/conditions: Terrain can be bumpy and variable. Some gates and gentle slopes.

How to get there: From Tring, head west on the old A41 (not bypass) towards Aston Clinton. Take a left turn (B4009) signposted to Wendover and take an immediate left for Dancersend. After one mile turn right at the T-junction. Continue to Water Works car park.

Walking time: At least 2 hours.

30-minute visit: Park at the small Water Works car park

then walk up the footpath across the road to enter the reserve.

Dancersend's different types of woodland reflect a chequered history. Most of the original wood was felled during WWII, but in the 1950s two large woods were replanted with mixed trees including beech, ash, cherry and oak. Now maturing, they have stunning displays of flowers throughout the year, including the white hanging bells of Solomon's-seal and the unusual winter-flowering stinking hellebore. Delicate fly orchids and spectacular greater butterfly-orchids grow in the grassy clearings, and you'll find Chiltern gentian and meadow clary in the chalk grassland. Dingy skipper, chalkhill blue, silver-washed fritillary and marbled white butterflies fill the air on sunny summer days. In autumn, the ground erupts with fungi, including the weird-looking collared earthstar.

In 2015, the BBOWT took on the management of Pavis Woods: 86 acres (35ha) of mature beech woodland, scrub and more recently planted woodland lying on the steep scarp facing Dancersend.

GREENHAM AND CROOKHAM COMMONS

Newbury, RG19 8DB; **OS Map** SU 499650; **Map Ref** F22

Access/conditions: Main tracks are level and accessible for those with limited mobility, off-road bikes and off-road mobility scooters. Other waymarked routes cross varying terrain. Keep to main paths during nesting season to protect ground-nesting birds.
How to get there: From A34 take A339 south through Newbury for 2.5 miles. At the roundabout, take first exit onto Greenham Road. Take third exit at next roundabout, still on Greenham Road, then first exit at next roundabout, onto Burys Bank Road. Continue to Control Tower car park.
Walking time: 3 hours.
30-minute visit: Park at Control Tower car park and explore the paths around the wide-open expanse of heathland and grassland ahead of you.

This unforgettable nature reserve is the largest single area of lowland heathland remaining in Berkshire. It also spans ancient woodland,

species-rich grassland, scrub and streams, meaning there is a huge diversity of wildlife to spot.

Weird and wonderful nightjars lie camouflaged on tree branches on the common floor during the day and fill the air with *churrs* as night falls. Woodlarks use lone trees as singing posts and you may be lucky enough to hear the rich and varied song of the nightingale. Keep your eyes peeled for Dartford warblers perched on vibrant yellow gorse bushes.

In summer, the heath comes alive with more than 30 species of butterfly, including the green hairstreak and expertly camouflaged grayling. You could even spot an adder slithering through the vegetation. When conditions are right, Greenham Common is host to a late-summer spectacle as hundreds of autumn lady's-tresses orchids come into flower. The best place to see these beautiful snow-white flowers twirling around soft grey stems is on the short, dry turf 100m east of the Control Tower car park, where they exude a coconut fragrance in the late afternoon.

BOWDOWN WOODS

Newbury, RG19 8DA; **OS Map** SU 505653; **Map Ref** F23

Access/conditions: Conditions are variable across the reserve's three areas. 'Bomb Site': flat, surfaced and accessible for robust mobility scooters and wheelchairs; Bowdown and Baynes: steep slopes and uneven underfoot with steps and boardwalks.
How to get there: Access to the main 'Bomb Site' car park is north of Burys Bank Road as you head east from Greenham towards Thatcham.
Walking time: 2.5 hours.
30-minute visit: From the 'Bomb Site' car park, follow the waymarked Wildlife Walk.

Stretching from the vast heathland at Greenham Common down to the River Kennet, Bowdown Woods forms part of the West Berkshire Living Landscape. The reserve has three distinct areas. The 'Bomb Site' was an ammunition store during WWII and has now been recolonised by birch and oak woodland. Bowdown is a dense ancient woodland giving views across the Kennet

Valley, and Baynes is the most secretive part of the wood, home to sparkling streams and elusive woodcock.

In spring, the woods are awash with bluebells and alive with birdsong, including that of the marsh tit. Listen for the drumming of great spotted woodpeckers and watch out for passing sparrowhawks as they dart through the trees after prey. In summer, more than 30 species of butterfly have been seen here and in the sunny glades of Bowdown in particular, you could spot the spectacular silver-washed fritillary or handsome white admiral. The open heathland is the domain of dragonflies. Giant four-inch-long 'hawker' species hunt for insects along the woodland edge and heathland clearings, and the smaller 'darter' dragonflies wait on perches, ready to pounce on unsuspecting victims. Autumn brings incredible fungi. Look out for the pipe club – spectacular in its strangeness, with long, thin fruiting bodies like breadsticks rising up from the ground – or the rare snakeskin grisette, which has a large yellow cap with blue, felty patches sitting on a stem resembling snakeskin.

COLLEGE LAKE

Tring, HP23 5QG; **OS Map** SP 935139; **Map Ref** F3

Opening hours: Visitor centre and café hours change with the seasons – check the BBOWT website for up-to-date opening hours before visiting.
Access/conditions: 90 per cent of paths are surfaced. Some gates and gentle slopes. Hides are wheelchair accessible. Two mobility tramper vehicles available to borrow – book in advance (01442 826774).
How to get there: By train to Tring station, then a two-mile walk. Buses from Aylesbury run to Tring several times a day. By car, it is two miles from Tring on the B488. After passing the canal bridge at Bulbourne, turn left into a signed entrance.
Walking time: 1.5 hours.
30-minute visit: Head along the southern rim of the quarry to the Marsh Hide for views over the whole reserve.

This transformation from chalk quarry to outstanding wetland nature reserve is a fantastic example of what passionate wildlife lovers can achieve through a shared vision and sheer

determination. The marshland is perhaps the most important of the reserve's homes for wildlife. During summer it supports breeding lapwings and redshanks; common terns nest on specially created islands in the lake; and you may catch a glimpse of hobbies hunting dragonflies. During winter the inhabitants of the water change, and wintering wildfowl such as wigeon and teal use the wetlands for feeding and roosting.

College Lake is also home to a charming chalk grassland, where hares box in spring and butterflies flourish during summer. Small blues and meadow browns twizzle around beautiful cornfield flowers that produce a glorious show of colour every June and July. The rough grassland areas provide a home for breeding skylarks, as well as shelter for small mammals, which in turn feed birds of prey such as kestrels and barn owls. Even winter is full of life, with redwings and fieldfares descending on the woodland, scrub and hedgerows.

WARBURG NATURE RESERVE

Near Henley-on-Thames, RG9 6BJ; **OS Map** SU 721878; **Map Ref** F19

🅿 ⓦⓒ ♿ ℹ ⛺ ♻ 🚶 ➡

Opening hours: Visitor centre open daily, 9am–5pm.
Access/conditions: Variable, mostly steep paths and loose flint as well as a flat grassy path. Bottom valley gets muddy after rain. Mobility vehicle available to hire – contact 01491 642001 or warburg@bbowt.org.uk.
How to get there: By train to Henley. By bus from Henley to Nettlebed, then a one-mile walk. By car it is four miles north-west of Henley-on-Thames. From A4130 turn into Bix Village. Turn left into Rectory Lane, go down the steep hill and turn left at the bottom, signposted Bix Bottom. Continue for about a mile before reaching the car park on the right.
Walking time: 30 minutes.

High up in the Chilterns AONB lies the magnificent Warburg Nature Reserve, rich in exciting plants and animals all through the year. It is the best BBOWT reserve for orchids, and from April–August fly, bird's-nest, narrow-lipped and violet orchids are just a handful of the species found blooming around the site.

But orchids aren't the only draw – in May and June the dawn chorus is second to none, with blackbirds, song thrushes, chiffchaffs and blackcaps vying for attention. There are several rare butterflies to search for too. Oak trees provide food for purple hairstreak caterpillars, while the silver-washed fritillary lays its eggs in bark crevices above violets on the ground below. At dusk, noctule and pipistrelle bats swoop and flutter in pursuit of insect prey. In autumn, an incredible 900 species of fungi speckle the floor beneath the russet canopy above, while in winter, the conifers provide welcome shelter for goldcrests and common crossbills. This is also a great time to spot mammals, with stoats, weasels and deer easier to see as they work hard to survive the lean months.

HERTS AND MIDDLESEX

About the Trust

Herts and Middlesex Wildlife Trust manages nearly 2,000 acres (800ha) of land for wildlife across the region, from rare patches of heathland to wonderful wetlands. Working in partnership with others fighting for a wilder future, the Trust leads countless conservation projects and inspires people to treasure the natural world and take their own action for nature's recovery.

Herts and Middlesex Wildlife Trust
01727 858901
hertswildlifetrust.org.uk

Aldbury Nowers
Tring, HP23 5QW
OS Map SP 951129;
Map Ref F5

Sitting on the Chiltern escarpment overlooking the Tring Gap and Vale of Aylesbury, Aldbury Nowers offers wildlife watching with a view. It's one of the best remaining areas of chalk downland in the county, with a stunning array of flowers flourishing on the warm south-west facing slopes, including clustered bellflower. Keep an eye out for solitary bees and brown argus, grizzled skipper, silver-washed fritillary and small blue butterflies. Dogs aren't permitted in the enclosures.

Thorley Wash
Spellbrook, CM22 7SE
OS Map TL 490181;
Map Ref F6

A reserve filled with birdsong and beautiful flowers. Cuckoos and whitethroats arrive in spring, casting their calls across the grassland. They're soon joined by garden and sedge warblers, whose eager song adds new layers to the unforgettable chorus. Ragged robin, marsh-marigolds, fen bedstraw and meadowsweet thrive in the wet conditions, offering perches to banded demoiselles. The long vegetation is also the perfect place for water voles to hide. They were reintroduced here in 2015.

Hexton Chalk Pit
Hexton, SG5 3JP
OS Map TL 107299;
Map Ref J14

Flower-rich grassland sits alongside an old chalk pit whose bare chalk has been reclaimed by five species of orchid, fine-leaved fescue grasses and slender tare, its delicate pink flowers blooming from July–August. The reserve has an impressive colony of chalkhill blue butterflies, which take to the wing in mid-July, filling the air with fluttering flashes of blue and bronze. If you can bear to look up from the flowers and insects, make sure you stop to take in the views.

Lemsford Springs

Lemsford, AL8 7TN
OS Map TL 222123;
Map Ref F10

Shallow spring-fed lagoons, marshes, willow woodland, hedgerows and meadows that are fantastic for winter birding. Settle into the hides to watch water rails, snipe, jack snipe and green sandpipers feeding on shrimps in the freshwater lagoons, which also support 50 species of water snail. Spring and summer highlights include kingfishers, little egrets, reed buntings and common frogs. The reserve is accessed by a key – contact the Herts and Middlesex Wildlife Trust on 01727 858901.

Old Park Wood

Harefield, UB9 6UX
OS Map TQ 049913;
Map Ref G3

A tranquil retreat tucked away on the edge of a bustling city. Old Park Wood is possibly the most varied patch of woodland in Middlesex, with fantastic wildflower displays in spring. Bluebells, yellow archangel, lesser celandines, wood anemones and rare coralroot bittercress create a spectacular rainbow of purple, yellow and white. Listen out for the *twit-twoo* of tawny owls, which nest in the wood, and the rhythmic drumming of male great spotted woodpeckers marking their territory.

Rye Meads

Hoddesdon, SG12 8JS
OS Map TL 389103;
Map Ref F12

Visitor centre open daily, 9am–5pm.

An ancient flood meadow with reedbeds, marshy grassland and fen. In spring, listen for reeling grasshopper warblers and watch the tumbling display flights of lapwings. In summer, dragonflies take to the air and the fragrance of meadowsweet drifts along the trails. In autumn and winter, green sandpipers drop by to feed, otters are more visible and peregrine falcons hunt over the reserve. Visitors can use the RSPB car park (9am–5pm) for a small fee.

TEWIN ORCHARD AND HOPKYNS WOOD

Tewin, AL6 0LZ; **OS Map** TL 268155; **Map Ref** F7

Access/conditions: Orchard is fairly flat. Woodland is steep in places and not as accessible.
How to get there: Buses run from Hertford and Welwyn Garden City to Upper Green (0.3 miles from reserve). On B1000 from Welwyn Garden City to Hertford turn left through Tewin. Continue to Burnham Green, passing Tewin cricket ground. Immediately after a bend in the road turn right into Tewin Orchard.
Walking time: 1 hour.
30-minute visit: Stroll around the orchard.

Tewin Orchard and Hopkyns Wood is a window into the past, when small village orchards were once common across the UK. Now, they're incredibly rare, but where

they do still stand, orchards like Tewin offer a vital refuge for wildlife. Apple and pear blossoms provide nectar for

insects in spring and summer, while the fruit satisfies hungry redwings, fieldfares and blackbirds when it falls

from the trees in autumn. Yellowhammers, greenfinches, linnets and goldfinches also use the orchard, and deep within the trees you'll find a mammal hide overlooking a sprawling badger sett. The Herts and Middlesex Wildlife Trust hosts badger-watching events here, so be sure to check the website for a night you'll never forget.

Hopkyns Wood has its own unique community of plants and animals. In spring, bluebells and wild garlic thrive in the dappled sunlight cast by shady oak and hornbeam trees. In autumn, weird and wonderful fungi catch your eye.

HERTFORD HEATH AND BALLS WOOD

Hertford, SG13 7PW; **OS Map** TL 351108; **Map Ref** F11

Access/conditions: Hertford Heath's paths are reasonably hard, with some muddy patches in wet weather. Main entrance of Balls Wood is flat and solid when dry, and has disabled parking.

How to get there: Buses run from Hatfield to The College Arms pub. From Hertford Heath village follow London Road (B1197) until The College Arms pub. Turn right into The Roundings. Hertford Heath is signposted in 0.1 miles – use the footpath to walk to the Balls Wood Entrance (0.3 miles).

Walking time: Allow a whole morning or afternoon to immerse yourself in both reserves.

30-minute visit: Park on Roundings Road to visit heathy clearings and pools on the Roundings section of Herford Heath, and to see Balls Wood.

Hertford Heath and Balls Wood are two separate Wildlife Trust nature reserves that sit opposite one another, offering even more opportunities for wildlife walks.

Hertford Heath is one of very few patches of surviving heathland in Hertfordshire and is split into two sections. The Roundings, at the south, is open heathland where reptiles bask among heather, heath

bedstraw, tormentil and gorse. Goldingtons, to the north, is home to coppiced hornbeams and an oak and birch wood.

Balls Wood is a wonderful mixed woodland with two waymarked trails, which guide you through the best parts of the reserve. The wide sunny rides are loved by birds, wildflowers and insects, with gatekeeper, speckled wood and white admiral butterflies luxuriating in the sunlight. The northern section of Balls Wood is a great place to find common spotted-orchids, herb-paris and wild service trees. Unusually, there are a number of ponds in Balls Wood, which are thought to have been created by WWII bombs – now a vital refuge for frogs, toads and newts.

KING'S MEADS

Ware, SG12 9XD; **OS Map** TL 349136; **Map Ref** F8

Access/conditions: Mostly flat grass paths that can be muddy in wet weather. Steep chalk bank in the southern section.
How to get there: Train to Ware station then walk 500m via Broadmeads Road. Buses stop at Hertford Regional College, 300m from the reserve. By car, park in Broadmeads car park (accessed from Amwell End Road) near Ware railway station, or Burgage Lane car park (accessed from Ware High Street – A1170).
Walking time: 2 hours.
30-minute visit: Walk along the towpath and stroll across the meadows to the main pool at Chadwell Springs.

Stretching from Hertford to Ware, King's Meads is one of the largest water meadows in Hertfordshire, crossed by waterways offering homes for 369 species of wildflower and 120 species of bird.

King's Meads is famous for its dragonflies and damselflies, with 21 of 27 species now found in Hertfordshire recorded hunting or breeding here. As well as more common but no less beautiful species like emperor dragonflies and banded demoiselles, you could see rare Norfolk hawker and southern migrant hawker dragonflies. There are countless birds too. Pochards, wigeon and gadwall flock here in winter and sedge and reed warblers breed during summer, singing from low in the reedbed. This is to say nothing of the ghostly barn owls, secretive grass snakes, chirping crickets and grasshoppers, aerobatic bats, and many other marvels of the Meads!

TRING RESERVOIRS

Tring, HP23 4PA; **OS Map** SP 904134; **Map Ref** F4

Access/conditions: Very steep steps from car park to top of the reservoir banks. Wear warm clothing as the reservoirs are exposed to the elements.
How to get there: Bus from Tring/Aylesbury stops at Crossroads, Tringford Road, then 0.9 miles to Wilstone and 0.4 miles to Startop's End. By car from Tring, take Tringford Road towards Long Marston. At the mini roundabout with B489, turn left for Wilstone Reservoir car park (0.9 miles) or right for Startop's End car park for access to Startop's End, Marsworth and Tringford Reservoir (0.3 miles).
Walking time: Allow 5 hours to explore all four reservoirs.
30-minute visit: Park at Wilstone Reservoir car park and see what you can see from the banks or walk along to the hide.

Tring Reservoirs nature reserve is made up of four individual reservoirs: Startop's End, Marsworth and Tringford reservoirs are all close together and Wilstone reservoir is just to the west. Together, they make up one of the best birdwatching spots in the south of England.

In winter, all four reservoirs become a stronghold for tufted ducks, pochards, teal, gadwall, wigeon and shovelers looking for a safe place to rest and refuel. If it's really cold you may even spot the occasional goldeneye, goosander or smew. Between December and February, Marsworth Reservoir is a great place to see overwintering bitterns that hide away in the reedbed.

Wilstone Reservoir boasts the rare plant mudwort, which you can see on the mudflats during autumn as the waters recede. In summer you can watch common terns raising their young on the tern rafts installed by the Herts and Middlesex Wildlife Trust, and don't forget your binoculars,

as Wilstone is also home to a fantastic heronry.

If you visit the reservoirs during late spring then you may spot a hobby hunting over the water, or hear a

cuckoo calling from the back of the reedbed at Wilstone or Marsworth. This is also the best place to listen for the reed and sedge warblers that breed deep within the reeds.

AMWELL

Ware, SG12 9SS; **OS Map** TL 376127; **Map Ref** F9

Access/conditions: Solid, steady paths when dry. Park on Amwell Lane and access the reserve along the track (very uneven), over the railway line to the main viewpoint. There is

also parking in a layby on Hollycross Road.
How to get there: Train to St Margaret's then walk 0.75 miles. Bus from Hertford stops at St Margaret's train station; reserve is 0.75 miles

from here. By car, from St Margaret's, just before the railway, turn left onto Amwell Lane. In 0.5 miles look out for the entrance sign on the reserve gate.
Walking time: 2 hours.

30-minute visit: Follow the track down to the viewpoint for a superb view of the reserve.

Amwell nature reserve is a haven for both wildlife and people. It forms part of the Lee Valley, which connects the site with other nature reserves and habitats along the River Lee, creating a wildlife corridor stretching from Hertford to the Thames.

In summer, Amwell is best known for its dragonflies. It is home to 21 species of dragonfly and damselfly and has its very own Dragonfly Trail (usually open from May–September), which gives you the best chance of seeing red-eyed damselflies, ruddy darters and more up close. However, winter is when Amwell really shines. Visit the viewpoint overlooking Great Hardmead Lake to see the spectacle of hundreds of wintering gulls flying in to roost in screeching, cawing groups. These are mostly black-headed and lesser black-backed gulls, but they're sometimes joined by more unusual Caspian and yellow-legged gulls. Large groups of gadwalls and shovelers also arrive on the lake in winter, sometimes joined by the odd smew.

Don't forget to drop by the Bittern Pool to spot another winter visitor, the bittern. They'll often sneak across the ride in front of the James Hide, where you can also watch garden birds, reed buntings and the occasional marsh tit filling up at the bird feeding station.

STOCKER'S LAKE

Rickmansworth, WD3 1NB; **OS Map** TQ 049939; **Map Ref** G2

Access/conditions: Good non-paved paths.
How to get there: Train to Rickmansworth, then a one-mile walk. Buses from Harefield and Rickmansworth stop at Tesco, 0.5 miles from the reserve. By car, head north from Harefield on Rickmansworth/Harefield Road. Turn left after one mile, then left after another mile onto Frogmore Lane. Park in Aquadrome car park.
Walking time: 1.5 hours.
30-minute visit: Turn left out of the Aquadrome car park, pass Bury Lake and the café on your right and continue to Stocker's Lake (0.2 miles on the right). Spend time seeing what you can spot on the lake before returning.

Get away from it all at this sparkling lake in the beautiful Colne Valley. It is one of the oldest gravel pits in the area, but what was once a bustling industrial hub is now a tranquil place to escape the hustle

and bustle. Stocker's Lake is nationally important for the huge groups of wintering birds that arrive to spend the winter each year. Goldeneyes, shovelers, wigeons and even smews seek refuge on the water, while bitterns hide in the reeds and siskins and redpolls rove through the trees.

Not all of the action happens in winter though. More than 60 species of breeding bird have been recorded here – including chiffchaffs and Cetti's warblers – and the heronry is the largest in the county. Mid-May is the best time to watch the young herons taking their flying lessons. In summer, the surrounding meadows are in full flower and attract countless insects. This is also the time when dragonflies fall prey to hobbies: agile falcons with a taste for swallows and martins too.

LONDON

About the Trust

London Wildlife Trust's vision is for a city alive with nature, where everyone can experience and enjoy wildlife. The Trust is protecting, restoring and creating wild places for nature; engaging, inspiring and enabling people to connect with nature; and championing, challenging and influencing people to stand up for nature.

London Wildlife Trust
020 7261 0447
wildlondon.org.uk

Bramley Bank

Croydon, CR2 7LG
OS Map TQ 353633;
Map Ref G13

A wonderful mix of enchanting oak wood, pretty heathland and peaceful grassland where you could see nuthatches, song thrushes and lesser spotted woodpeckers; purple hairstreaks, stag beetles and yellow meadow ants; common dog-violets, bluebells and heathers. The reserve also boasts the largest woodland pond in Croydon.

Crane Park Island

Whitton, TW2 6AA
OS Map TQ 128717;
Map Ref G11

It's hard to believe that this wonderful wetland was once a hub for gunpowder production. Now, treecreepers, kingfishers and water voles live above the water, while fish – including sticklebacks, minnows and

bullheads – thrive below. There is a wonderful nature trail and fantastic family events throughout the year.

Frays Farm Meadows

Hillingdon, UB9 4NA
OS Map TQ 058860;
Map Ref G5

Frays Farm Meadows borders another London Wildlife Trust reserve, Denham Lock Wood, to provide refuge for some of London's most threatened species. Look out for snipe and lapwings; banded demoiselles and water voles; slow worms and grass snakes. Ragged robin and marsh-marigolds add stunning splashes of pink and yellow.

Denham Lock Wood

Hillingdon, UB9 4NA
OS Map TQ 054863;
Map Ref G6

This wonderful wet woodland and fen is home to unusual species like pygmy shrews

and glow-worms as well as little egrets, great spotted woodpeckers and bank voles. Meadowsweet scents the air in summer and guelder roses feed birds with plump red berries in autumn.

Braeburn Park

Crayford, DA1 3RG
OS Map TQ 569720;
Map Ref G10

A thriving oasis, home to green woodpeckers and unusual insects. The south-facing banks are great places to watch reptiles basking and ivy bees returning to their nest holes on sunny days. Blackcaps and lesser whitethroats arrive in spring, while pyramidal orchids bloom in summer.

Gunnersbury Triangle

Chiswick, W4 5LN
OS Map TQ 201786;
Map Ref G9

A green oasis created by intersecting railway lines,

saved from development and managed for wildlife and people. Birds and small mammals take advantage of the sheltered birch and willow, while walkways and footpaths guide visitors around this wild retreat.

Totteridge Fields
Barnet, NW7 4HR
OS Map TQ 223940;
Map Ref G1

A leafy patch of traditional London countryside. Spring and summer walks are a riot of colour, birdsong and buzzing insects. The ancient hay meadows are criss-crossed by old hawthorn and blackthorn hedgerows that shelter whitethroats, bullfinches and long-tailed tits. Stoats bound through the grassland and noctule bats hunt above as night falls.

HUTCHINSON'S BANK
Croydon, CR0 0LD; **OS Map** TQ 381616; **Map Ref** G14

Access/conditions: Footpaths are sometimes steep and stepped. There are occasional benches.
How to get there: Enter from Featherbed Lane, Farleigh Dean Crescent or the Croydon Tramlink terminus at New Addington, which is a short walk away via a footpath leading from North Downs Road to Featherbed Lane. Very limited parking at the bottom of Farleigh Dean Crescent or in North Downs Way in New Addington.

Walking time: 45 minutes to 1 hour.
30-minute visit: The nature trail can be cut at several points.

A secluded chalk grassland and woodland adored by butterfly lovers, orchid fanatics and wildflower fans alike. Pyramidal orchids, common spotted-orchids and common twayblades fill the grassland in summer, adding brilliant layers of colour alongside kidney vetch: the sole foodplant of the rare small blue butterfly.

But this isn't the only beautiful butterfly to look out for – dingy skippers, green hairstreaks and dark green fritillaries feed here too. In spring, bluebells and wild garlic bloom beneath the whitebeam, cherry and hazel canopy of the spectacular ancient woodland until yellow archangel takes over in summer. Common lizards and slow worms bask on the exposed chalk banks and secretive badgers wait until nightfall to snuffle around the reserve on the hunt for food.

SYDENHAM HILL WOOD

Sydenham Hill, SE26 6LS; **OS Map** TQ 344725; **Map Ref** G12

Access/conditions: Uneven paths and lots of steps.
How to get there: Entrance at Crescent Wood Road. Buses stop along Sydenham Hill or near Cox's Walk entrance on London Road. By train, Sydenham Hill station is a five-minute walk from the entrance. By car, park in Crescent Wood Road.
Walking time: 1 hour.
30-minute visit: Explore some of the nature trail or just find a quiet place to sit and enjoy the sights and sounds.

Sydenham Hill Wood forms part of the largest remaining tract of the old Great North Wood. Though smaller than in its heyday, it certainly isn't short of wildlife – there are an incredible 200 species of trees and plants alone, plus rare fungi, insects, birds and mammals.

Old oaks and hornbeams mix with Victorian garden survivors and more recently planted trees to create a range of different habitats. Tawny owls and kestrels nest in the old tree holes, firecrests hop through the branches and stag beetles thrive among the pieces of rotting wood, which their larvae munch on as they grow. The sunny glades attract green woodpeckers and butterflies, including brown argus, speckled woods and commas. Bluebells, common dog-violets and wood anemones grow on the woodland floor – keep to the paths so they don't get trampled.

CAMLEY STREET NATURAL PARK

London, N1C 4PW; **OS Map** TQ 299834; **Map Ref** G8

Opening hours: Visitor centre open 10.30am–5pm summer; 10.30am–4pm winter.
Access/conditions: Accessible surfaces around the visitor centre and main path to the pond-dipping platform. Other paths surfaced in woodchip. Steep steps with handrails at the southern end of the reserve lead to a canal viewpoint.
How to get there: By tube or train to King's Cross, then a 10-minute walk. Bus to King's Cross or Pancras Road. No car park.

Walking time: A walk only takes around 20 minutes, but linger longer to enjoy the peace and wildlife.

This unique urban nature reserve offers relief from the bustling streets around King's Cross and St Pancras. As you explore the woodland, grassland, ponds and reedbed you'll soon forget that you're right in the centre of London.

Nature rolls through its glorious seasons unhindered by the urban backdrop. In spring, frogspawn fills the ponds, reed warblers sing from the reedbed and bright yellow flag irises blaze in the marsh. Summer brings a surge of bees and butterflies flitting among the grasses and meadow flowers including stunning snake's-head fritillaries. Autumn arrives in a riot of berries, which feed blackbirds and visiting redwings and fieldfares. Then, of course, there are the fungi: from wobbly jelly ear to subtly beautiful turkeytail. On a midwinter's day, stand at the top of the reserve and look out through the gentle architecture of trees to the city beyond.

Before you leave, pop into the visitor centre to hear more about the reserve's amazing floating reedbeds, which don't just provide homes for birds, fish and invertebrates, but also clean the water and help prevent canal pollution.

WOODBERRY WETLANDS

London, N16 5HQ; **OS Map** TQ 350893; **Map Ref** G7

Opening hours: Visitor centre open 9am–4.30pm summer; 9am–4pm winter.
Access/conditions: Level access with a wheelchair-accessible path. Disabled parking bays outside each entrance.
How to get there: Entrances on New River Path from Lordship Road and on Newnton Close. Manor House underground station (Piccadilly line) is a five-minute walk from the west entrance; Stamford Hill station is a five-minute walk from the northern entrance. Buses stop in Seven Sisters Road.
Walking time: Around 30 minutes.

Woodberry Wetlands was opened by Sir David Attenborough in 2016, the Stoke Newington East Reservoir given a new lease of life. This metamorphosis began when London Wildlife Trust proposed to enrich the reservoir for wildlife and to give people access to vital green space in the urban

sprawl. Now, Woodberry Wetlands is a thriving retreat for migratory birds and a haven for insects. Reed warblers and Cetti's warblers arrive to breed in spring, joined later by hungry swifts and swallows that snatch insects from above the water. Hedgerows and wildflowers line the grassy banks, offering food to holly blue butterflies and perches to red-eyed damselflies. The reedbed is perfect shelter for all kinds of waterbirds – especially winter ducks – with gadwall, shovelers, shelducks and tufted ducks feeding among the stems. You may also spot a kingfisher perched on a reed-top or hear the squeal of a water rail from within the vegetation.

Pop into the Coal House Café and take a drink onto the terrace for the best views over the reserve.

WALTHAMSTOW WETLANDS

Walthamstow, N17 9NH; **OS Map** TQ 350893; **Map Ref** G4

Opening hours: 9.30am–5pm summer, 9.30am–4pm winter. Last entry 3.30pm on weekends and bank holidays. Open every day except Christmas Day and Boxing Day.
Access/conditions: Visitor centre is fully accessible. Unpaved paths can be muddy after wet weather.
How to get there: Main entrance (Ferry Lane/Forest Road) is a 10-minute walk from Tottenham Hale and Blackhorse Road stations (Victoria Line) and served by buses. (Further information on bus routes and numbers can be found at the Transport for London website.) There is also an entrance at Coppermill Lane next to Walthamstow Marshes, and one at Lockwood Way, off Blackhorse Lane.
Walking time: 1 hour.
30-minute visit: Wander around the reservoir and see what birds you can spot, then enjoy a coffee in the Victorian-era Engine House visitor centre and café.

In the Lee Valley a cluster of 10 reservoirs has been transformed into Europe's largest urban wetland reserve: Walthamstow Wetlands. As well as providing drinking water for London, the reserve is internationally important for migrating birds in desperate need of somewhere to rest and feed, particularly in winter. The plunging temperature brings gadwall, shovelers, tufted ducks, grey herons and cormorants in their droves. New reedbeds have even attracted bitterns.

The reedbeds also provide shelter for fish. Brown and rainbow trout, bream and perch swim among the stems alongside smaller fish, which fall prey to waiting kingfishers and little egrets. In summer, dragons emerge: southern hawkers and common hawkers perch on the vegetation before darting after prey.

But the reservoirs themselves aren't the only wildlife havens. London Wildlife Trust is installing bat boxes, bird nest boxes and bird feeding stations to attract even more wildlife. The dense scrub-lined banks are perfect for small birds and hedgehogs, while in summer, the wide-open skies fill with swifts, eager to take advantage of the bounty of flies. Peregrine falcons are year-round visitors, so keep your eyes to the skies and you may just spot one!

SURREY

Chinthurst Hill

Wonersh Common, GU5 0PR
OS Map TQ 014458;
Map Ref G21

A steep hillside woodland with a folly and heart-swelling views at its summit. Look out for buzzards and red kites soaring above, and sparrowhawks streaking through the wood. Wood sorrel, yellow archangel and butcher's broom grow on the woodland floor while ringlet, meadow brown and brimstone butterflies dance around the plants. Watch bats hunting on summer evenings.

Cucknell's Wood

Cranleigh, GU5 0ST
OS Map TQ 041430;
Map Ref G23

A 400-year-old wildlife haven where white clusters of wild garlic and glorious carpets of bluebells emerge in spring. Marsh-marigolds grow near two short bridges and April sees the flowering of early purple orchids. The wood's most secretive residents are dormice and woodcock, but thankfully, the treecreepers, lesser spotted woodpeckers and willow tits are much more accommodating.

Priest Hill

Epsom, KT17 3BZ
OS Map TQ 230615;
Map Ref G17

Abandoned playing fields transformed into a home for wildlife. Conservation grazing and green hay spreading has returned kidney vetch, yellow rattle and wild thyme to the chalk grassland. As a result, insects thrive, and the rare small blue butterfly has been recorded here. As well as the grassland there are three ponds – perfect for dragonflies and amphibians.

Sheepleas

East Horsley, Surrey
OS Map TQ 090515;
Map Ref G20

A mosaic of ancient woodland, chalk grassland and extraordinary wildflower displays in Cowslip Meadow – Surrey's 'Coronation Meadow'. More than 30 species of butterfly include the brown argus, silver-washed fritillary and purple emperor. Hazel coppicing is improving the reserve for dormice as well as encouraging more plants to thrive – look out for fly, greater butterfly and chalk fragrant orchids. July brings the sweet scent of wild marjoram and dreamy blue hue of harebells.

Thundry Meadows
Elstead, GU8 6LE
OS Map SU 895441;
Map Ref G22

These special water meadows are grazed by belted Galloway cattle, whose selective munching is helping harvest mice to thrive. Grass snakes and common lizards use the reserve as a winter refuge, while devil's-bit scabious offers important late-summer nectar. Thundry's most remarkable habitat lies near the reserve entrance: one of the few examples of quaking mire in Surrey. This is a mat of vegetation floating in liquid peat, which is home to bogbean, marsh cinquefoil and raft spiders.

BRENTMOOR HEATH AND FOLLY BOG
Woking, GU24 9PY; **OS Map** SU 936610; **Map Ref** G16

Access/conditions: Not suitable for wheelchair users or those with limited mobility.
How to get there: Open access via several public footpaths running off the A322 Guildford/Bagshot Road, near West End. By car, use the car park off Red Road.
Walking time: 45 minutes to 1 hour.
30-minute visit: From the car park, follow the public footpath around New England Hill.

A patchwork of different habitats that brim with life. The dry heath is blanketed in ling heather that transforms the ground into a vibrant pink carpet when the flowers bloom in late summer. The wet areas harbour teeny-tiny carnivores: insect-eating plants called sundews, which trap prey with a sticky dew that clings to their filaments. Cotton-grass, white beak sedge and cross-leaved heath also grows here, adding layers of texture and colour.

But plants aren't the only draw. This reserve is a haven for reptiles with grass snakes, common lizards, slow worms and adders all found here. Dartford warblers breed in the gorse bushes, woodlarks sing from the trees and hobbies drop by to hunt dragonflies.

NORBURY PARK
Dorking, KT22 9DX; **OS Map** TQ 158538; **Map Ref** G19

Access/conditions:
Public access managed by Surrey County Council. Not suitable for wheelchair users or those with limited mobility.
How to get there: Fetcham and Young Street car parks located off the A246. Crabtree car park situated off Crabtree Lane in Westhumble.
Walking time: Self-guided trail from Young Street car park takes about 1.5 hours.
30-minute visit: Park at Fetcham car park and follow the circuit of tracks around the woodland.

A varied natural landscape with grassland, farmland, and woodland harbouring some yew trees almost 3,000 years old. Surrey Wildlife Trust manages the woodland by coppicing the hazel and sweet chestnut trees, which provides vital habitat for rare

hazel dormice and encourages beautiful spring flowers to thrive in the resulting sunny patches.

There is so much wildlife to see, including all three species of woodpecker. The veteran trees harbour roosting long-eared bats and the chalk grassland nurtures a wide variety of butterflies, with more than 40 species of flowering plants. Skylarks nest in the fields of the park's three farms, while linnets, yellowhammers and hedgehogs shelter and forage in the hedges.

CHOBHAM COMMON

Chobham, KT16 0ED; **OS Map** SU 974648; **Map Ref** G15

Access/conditions: During summer a hard track is available from Longcross car park for suitable mobility vehicles.
How to get there: Use one of six car parks serving the common.
Walking time: 2 hours.
30-minute visit: Follow the green waymarked route from Staple Hill car park, but cut across from Point Five back to the car park for a shorter walk.

Chobham Common isn't just beautiful, it's formidable. Its sprawling 1,400 acres (560ha) make it the largest National Nature Reserve in the south-east of England, while its stunning heathland is one of the finest remaining examples of lowland heath in the whole world. Originally created by prehistoric farmers, this stunning open countryside was carefully managed by rural communities for more than 200 generations, creating a wonderfully wild patchwork of mini habitats.

Bring your binoculars and see how many of the 100 different bird species you can spot. From the stunning Dartford warbler and bizarre nightjar to stonechats, cuckoos and hobbies, the trees, air and ground seem constantly alive with movement and song. If flowers are more your thing there are more than 300 species to go at! Sweeps of purple heather and sweet-scented gorse bloom on the heath, while sundews and rare marsh gentian thrive in the wetlands. Look out for orchids around the heathland verges in summer.

If that wasn't enough you could spot adders, grass snakes, common lizards, sand lizards and slow worms, as well as countless insects. Spiders, ladybirds, bees, wasps – Chobham Common has it all, including the rare silver-studded blue butterfly, 22 types of dragonfly and glistening green tiger beetles.

WISLEY AND OCKHAM COMMONS AND CHATLEY HEATH

Wisley, KT11 1NR/GU23 6QA; **OS Map** TQ 080590; **Map Ref** G18

Access/conditions: Soft, sandy surfaces with some steep slopes. Not suitable for wheelchair users or those with limited mobility.
How to get there: Reserve is off the main London to Portsmouth road (A3), south of J10 of M25. Park at Boldermere Car Park, Pond Car Park or Wren's Nest Car Park.
Walking time: 1 hour.
30-minute visit: Follow the blue sailor waymarkers from Boldermere Car Park up to the tower and back.

More than 800 acres (320ha) of heathland and woodland right by the side of the M25. Surrey has lost 85 per cent of its heaths in the last 200 years, but this precious fragment is in good hands. The Surrey Wildlife Trust uses grazing cattle to keep the harsher vegetation in check and clears some of the birch and pine trees to make way for more purple heather, and to expand the heath. The reserve is renowned for dragonflies and damselflies, with 20 species – including emperor and southern hawker – recorded here. Then there are the birds, with iconic species including Dartford warblers, hobbies and nightjars either breeding or feeding here. The wetter ground harbours round-leaved sundew, while drier areas are patrolled by green tiger beetles – watch out for them soaking up the sunshine on the sand or speeding after prey.

Make sure you visit the Semaphore Tower on Chatley Heath before you leave this wild refuge. Built in 1822, it was once part of a chain that was used to pass messages between the Admiralty in Whitehall and the Royal Naval Dockyard in Portsmouth.

KENT

About the Trust

Kent Wildlife Trust has been protecting wild places, helping wildlife thrive and inspiring people to connect with nature since 1958. It cares for 80 nature reserves and more than 55 miles of roadside reserves, influences decision-makers, and works with the local community to make Kent's towns, cities, countryside and coast wilder.

Kent Wildlife Trust
01622 662012
kentwildlifetrust.org.uk

East Blean Wood

Canterbury, CT3 4JS
OS Map TR 194642;
Map Ref G25

Lying between Canterbury and the sea, East Blean Wood is one of Kent's richest woods. Rare heath fritillary butterflies feed on cow-wheat in the sunny glades and wide rides. Carpets of bluebells appear under coppiced trees in spring and woodpeckers nest in the trunks of old oaks. Visit on spring evenings to hear a sweet nightingale serenade.

Lydden Temple Ewell – The James Teacher Reserve

Temple Ewell, CT16 3DE
OS Map TR 287444;
Map Ref G31

A sight to behold, these chalk downland slopes are decorated with early spider, twayblade, autumn lady's-tresses, fragrant, pyramidal and bee orchids through spring and summer. Marbled white, silver-spotted skipper, Adonis blue and chalkhill blue butterflies erupt from the grass as you walk. Keep an eye out for the wart-biter cricket: a flightless cricket the size of your thumb! Car park behind George and Dragon pub.

Queendown Warren

Hartlip, ME9 7XH
OS Map TQ 827629;
Map Ref G28

Chalk grassland, open pasture and woodland where you can admire 10 species of orchid, including the fantastic lizard orchid. Countless other plants nurture butterflies such as the Adonis blue, which was reintroduced here in 2002. Adders bask in woodland glades and buzzards call overhead. As dusk approaches, barn owls float silently over the grassland.

Romney Marsh Visitor Centre and Nature Reserve

New Romney, TN28 8AY
OS Map TR 078261;
Map Ref G32

Visitor centre open 11am–3pm, Wednesday–Sunday.

Dune grassland and ponds are home to great crested newts and great silver water beetles – both under threat in the UK. Dragonflies and damselflies fill the air with colour and three exciting reptiles can be found: grass snakes, slow worms and common lizards. Keep an eye out for tree sparrows as you stroll around the gardens of the eco-friendly visitor centre, where you'll also find a reconstructed Looker's Hut.

SEVENOAKS WILDLIFE RESERVE AND JEFFERY HARRISON VISITOR CENTRE

Sevenoaks, TN13 3DH; **OS Map** TQ 521563; **Map Ref** G30

Opening hours: 10.30am– 3.30pm, Thursday–Sunday, (Tuesday–Sunday from June). **Access/conditions:** Visitor centre, three hides and most of the trails are wheelchair accessible.
How to get there: Train to Bat & Ball, then a 20-minute walk. Buses from Gravesend and Tunbridge Wells stop at Knole Academy, next to the reserve. By car, take M25 towards Sevenoaks/Hastings. Exit at J5 onto A25 towards Sevenoaks/ Riverhead and follow this road for just under two miles before turning left. Drive straight to reach the car park.
Walking time: 3 hours.

30-minute visit: Grab a brew from the café and walk to Tyler Hide to watch waders loafing on the islands.

Sevenoaks is a piece of conservation history – the first example of a former gravel pit being transformed by nature conservation. More than 2,000 species have been recorded so far, with more being added to the list every year. With woodland, ponds, reedbeds, grassland and five lakes to take advantage of, it's little surprise that Sevenoaks is such a wildlife hotspot.

Dragonflies and damselflies hunt over the water and

reed buntings and reed warblers breed in the reedbed. The lakes are brilliant places to count teal and shovelers in winter, while in summer, they're visited by green and common sandpipers, greenshanks, lapwings and little-ringed plovers.

It's easy to overlook the trees and scrub with so much activity on the water, but with quiet patience you could spot chiffchaffs, blackcaps, bullfinches and all three species of woodpecker. Siskins and redpolls descend on the alder trees in winter, tweezing seeds from the cones.

TYLAND BARN VISITOR CENTRE AND NATURE PARK

Sandling, ME14 3BD; **OS Map** TQ 754593; **Map Ref** G29

Opening hours: Check the Kent Wildlife Trust website for up-to-date opening hours before visiting.

Access/conditions: Wheelchair accessible with all-surface path around the wildlife garden, and accessible

platform at the ponds.
How to get there: Trains run to Maidstone East station. Bus from Maidstone/Chatham

stops at Cobtree Golf Course, close to the reserve. By car, follow 'brown badger' signs on the Maidstone to Chatham Bluebell Hill Road (A229) between M2 (J3) and M20 (J6).

Walking time: Exploring the nature trail takes less than 30 minutes, but allow time to sit and relax by the ponds and head into the visitor centre.

The Nature Park at Tyland Barn is a fantastic way to experience the wonders of the Kentish countryside. It was created to be a 'little Kent' and now has woodlands, colourful wildflower meadows and a large pond full of life. Wheelchair and pushchair-accessible paths guide you through a peaceful retreat where you could spot spectacular orchids in the grass, powerful stag beetles in the log piles and dragonflies flitting over the ponds. Brightly coloured wasp spiders cling to webs strung between the vegetation and shy adders bask in sunny patches, slithering into secret shelters when they feel your footsteps approaching. Tread lightly and you might catch a glimpse of one!

The area around the Barn itself is an inspirational wildlife garden, offering ideas for your own outdoor space. There are logs to peer under, compost heaps to delve into and bug hotels buzzing with solitary bees to enchant visitors of all ages.

OARE MARSHES

Oare, ME13 0QD; **OS Map** TR 013647; **Map Ref** G24

Access/conditions: Level, surfaced footpath and RADAR gates. Some paths muddy in wet weather.
How to get there: Train to Faversham. Bus from Faversham and Ashford stops in Oare village. By car, from A2 just west of Faversham follow signs to Oare and turn right to 'Harty Ferry' at Three Mariners pub. Park at the end of the road and continue to the bank of the Swale Estuary.
Walking time: 2 hours.

30-minute visit: Look out over the sea or mudflats (tide dependent) from the sea wall near the car park.

A refuge for birds so important it is renowned across the world. Whether on migration, spending the winter or settling down to breed, the birds that arrive at Oare Marshes find a safe refuge.

As well as being one of the last few grazing marshes left in Kent, the reserve boasts freshwater dykes, open water scrapes, reedbeds and saltmarsh, providing homes for fantastically diverse birdlife. Brent geese, dunlins, curlews and wigeons flock here to fill up on salty sea grasses and nutritious mud-dwelling invertebrates in winter. They're joined by merlins, hen harriers, short-eared owls and sometimes bitterns. In summer, the reedbeds are alive with reed buntings, warblers and bearded tits singing beautifully and raising

feathered families. But songbirds aren't the only breeding birds – avocets, redshanks, snipe, lapwings and water rails breed here too.

While the birdlife is incredible, don't underestimate Oare Marshes' other wildlife. Sea clover, spiny restharrow, sea lavender and golden samphire add splashes of colour, competing with the bright flashes of passing dragonflies. Don't forget to scan the sandbanks for snoozing seals.

SANDWICH AND PEGWELL BAY

Ramsgate, CT12 5JB; **OS Map** TR 341632; **Map Ref** G26

Access/conditions: Circular solid path around Pegwell Bay sea wall. Sandy unsurfaced paths at Sandwich Bay.
How to get there: Bus stops at The Sportsman. Trains run to Sandwich town. By car, Pegwell Bay car park is on the north side of the Stour on the A256 and is well signposted. Sandwich Bay has a toll gate.
Walking time: At least 1 hour.
30-minute visit: Walk down to enjoy the view over the sea or mudflats (tide dependent).

A magical mosaic of habitats (including Kent's only ancient dune pasture) where rare plants and animals wait to cast a spell over all who visit. Nightingales stop by on their spring migration, bewitching visitors with their melodious song. Cuckoos signal their territories from the treetops and warblers create a lyrical chorus that will stop you in your tracks. In summer, ringed plovers nest on the shingle beach and butterflies flit around duneland flowers

including lizard orchids and sea holly.

Autumn brings an influx of waders and wildfowl on its chilly winds, including sanderlings and grey plovers desperate to rest after their long migrations. Winter is the best time to see seals – you can watch them from the end of Stonelees after walking through Pegwell Bay Country Park. You might even be lucky enough to catch the odd winter waxwing that comes to feed on juicy berries.

WEST BLEAN AND THORNDEN WOODS

Canterbury, CT6 7NZ; **OS Map** TR 143632; **Map Ref** G27

Access/conditions: Level paths from the car park, including a two-mile hard track running the length of the reserve.

How to get there: From Whitstable, get onto A2990 until Millstrood Road roundabout. Take first exit then right onto South Street. Turn right onto Radfall Hill then left onto Thornden Wood Road after around 1.5 miles. Drive until you reach the car park (on the right).

Walking time: Five waymarked trails offer at least 2 hours of adventure time.

30-minute visit: Take a brisk walk along the one-mile all-weather circular walk.

An ever-changing ancient woodland almost 1,000 years old. Before Kent Wildlife Trust bought the wood it was managed for commercial timber production, with plantations of non-native conifer trees. Now, the Trust is removing the pines and regenerating the woodland with help from coppicing: a traditional management technique that is great for sensitive wildlife. As well as creating sunny glades perfect for sun-loving plants and heath fritillary butterflies, as the trees regenerate, they form a thicket, which is perfect cover for hazel dormice and nightingales.

Thankfully there are still mature oaks and veteran trees thriving in the wood, with carpets of bluebells decorating the base of their trunks in spring. Lesser spotted woodpeckers bore into the wood to perfect their nest-holes, tawny owls perch sleepily on inconspicuous branches and bats roost behind the bark until nightfall. Why not challenge yourself to find the rare wild service trees?

SUSSEX

Amberley Wildbrooks
Amberley, BN18 9NT
OS Map TQ 030136;
Map Ref G39

Bewick's swans take refuge here during winter; lapwings display and snipe drum during spring; and hobbies hunt dragonflies over the ditches in summer. Access is restricted to the Wey South Path, which runs through the middle of the brooks from Hog Lane in Amberley.

Burton and Chingford Ponds
Duncton, GU28 0JR
OS Map SU 978180;
Map Ref G38

Start at the Mill and follow the circular trail to experience the best of this reserve. Lesser spotted woodpeckers, kingfishers and blackcaps are birding highlights, while

golden-ringed and emperor dragonflies can also be seen. Rarities include the recently reintroduced field cricket, and cowbane, a poisonous member of the carrot family not found anywhere else in Sussex.

Eridge Rocks
Eridge Green, TN3 9JW
OS Map TQ 554355;
Map Ref G33

The going is flat at Eridge Rocks, with no stiles or gates. Cretaceous sandstone outcrops are home to rare mosses, liverworts and ferns. In winter, impressive icicles form as water escapes through the porous rock. Monolithic veteran trees attract wasp beetles, while the wider rides and coppiced areas encourage silver-washed fritillary and white admiral butterflies. Adders bask among the bracken.

Iping and Stedham Commons
Stedham, GU29 0PB
OS Map SU 852219;
Map Ref G37

A heathland as rich in atmosphere as it is in wildlife. See heath sand wasps, black darter dragonflies, heath tiger beetles and minotaur beetles as well as woodlarks, nightjars and Dartford warblers. Summer is the peak time to see carpets of purple heather in bloom.

Levin Down
Charlton, PO18 0HU
OS Map SU 887130;
Map Ref G40

You'll find butterflies aplenty at this chalk grassland: brown hairstreak, green hairstreak and chalkhill blue being highlights. The wildflowers are dizzying, including clustered bellflower, pyramidal orchids and harebells.

Yellowhammers, garden warblers and hazel dormice are also here. There's an uphill climb to enter Levin Down, with stiles at each entrance.

The Mens
Billingshurst, RH14 0HR
OS Map TQ 023236;
Map Ref G36

A 395-acre (160ha) ancient woodland with an untamed, mysterious atmosphere. Towering cathedrals of beech grow alongside veteran oaks, spindle and midland hawthorn. Fungal highlights include horn of plenty, magpie inkcap and white saddle. In Badlands Meadow you can see zigzag clover, dyer's greenweed and devil's-bit scabious.

Woods Mill
Henfield, BN5 9SD
OS Map TQ 218137;
Map Ref G41

This flagship environmental education reserve offers an unmissable spring/summer highlight: the fantastic song of the nightingale. Woodpeckers, barn owls and gently purring turtle doves live here, and you'll find dragonflies in abundance around the lake. If you're lucky you may catch a glimpse of brown trout swimming up Woods Mill stream, or water shrews paddling from bank to bank.

FILSHAM REEDBED
Hastings, TN38 8DY; **OS Map** TQ 775088; **Map Ref** G43

Access/conditions: Boardwalks suitable for wheelchair access, with passing places and viewpoints over the reserve. Narrow riverside path connecting the car park to the reedbed is uneven.
How to get there: From Bulverhythe recreation ground, just off the A259 in St Leonards, take the footpath that runs alongside Combe Haven river. After 0.6 miles there is a stepped footbridge over the river.
Walking time: 1–2 hours.
30-minute visit: Walk up from Bulverhythe recreation ground alongside the river to view the reserve from the bridge.

One of the largest reedbeds in Sussex, sitting at the southern end of the Combe Haven Valley. Its mixture of reedbeds, meadows and fens has earned the reserve SSSI status – little surprise when you experience the wildlife.

Winter visits have a soundtrack of squealing water rails and singing Cetti's warblers, while marsh harriers and bitterns glide above the reeds. Spring arrives with reed warblers, sedge warblers and cuckoos fresh from Africa. Bearded tits breed, and you may even spot some rare migratory birds. Filsham Reedbed sits on an important migration route that has seen purple herons, red-backed shrikes and bee-eaters visit.

Filsham's fenland blossoms with blunt-flowered rush, ragged robin, water mint and marsh pennywort. Such botanical diversity has encouraged around 1,000 species of insect to thrive, including reed dagger and flame wainscot moths, hairy dragonflies and yellow-faced bees.

OLD LODGE

Uckfield, TN22 3JD; **OS Map** TQ 469306; **Map Ref** G34

Access/conditions: A well-marked nature trail leads around the reserve. Some steep slopes, with steps at the reserve entrance.
How to get there: Four miles north of Maresfield on the B2026 to Hartfield, about 500m north of the junction with the B2188.
Walking time: 1–2 hours.
30-minute visit: Walk along the first section of the nature trail for spectacular views over Ashdown Forest.

Old Lodge offers sweeping vistas of heather and pine woodland in the middle of the much larger Ashdown Forest. The year starts early here, with fluting woodlark song sounding in January. This is joined in spring by tree pipits, cuckoos and beautiful redstarts, which constantly twang their russet-red tails as though they're attached by springs. The small plantations of Scots pine are good places to spot marauding gangs of common crossbills: curious finches with bills that are specially adapted for extracting seeds from pine cones.

The heathlands are at their best in summer when the heady mix of heathers bloom, the landscape flowing with pink and purple. Keep an eye on the ponds and wet areas for keeled skimmer, golden-ringed and black darter dragonflies.

CASTLE WATER AND RYE HARBOUR

Rye Harbour, TN31 7TX; **OS Map** TQ 942189; **Map Ref** G44

Opening hours: Rye Harbour Discovery Centre and Lime Kiln Café open daily, 10am–4pm.
Access/conditions: The ground is level and most footpaths have a good surface. Bird hides are accessible to some wheelchairs. Toilets have facilities for disabled visitors with a RADAR key
How to get there: By car, it is 2.5 miles south-east of Rye along Harbour Road, near the settlement of Rye Harbour. There is a car park with toilets here.
Walking time: 3–4 hours.
30-minute visit: Park near the industrial complex on Harbour Road to see roosting cormorants, little egrets and, in winter, bitterns.

Shingle, saltmarsh, gravel pits and grassland combine to create the coastal wonderland of Castle Water and Rye Harbour. Now with the newly opened Rye Harbour Discovery Centre, it's the perfect place for a whole day of exploring complete with a bite to eat in the café and browse of the shop.

The reserve is great for birdwatching at any time of year. Bitterns boom during summer, while winter brings hundreds of ducks to Castle Water, including pochards, wigeon, teal, gadwall, pintails and more unusual visitors like smew. Rare Lapland buntings, snow buntings and shorelarks can be seen on the saltmarsh in winter, and roosting flocks of golden plovers may number

into the thousands. Spring brings breeding colonies of little, common and Sandwich terns plus ringed plovers, avocets and lapwings. You may also spot a water vole, as this reserve is one of the few remaining places in Sussex where you can still see them.

The Beach Reserve is transformed by a colourful cast of wildflowers in late May and June: sea kale, viper's-bugloss, yellow horned-poppy and sea pea, to name a few. Look out for the endangered least lettuce and stinking hawksbeard. Such incredible plant life in turn supports a spectacular range of invertebrates, including the spangled button beetle and medicinal leech – both threatened species.

EBERNOE COMMON

Ebernoe, GU28 9LD; **OS Map** SU 975278; **Map Ref** G35

Access/conditions: The ground is flat but can be muddy. There are some stiles.
How to get there: About five miles north of Petworth. Take the first right for Gunters Bridge and Balls Cross, onto Streel's Lane. Opposite the telephone box, turn right down the track. Small car park near Ebernoe Church at the bottom of the track.
Walking time: 3–4 hours.
30-minute visit: Park at the church and explore some of the northern part of the reserve, taking in Furnace Pond and Furnace Meadow.

A superb Low Weald woodland with a long and interesting history. The ruins of clay pits, furnaces and Victorian cottages contrast with a magical natural landscape where rare bats hide away and colourful flowers take centre-stage. Carpets of bluebells, wild daffodils and orchids herald the arrival of spring, while cowslips, pepper saxifrage and betony colour Furnace Meadow through summer. Sussex Wildlife Trust's careful raking of areas previously overgrown with bracken and brambles has resulted in pretty glades full of primroses, devil's-bit scabious and sneezewort.

Wherever you walk you'll find an array of trees and shrubs: oak and ash on the sticky clay soils to the north and beech on the more acidic, sandy soils to the south. Field maple, hazel and wild service trees also grow at Ebernoe Common, with the proliferation of dead wood an enticing precursor to autumn's fungi bonanza. Common stinkhorn, magpie inkcap and beefsteak fungus are just a few of the weird and wonderful species that emerge. Bats are at home in the cracks and hollows of the trees, including thriving colonies of rare barbastelle and Bechstein's bats. More than 70 bird species have been recorded at the reserve, including nightingales and turtle doves. In summer, woodland butterflies emerge – look out for the resplendent purple emperor, purple hairstreak and white admiral. You may also spot the delicate white-legged damselfly in the glades.

MALLING DOWN

Lewes, BN7 2RU; **OS Map** TQ 423112; **Map Ref** G42

Access/conditions: There are fences, gates and stiles, and some paths are very steep. The gentlest route to the top is from Mill Road.

How to get there: Easily reached on foot from Lewes town centre – head east and there is a small entrance in Wheatsheaf Gardens opposite the petrol station, but no parking. Other access points from Mill Road or the layby on the B2192 Ringmer Road.

Walking time: 4–5 hours.

30-minute visit: From Wheatsheaf Gardens, walk up the Coombe towards the 'snout' for fabulous summer flowers and butterflies.

A superb chalk grassland brimming with butterflies and wildflowers. It's hard to believe this endangered habitat is within easy walking distance of Lewes town centre.

Sussex Wildlife Trust uses traditional grazing and an army of passionate volunteers to preserve the incredible floral diversity. In June, parts of the Coombe are painted yellow with horseshoe vetch. Later, they glow pink with centaury or creamy-white with the frothy heads of dropwort. Orchids are a speciality, with common spotted-orchids numbering in their thousands on north-facing slopes. Rare musk orchids and frog orchids, barely two inches tall, can be found – remember to look before sitting down!

Summer belongs to the butterflies, with thousands enjoying the nectar of the grassland flowers. The 'snout' is a great place to look for the rare Adonis blue between May and mid-June, then again from early August to mid-September. You can't miss the brilliant blue males as they sip nectar from horseshoe vetch, which is also where the females lay their eggs.

WILDLIFE FACT: ADONIS BLUE

This specialist of chalk grassland has an unusual life cycle. It lays its eggs almost exclusively on horseshoe vetch. When the green larvae hatch, they are looked after by ants, which are attracted by the honey-like secretions expelled from its glands. The ants will protect the larvae from predators and often bury them at night.

Home to some of the most precious wetlands and best birdwatching in the country, the east of England has something extra special. It was on the north Norfolk coast that, in 1926, the very first county Wildlife Trust came into being. The passionate group of naturalists came together to purchase 400 acres (162ha) of marsh at Cley, and to this day, Cley Marshes remains a shining example of the power of nature conservation. Bitterns, avocets, pink-footed geese, wigeon, teal and unusual rarities attract a stream of visitors from all over the country.

Summer brings booming bitterns, breeding bearded tits and magnificent marsh harriers to the marshes, reedbeds and shallow lakes of the Broads. This rich tapestry of both human and natural history is also the only place in the UK to find two particularly special insects: the flamboyant swallowtail butterfly and dashing Norfolk hawker dragonfly. The first, butter-yellow splashed with black, blue and crimson; and the second, golden-brown with emerald eyes.

Further inland you'll find the Fens, a landscape once shaped and maintained by reed cutters traversing the waterways on poles. As the need for thatch declined, much of the Fens was drained and converted to farmland, and today, less than one per cent of the original fen wetlands remain. Thankfully, the Wildlife Trusts are pioneering one of the most exciting habitat restoration projects ever undertaken in Britain. The Great Fen Restoration Project is returning a 9,100-acre (3,700ha) wetland between Huntingdon and Peterborough to its former glory, creating homes for marsh harriers, water voles and countless other wildlife.

While the wetlands of the East are breathtaking, don't discount its other wild refuges. The Brecks, a 393-square-mile ancient heathland stretching across Norfolk and Suffolk, is home to rare plants, relic glacial ponds known as 'pingos' and more than 65 per cent of the UK's stone curlews. In Bedfordshire, chalk grasslands throng with chalkhill blue and Duke of Burgundy butterflies, while in north Northamptonshire,

you could while away a whole day roaming the limestone grassland and ancient woodlands of Old Sulehay.

NOT TO BE MISSED

- **Cley and Salthouse Marshes, Norfolk**
  The oldest Wildlife Trust nature reserve and one of the best birdwatching spots in the UK.

- **Nene Wetlands, Northamptonshire**
  A unique mosaic of flooded gravel pits, wet meadows, wet woodland and reedbeds right outside a busy retail park.

- **Brampton Wood, Cambridgeshire**
  One of the largest and oldest ancient woods in Cambridgeshire. Look for orchids, listen for woodpeckers and keep an eye out for black hairstreak butterflies.

- **Langdon Nature Discovery Park, Essex**
  Natural history meets social history at this enchanting reserve. It shows that countryside once threatened by intensive farming can be restored to its former glory with woodcock, turtle doves and nightingales thriving.

- **Carlton Marshes, Suffolk**
  The southern gateway to the Broads National Park and a home for marsh harriers, raft spiders and grasshopper warblers.

Opposite: Swallowtail butterfly, Norfolk

BEDS, CAMBS AND NORTHANTS

About the Trust

The Wildlife Trust for Beds, Cambs and Northants (BCN) has a big mission: to stop wildlife declining in Bedfordshire, Cambridgeshire and Northamptonshire. As well as caring for more than 100 nature reserves encompassing ancient woods, wild fens, heathlands, wetlands and wildflower meadows, the Trust advises landowners and manages other wild spaces to help create a nature recovery network across the landscape.

The Wildlife Trust for Beds, Cambs and Northants (BCN)
01954 713500
wildlifebcn.org

Beechwoods

Cambridge, CB22 3BF
OS Map TL 485547;
Map Ref J11

Beechwoods was originally planted in the 1840s, and today, delicate white helleborines thrive on the dry chalky soil. Their flowering spikes emerge in spring before the budding beech leaves cast their deep, cool shade. In years with a good beech-mast crop, large flocks of bramblings gather to exploit the rich food source.

Blow's Downs

Near Luton, LU5 4AE
OS Map TL 030215;
Map Ref J17

The steep chalk hills rising from the edges of Luton and

Dunstable have protected this colourful, wildlife-rich grassland. Great pignut, orchids, scabious and knapweeds grow alongside butterfly favourites, including horseshoe vetch, common rock-rose and kidney vetch, which help chalkhill blue, brown argus and small blue butterflies to thrive. In spring and autumn, migrant birds include wheatears, whinchats and ring ouzels.

Collyweston Quarries

Stamford, PE9 3PA
OS Map TF 005037;
Map Ref J1

In June, the grassland glows with the golden-yellow flowers of common rock-rose, common bird's-foot trefoil and dyer's greenweed. This

colourful display continues with pinks and purples when pyramidal orchids, greater knapweed, wild thyme and clustered bellflower bloom. Glow-worms beam from the long grass on June nights. Common lizards bask on the dry-stone walls.

Cooper's Hill

Near Ampthill, MK45 2HX
OS Map TL 028376;
Map Ref J13

Rare and endangered open heath surrounded by trees on the Greensand Ridge. A small area of acidic mire and ponds nestles in the north-west corner of the reserve, where marsh violets grow and willow carr gently shades the water. Lizards, green tiger beetles and solitary bees and wasps live on the open heath.

Birds nest in the spiky gorse, which gives off a wonderful scent in summer.

Glapthorn Cow Pastures
Near Oundle, PE8 5BH
OS Map TL 005903;
Map Ref J5

A mix of blackthorn scrub and mature woodland that nurtures black hairstreak butterflies and nightingales. Primroses, bluebells and orchids bloom in the mature woodland covering the northern half of the reserve. Nuthatches and warblers sing loudly, and you may be lucky enough to see roding woodcock on still summer evenings.

King's Wood and Rammamere Heath
Near Stockgrove, LU7 0BA
OS Map SP 920294;
Map Ref J16

This magnificent wood and adjoining heath are the perfect place to lose yourself in nature. Small-leaved lime and hornbeam trees grow in the wood where woodpeckers drum, bluebells bloom and white admiral and silver-washed fritillary butterflies feed on bramble flowers. On the open heath, tree pipits sing and adders bask in the sunshine.

Pegsdon Hills and Hoo Bit
Pegsdon, SG5 3GS
OS Map TL 120295;
Map Ref J15

A jewel of the Chilterns AONB, with steep chalk hills offering some of the best views in the county. In spring, look for moschatel in the woodland and dingy and grizzled skippers in the grassland. In summer, skylarks provide a wonderful soundtrack and glow-worms glimmer in the dark. In the woods, white helleborine flowers in large numbers beneath the dense beeches.

Stanground Wash
Peterborough, PE2 8HZ
OS Map TL 208975;
Map Ref J4

A distinctive part of the Nene Washes where annual winter flooding provides a winter refuge for wildfowl and spring nesting space for waders. The ditches host rare beetles and scarce plants, including fringed water lilies and grass-wrack pondweed, as well as a rare European fish: the spined loach. There is no shortage of birds, so bring your binoculars to watch snipe, redshanks, sandpipers, and maybe even a peregrine falcon on the hunt.

Thorpe Wood
Peterborough, PE3 6SZ
OS Map TL 159986;
Map Ref J2

An unexpected ancient woodland treasure among the urban hustle and bustle. Wood anemones, wild garlic and a spectacular bluebell display add fairy-tale magic to spring walks. The mature oaks are home to countless invertebrates, as well as great spotted woodpeckers, whose drumming echoes around the trees in spring.

Gamlinglay Wood
Near Gamlinglay, SG19 3DH
OS Map TL 240537;
Map Ref J12

A wonderfully diverse woodland that has stood for at least 1,000 years. The Wildlife Trust BCN is gradually removing conifers planted after WWII and coppices the woodland to help wildlife thrive. Myriad insects live in the wood, including purple hairstreak butterflies, longhorn beetles and several species of dragonfly. Clouds of butterflies drink from flowers along the grassy rides, then as dusk descends, bats take over, taking advantage of the abundant moths.

SUMMER LEYS
Near Wollaston, NN29 7TD; **OS Map** SP 886634; **Map Ref** J10

Access/conditions: Can be muddy in winter and after rain. Some paths and hides are wheelchair accessible.
How to get there: South of Wellingborough on the road between Great Doddington and Wollaston. Train to Wellingborough (three miles). No direct bus to Summer Leys but buses run to Great Doddington and Wollaston. Parking is free for Trust members.
Walking time: 1 hour.
30-minute visit: Visit the

Marigold pond and the hides overlooking the main lake and wader scrape.

Summer Leys is one of the best birdwatching spots in the Nene Valley. An ex-gravel pit, its shallow waters, low-lying islands, large scrape and reeds make it perfect for breeding and wading birds.

In winter, goosanders, wigeon and gadwall arrive to take refuge from the worst of the weather, joined by large numbers of roosting lapwings and golden plovers that fill the air with urgent peeping and piping. Oystercatchers, ringed plovers, little ringed plovers and redshanks breed on the scrape, while whimbrels, turnstones and common

sandpipers pass through on migration. Common terns nest in a colony on the islands. Otters are seldom seen but are regular visitors, while the taller reeds and rushes may reveal the ball-shaped woven

nests of harvest mice. The Marigold pond is one of the best places to see the hairy dragonfly, and Kim's Corner – a fragment of species-rich grassland – is alive with butterflies in summer.

NENE WETLANDS

Rushden Lakes, NN10 6FA; **OS Map** SP 938679; **Map Ref** J8

Opening hours: Visitor centre open 10am–4pm daily (except Christmas holidays). **Access/conditions:** Many wide, smooth trails. Wheelchair and pushchair-friendly. Mobility scooter available for hire at the visitor

centre (book in advance). **How to get there:** Reserve sits off A45 opposite Rushden Lakes Retail Park. There is a 5-hour parking limit at Rushden Lakes. **Walking time:** Five walking trails and a number of

other footpaths range from 20-minute to 2.5-hour walks. Set aside an entire day to explore the whole reserve and relax in the visitor centre. **30-minute visit:** Take the Nature Trail walk around Skew Bridge Lake.

You'd never know that Nene Wetlands sat right outside a busy retail park. Four Wildlife Trust nature reserves – Irthlingborough Lakes and Meadows, Ditchford Lakes and Meadows, Higham Ferrers Pits and Wilson's Pits – are linked up with Skew Bridge Lake, Delta Pit and Higham Lake, creating a thriving mosaic of flooded gravel pits, wet meadows, wet woodland and reedbeds at the heart of the Trust's Nene Valley Living Landscape.

This is a wonderful place to while away an entire day watching and listening to a fantastic array of birds. An amazing 20,000 waterbirds use the reserve every year, either to breed, spend the winter or refuel on their long migration. Cuckoos arrive in spring to seize the nests of unlucky reed warblers. Cetti's warblers sing from deep in the reeds and kingfishers hunt from strategic perches above the water. Summer is the best time to watch dragons and damsels, including common darters and banded demoiselles, hunting over the lagoons. You may even spot a barn owl quartering the grassland at dusk. In winter, the lakes fill with ducks like wigeon, gadwall and tufted ducks, while golden plovers feed along the shallow fringes.

BRAMPTON WOOD

Brampton, PE28 0DB; **OS Map** TL 184698; **Map Ref** J6

Access/conditions: More than two miles of wide rides and some difficult minor paths with steep gradients. Paths can be muddy. Check the Wildlife Trust BCN's website for closures after wet weather.
How to get there: Small car park at reserve off Brampton Road. From the A1 take the exit for Brampton and head west for 0.75 miles.
Walking time: The network of paths and rides offers walks from 20 minutes to a whole day – the choice is yours!
30-minute visit: Walk up the main ride, between the two large oaks and to the main cross rides to see down the length of the wood.

Brampton Wood isn't only the second largest ancient woodland in Cambridgeshire, but also one of the oldest. At around 900 years old, it is mentioned in the Domesday Book, and protects a fantastic diversity of plants and animals. Primroses, water purslane, wood spurge, common spotted-orchids and devil's-bit scabious grow around oak, ash, field maple and birch trees. You can even find common pear trees, the fallen fruits of which offer tasty snacks to blackbirds and thrushes.

In spring you can be swept away by the heady scent of bluebells and the beautiful freshness of wood anemones and oxlips. You may hear the drumming of woodpeckers preparing to nest or the joyful, repetitive tune of a song thrush drifting down from a high perch. The woodland rides hum with insects in summer, including black hairstreak and white admiral butterflies.

Wildlife Trust BCN is hard at work restoring areas of the wood that have struggled to recover from being clear-felled. Each year the charity coppices different sections of the wood (providing perfect habitat for the reserve's hazel dormice) while also clearing conifers to allow the natural regeneration of native trees and shrubs. Trees are felled beside the rides to improve the 'edge habitat', while the grassy areas of the rides are mowed biennially to encourage more wildflowers to flourish.

Huntingdon, PE28 0BX; **OS Map** TL 143671; **Map Ref** J9

Opening hours: Anglian Water car park open 8am–dusk.
Access/conditions: Surfaced cycle track around reservoir. Surfaced paths to Mander Hide and Valley Creek Hide. Other paths more awkward.
How to get there: Between Huntingdon and St Neots on the A1. Leave B661 at Buckden or A14 at Ellington. Nearest train station is Huntingdon.
Walking time: The full circuit is eight miles, but a network of shorter paths and trails takes around 30 minutes.
30-minute visit: Walk through the wildlife garden and along the track to Dudney hide, where you can watch the birds on the water.

Grafham Water nature reserve surrounds the western side of Grafham Reservoir and contains a mix of ancient and plantation woodlands, wildlife-rich grasslands and wetland habitats including reedbeds, willow and open water – all home to bountiful birdlife. Each year 170 species are recorded here, including rarer visitors like ospreys and the occasional Slavonian grebe.

There is something different to see from each of the hides. On evening walks you may hear a nightingale singing from the scrubby stands of blackthorn, dog-rose and hawthorn around Dudney

hide. The Lagoons hide overlooking the mudflats is a brilliant place to watch redshanks, snipe and green sandpipers digging into the rich mud for invertebrates.

The plantation surrounding Littless hide is a haven for orchids, as well as butterflies including speckled woods and ringlets. As you venture deeper into the wood, the plantation transforms into ancient woodland where badgers roam and bats swoop. Grafham even has a wildlife garden, where you can simply sit and take in the peaceful atmosphere among flowers, insects, reptiles and amphibians.

OLD SULEHAY

Yarwell Village, PE8 6PA; **OS Map** TL 054980; **Map Ref** J3

Access/conditions: Main ride is surfaced in woodland though other paths can be muddy. Quarry has uneven paths and steep slopes.

How to get there: Near Yarwell on Old Sulehay Road, just off the Wansford junction of A1/A47 west of Peterborough. Limited layby parking along Old Sulehay Road; many public rights of way from surrounding villages. Please park considerately.

Walking time: 5 hours.

30-minute visit: Take one of the circular walks around the wood, quarry or grassland surrounding the lodge.

A precious remnant of the ancient Rockingham Forest where you could spend a whole day immersing yourself in the wild wonders to be found. Many of the wildflowers are rare in Northamptonshire, including ploughman's-spikenard, wild thyme, viper's-bugloss, common cudweed and yellow-wort. These floral displays attract a wide range of butterflies eager to fill up on nectar, including common blues, brown argus and dingy skippers. On warm spring days look out for energetic grizzled skippers in Stonepit Close, on the disused railway, or the Calcining Banks. In summer, one of the UK's most memorable wild spectacles unfolds after dark as glow-worms glimmer in the long grass.

There are birds aplenty, too. Whitethroats and bullfinches feed and breed in the scrub, and great spotted and lesser spotted woodpeckers live in the woodland alongside nuthatches and treecreepers, which scamper up the trees like little mice. Invertebrates thrive on the sun-warmed paths and rides, including green tiger beetles, whose jewel-green bodies shimmer in the sunlight. Old Sulehay also has some more secretive residents: grass snakes, badgers and woodcock.

The Wildlife Trust BCN has restored a former arable area of the reserve called Sammock's Hill. Now, after spreading wildflower seeds collected from other local grasslands, this peaceful patch brims with cowslips, bird's-foot trefoil, broomrape and pyramidal orchids.

PITSFORD WATER NATURE RESERVE

Near Northampton, NN6 9SJ; **OS Map** SP 787699; **Map Ref** J7

Access/conditions: Permit required: free for Wildlife Trust BCN members; £6 non-members (£4 concession); £45 annual family season ticket. Wildlife Trust BCN members can get a permit by calling 01604 405285 or emailing northamptonshire@ wildlifebcn.org. Non-members can buy a permit from the Pitsford Water Fishing Lodge (opening hours vary) or permit hut at the main gate of the Lodge. Wheelchair access to one hide. Paths mainly grass and can get muddy.
How to get there: Five miles from Northampton between A43 and A508, on the Holcot and Brixworth Road. Buses run from Northampton to both villages but the remaining one to two miles have no public transport.

Walking time: The seven-mile circular walk takes 3–4 hours with no hide visits.
30-minute visit: Head north of the Fishing Lodge and follow the circuit around the blocks of woodland.

Pitsford Water Nature Reserve is the perfect place to get away from it all. Quiet pathways, wide-open reservoir views and peaceful bird hides dotted along the lakeshore will wash away your cares and introduce you to a wealth of wildlife.

Large shallow bays attract a range of wildfowl searching for a safe place to feed and shelter. Wigeon, gadwall, pintails and teal join up to 10,000 birds, including three species of diver and five species of grebe. The scrubby

areas offer a rich berry crop to hungry flocks of fieldfares and redwings.

When spring arrives, more than 40 species of bird choose to breed here, from prehistoric-looking herons to tiny goldcrests. Make sure you drop by the feeding station on the Old Scaldwell Road to watch tree sparrows, yellowhammers and many other small birds filling up on seeds.

In summer, the reserve comes alive with insects. Common blue and emerald damselflies fly alongside ruddy darter dragonflies and a dazzling array of butterflies. Commas, orange-tips and small tortoiseshells, as well as six-spot burnet moths, seem to perch on every flowerhead on the brightest summer days.

NORFOLK

About the Trust

Norfolk is the oldest Wildlife Trust, formed in 1926 to protect Cley Marshes. Supported by more than 35,500 members, the Norfolk Wildlife Trust cares for more than 60 nature reserves encompassing wetlands, woodlands, heathlands and breathtaking coastline. From water voles and natterjack toads to bitterns, bearded tits and spectacular swallowtail butterflies, the Trust is reversing the fortunes of struggling wildlife and connecting more people with the wild wonders on their doorstep.

Norfolk Wildlife Trust
01603 625540
norfolkwildlifetrust.org.uk

Upton Broad, Marshes and Fen

Upton, NR13 6EQ
OS Map TG 380137;
Map Ref H6

A tranquil haven for some of Norfolk's rarest wildlife, including swallowtail butterflies and Norfolk hawker dragonflies. There is a staggering array of wetland plants, with fen orchids, marsh ferns, marsh pea, cowbane and fen pondweed being some of the highlights. Lapwings and redshanks feed on the grazing marshes and majestic marsh harriers drift across the reedbeds in summer.

Hethel Old Thorn

Norwich, NR14 8HE
OS Map TG 171005;
Map Ref H7

This might be the smallest Wildlife Trust nature reserve,

but size doesn't matter. Hethel Old Thorn comprises a single hawthorn tree dating back to the 13th century. Though decayed to a remnant of its former nine-foot girth, this ancient tree has something special and defiantly continues to grow. Legend tells that the hawthorn grew from the staff of Joseph of Arimathea.

Lower Wood, Ashwellthorpe

Wymondham, NR16 1HB
OS Map TM 138976;
Map Ref H8

A beautiful ancient woodland refuge. Lower Wood was recorded in the Domesday Book and is dominated by towering oaks. Bluebells carpet the ground in spring and are followed by herb-paris, twayblades and a profusion of early purple

orchids. Butterflies including white admirals bask in sunny patches and more than 200 species of fungi have been recorded. This is a dog-free reserve.

East Wretham Heath

Thetford, IP24 1RU
OS Map TL 913887;
Map Ref H10

Open heath that's great for birdwatching. Woodlarks and redstarts breed here and two meres attract migrating wading birds, ducks and geese in spring and autumn. Pop into the Langmere hide to watch them. With an abundance of rabbits to hunt, stoats are regular visitors and you may spot one scampering across the open grassland. Keep your eyes peeled for adders and grass snakes on sunny spring mornings.

FOXLEY WOOD

Foxley, NR20 4QR; **OS Map** TG 049229; **Map Ref** H2

Access/conditions: Paths can be wet and muddy. Reserve closed every Thursday for important habitat management works.
How to get there: By car, leave Norwich on the A1067 Fakenham Road, from where the wood is signposted on the right.
Walking time: 2 hours.
30-minute visit: Venture down one of the rides as far as you like and retrace your steps when time runs out.

A glorious ancient woodland thought to be more than 6,000 years old. In early spring, primroses peek out from the banks of ditches – a prelude to the riot of colour that follows with the April/May bluebell display. Greater butterfly-orchids, delicate pink water avens and the unusual herb-paris add yet more colour and texture, with birds including green woodpeckers, garden warblers, chiffchaffs and sometimes even turtle doves providing the soundtrack to your wildflower walk.

By midsummer, masses of meadowsweet fills the woodland rides with a vanilla fragrance that attracts humming, fluttering and hovering throngs of insects. Purple emperor butterflies have returned to Foxley, 50 years after they were declared extinct in Norfolk.

If autumn isn't too dry, the displays of fungi can appear literally overnight, before succumbing to the first frosts. Winter walks will take your breath away, with the tallest oaks casting a cathedral-like majesty through the woodland. Please note that this is a dog-free reserve.

THOMPSON COMMON

Attleborough, NR17 1DP; **OS Map** TL 941966; **Map Ref** H9

Access/conditions: Enter from the car park via a kissing gate.
How to get there: Leave Watton on A1075 to Thetford Road. Look out for the Great Eastern Pingo Trail car park located behind the layby as the road bends to the left just before you reach Stow Bedon.
Walking time: 2 hours.
30-minute visit: Visit the first few pingos along the Great Eastern Pingo Trail then retrace your steps.

Thompson Common is famous for its pingos: a series of around 400 shallow pools, which formed 9,000 years ago at the end of the last ice age. Water violets, fen pondweed, marsh cinquefoil, bladderwort and marsh orchids all bloom in spring and are joined by bogbean, heather and dwarf thistles in summer. The reserve is one of the most important in the UK for dragonflies and damselflies, with huge numbers swooping and darting over the larger pingos in July and August. The hairy dragonfly, ruddy darter, brown hawker, blue-tailed damselfly, scarce emerald damselfly and red-eyed damselfly are just a handful of the species you could spot.

One of Thompson Common's most exciting residents is the northern pool frog. It became extinct in England at the end of the 20th century but has now been released back onto this nature reserve.

WEETING HEATH

Weeting, IP27 0QF; **OS Map** TL 757881; **Map Ref** H11

Opening hours: Opening hours change annually. Check Norfolk Wildlife Trust's website before visiting. Closed during autumn and winter.
Access/conditions: Visitor centre, hides and paths are wheelchair accessible. £4.50 entry with Gift Aid, £4 standard price.
How to get there: Bus departs from Brandon and stops at Weeting. By car, leave Brandon, going north on A1065 to Mundford. Turn left to Weeting and left to Hockwold-cum-Wilton. Car park and visitor centre signed 1.5 miles west of Weeting.
Walking time: 3–4 hours.
30-minute visit: Sit quietly in one of the hides and watch the birds.

Though wonderful for wildflowers, insects and birds of prey, the real stars of Weeting Heath are its stone curlews. They are the only European member of the 'Thick-knee' family of birds and do indeed have rather knobbly knees! They are as rare as they are strange and have suffered tragically through habitat loss. They breed on open, stony ground with short vegetation, making the close-cropped turf of Weeting the perfect spot. Grazing sheep and a willing army of wild rabbits help to keep the heath in check and the curlews happy. You can watch them on their nests from the hides or via cameras in the visitor centre.

This reserve is also home to woodlarks, green woodpeckers and lapwings.

In summer, hobbies feed on clouds of dragonflies and are a joy to watch from the hides. Keep your eyes peeled for hovering kestrels, grumpy-looking little owls and soaring sparrowhawks too. A stroll through the woods offers the best chance of seeing crossbills, tree pipits and spotted flycatchers.

WILDLIFE FACT: STONE CURLEW

With long, almost reptilian legs and staring yellow eyes, these peculiar waders have long inspired local folklore and earned themselves the less-than-flattering nickname 'goggle-eyed plover'. They were once caught and hired out to people suffering from jaundice, who believed that looking into a stone-curlew's eye would cure them.

King's Lynn, PE32 1AT; **OS Map** TF 680229/TF 698229; **Map Ref** H4

Access/conditions: Sandy tracks lead across the heath.
How to get there: From A149 roundabout at King's Lynn take A148 to Fakenham. After 300m turn right on the minor road towards Roydon village. Main car park is 950m on the right.
Walking time: 2–3 hours.
30-minute visit: Park at the eastern car park and walk the small circular trail.

These two adjacent reserves form part of Norfolk Wildlife Trust's Gaywood Valley Living Landscape. In spring, woodlarks, tree pipits and yellowhammers sing on the heath, where nightjars nest in summer. These bizarre-looking birds lie camouflaged on the ground by day, but at night, they take to the air with a jerky, fluttering flight like giant moths.

While balmy summer nights belong to the nightjars, bright summer days are dominated by an incredible range of invertebrates. At least 15 species of dragonfly are regularly recorded at Roydon Common, including the striking black darter, for which Roydon is one of only three breeding sites in Norfolk. If that wasn't enough you could spot more than 30 species of butterfly, including white admiral, brown argus and green and purple hairstreak. Roydon is the only place in East Anglia where you can see raft spiders, which lurk at the edge of dykes and ponds until they feel the tell-tale vibrations of potential prey and dart out onto the water.

Winter here is anything but lifeless. Merlins hunt across the heath and hen harriers arrive to roost. Barn owls quarter the reserve in the evening and a single great grey shrike is known to spend some winters here.

CLEY AND SALTHOUSE MARSHES

Cley-next-the-Sea, NR25 7SA; **OS Map** TG 054440; **Map Ref** H1

Opening hours: Visitor centre open 10am–5pm, March–November; 10am–4pm, November–February. Closed Christmas Eve and Christmas Day.

Access conditions: Members and children go free. Non-members £5.50 (with gift aid) or £5 (standard price). The visitor centre is free to enter; parking and bird hides are free for members and children. Visitor centre, hides and some paths are wheelchair accessible. Please note that apart from the decking and outside the visitor centre, this is a dog-free reserve.

How to get there:
Coasthopper bus service stops just outside the reserve, which is on the A149 coast road, 3.7 miles north of Holt. By car, the visitor centre and car park are easily accessible on the landward side of the road. The entrance is located directly across the A419 coast road from the car park.

Walking time: 4 hours.

30-minute visit: Cross over the road from the visitor centre and onto the reserve. Wander along the boardwalk through the reedbed and slip into any of the hides that catch your fancy.

Cley Marshes is the oldest Wildlife Trust nature reserve in the UK, purchased in 1926 to be held 'in perpetuity as a bird breeding sanctuary'. A 2012 appeal helped the Trust purchase a further 140 acres (57ha) of land, now linking Cley with its neighbouring nature reserve, Salthouse Marshes.

The five hides are a window into the lives of the thousands of birds that congregate on the pools and scrapes. Elegant avocets breed alongside ringed plovers, lapwings and redshanks. Bitterns hide in the safety of the reeds – listen out for their 'booming' call, which sounds like air being blown across the top of a glass bottle. Spoonbills have been known to drop by from nearby Holkham Marshes and there is always the chance of spotting a rare bird on passage in spring. Cley has been a stopping off point for a huge number of rarities over the years, including a white-crowned sparrow from North America and a red-necked stint from Asia. Winter is prime time for rare visitors, particularly snow buntings. The best place to spot them is Salthouse beach, where they're sometimes joined by Lapland buntings and shorelarks. Winter also brings breathtaking gatherings of wildfowl including pintails, Brent geese and wigeon. Watch for a sudden scattering of ducks and wading birds – a tell-tale sign that a marsh harrier has drifted into view.

HICKLING BROAD AND MARSHES

Norwich, NR12 0BW; **OS Map** TG 428222; **Map Ref** H3

Opening hours: Visitor centre open 10am–5pm, spring to autumn half-term; 10am–4pm, November to new season (Friday–Sunday only, including Boxing Day and Near Year's Day).

Access/conditions: Members and children go free. Non-members £5 (with gift aid) or £4.50 (standard price). There is disabled parking and a rough surface leading to the visitor centre where there is a disabled toilet and hearing loop. There are a number of accessible trails. Track to Stubb Mill raptor viewpoint can be wet, uneven and muddy.

How to get there: Reserve is around 2.5 miles south of Stalham off the A149 Stalham to Caister-on-Sea road. From Hickling village, follow the 'brown badger' tourist signs into Stubb Road and on to the nature reserve.

Walking time: The walk around the reserve and a ride on the Water Trail boat takes at least 3 hours.

30-minute visit: Follow the Swallowtail Trail (green markers) for the best chance of seeing waders, wildfowl and bitterns.

As the largest of the Broads, Hickling Broad is a true wildlife refuge, where you can easily while away a whole day exploring the trails, watching the birds and peeking into the Broad's hidden corners on one of Norfolk Wildlife Trust's summer boat tours.

Hickling is home to some of England's most iconic birds, including the common crane. The best place to see them is the Stubb Mill viewing platform in winter, when they fly in each evening to roost with a haunting bugle-like call. But this isn't the only spectacle you can see from the viewpoint – Stubb Mill is the gateway to an unforgettable raptor roost. Marsh harriers (sometimes numbering more than 100), hen harriers and merlins regularly soar overhead on their way to bed.

But birds aren't the only star species at Hickling Broad. Between late May and early July, swallowtail butterflies take to the air on huge black and yellow wings measuring in at around 9cm across. They're joined by equally rare but lesser-known insects like the fen mason wasp and Norfolk hawker dragonfly.

RANWORTH BROAD AND MARSHES

Ranworth, NR13 6HY; **OS Map** TG 358151; **Map Ref** H5

Opening hours: Visitor centre open 10am–5pm, spring to autumn half-term. Car park open 10am–5pm, 30 March–1 November (open intermittently between November and April).

Access/conditions: Limited disabled parking available off Broad Road. A boardwalk leads through the reserve to the visitor centre.

How to get there: Bus runs from Norwich city centre through Panxworth and South Walsham (both around a mile's walk from the reserve). By car, the Broad is signed from B1140 (Norwich to Acle) at South Walsham. At Ranworth, look for signs to Ranworth Broad car park.

Walking time: Allow at least 3 hours to enjoy everything the reserve, visitor centre and boat trip have to offer.

30-minute visit: Walk down the boardwalk nature trail to learn about the ecology of the Broads, then see what you can spot through the binoculars on the top floor of the visitor centre.

Start your adventure at the Broads Wildlife Centre, where you can see a wonderful wealth of wildlife including winter gatherings of wigeon, gadwall, teal, shovelers and pochards. Great crested grebes paddle across the water all year round and kingfishers occasionally zip by in a dazzling flash of blue. In winter, hundreds of cormorants roost in the skeletal dead trees and then, as the days lengthen, common terns nest right in front of the centre. The boardwalk passes through a tranquil woodland

and whispering reeds where Cetti's warblers and sedge warblers project their explosive song in spring and summer. Ospreys sometimes drop by for a fish supper and, if you're lucky, you may spot an otter twisting through the water. Ranworth's swallowtail butterflies are much easier to spot as they flutter through the air or lay eggs on their caterpillars' sole foodplant, milk parsley.

Much of the reserve is inaccessible by foot, so the best way to enjoy Ranworth is by joining one of the Norfolk Widlife Trust's water trail boat trips, from April–October. As well as abundant wildlife you'll also see the wrecks of wherries sunk in WWII to prevent German seaplanes from landing on the water.

SUFFOLK

About the Trust

Suffolk Wildlife Trust is the only organisation solely dedicated to safeguarding Suffolk's wildlife and countryside. The charity cares for nearly 8,000 acres (3,238ha) of precious wild space – including 49 nature reserves – and works with farmers and local communities to improve their land for wildlife. From dormice to hedgehogs, swifts to skylarks, the Trust is dedicated to helping vulnerable wildlife thrive across Suffolk.

Suffolk Wildlife Trust
01473 890089
suffolkwildlifetrust.org

Dingle Marshes

Southwold, IP17 3DZ
OS Map TM 479708;
Map Ref H17

A genuine wilderness where coast, fresh water, moody heathland and atmospheric forest meet. Salty lagoons attract redshanks, grey plovers, wigeon and, in winter, flocks of twite. Bitterns, marsh harriers and bearded tits thrive in the reedbeds. You may spot crossbills, goldcrests and siskins in the wood and hear woodlarks singing sweetly in spring.

Newbourne Springs

Ipswich, IP12 4NY
OS Map TM 274433;
Map Ref H20

A small wooded valley home to all three woodpeckers.

The woodland is like a secret garden where water avens and spectacular displays of marsh-marigolds brighten up the stream-banks. Common twayblades and common spotted-orchids grow here too, but the most magical thing about this reserve isn't the sights but, rather, a sound – the song of the nightingale.

Hen Reedbeds

Southwold, IP18 6SH
OS Map TM 471771;
Map Ref H15

A rich mosaic of wonderful wetland habitats where you can see marsh harriers, bitterns and hobbies in summer. It's a haven for dragon and damselflies including four-spotted chasers, hairy dragonflies and Norfolk hawkers. Otters and water

voles live here but are much more secretive. The mudflats at Wolsey Creek Marshes are a great place to watch avocets and sandpipers feeding, while further along Wolsey Creek, two hides overlook scrapes and islands that fill with godwits, oystercatchers and little egrets.

Redgrave and Lopham Fen

Diss, IP22 2HX
OS Map TM 052802;
Map Ref H14

Tranquil fen, woodland and heath with something for everyone. Hobbies snatch dragonflies from above the pools and evening walks are often accompanied by barn owls. In winter you can watch starling murmurations. More than 270 species of plant will delight botanists, while invertebrate-obsessives will want to check the water's edge for fen raft spiders.

Black Bourn Valley
Stowmarket, IP31 3SQ
OS Map TL 942650;
Map Ref H18

Former arable fields reclaimed by nature. Hawthorn, blackthorn and dog-rose thickets offer hiding places for blackcaps and warblers, while pyramidal and common spotted-orchids grow in the grassland. The seed-heads of bristly oxtongue and thistles attract yellowhammers, linnets and goldfinches. Slow worms and grass snakes slither through the vegetation and teal and snipe feed on the watery grazing marshes.

KNETTISHALL HEATH
Thetford, IP22 2TQ; **OS Map** TL 966806; **Map Ref** H13

Access/conditions: Generally good paths but can be muddy in winter. Some parts suitable for wheelchairs and mobility scooters.
How to get there: From Thetford, take A1066 for around seven miles. Turn right and follow this road to the reserve entrance.
Walking time: Exploring all four trails takes around 5 hours.
30-minute visit: Explore the Short Heathland Trail (red trail).

Despite its name, Knettishall Heath is a diverse mosaic of habitats that includes woodland and riverside meadows as well as stunning heathland.

A Bronze Age burial mound and Hut Hill evidence thousands of years of human occupation, while the 'patterned ground' at the western end of the heath is even older – the result of ice-age freezing and thawing. Today, grazing Exmoor ponies keep this wild sense of the past alive and help the reserve's wildlife to thrive. Stonechats perch on top of bushes and skylarks sing from high in the sky. Slow worms, common lizards and grass snakes bask on patches of open ground, and plants including common rock-rose, purple milk vetch and the rare dropwort add beautiful colour before blooming heather steals the show at the end of summer. More than 1,000 species of moth have been recorded here, including the grey carpet and lunar yellow underwing.

BRADFIELD WOODS

Access/conditions:
Wheelchairs can be pushed
from the car park along
several rides and paths
in drier conditions. Some
parts accessible by mobility
scooter. Can be muddy after
wet weather.
How to get there: Turn off
A134 (Sudbury to Bury St
Edmunds) towards Little
Welnetham. Bradfield Woods
is between Bradfield St
George and Felsham.
Walking time: Allow 4–5
hours to properly explore.
30-minute visit: Stay on
the main wide ride. Linger
on a bench to enjoy the
nightingales or butterflies
before heading back.

Bradfield Woods offers a
window into the past – it has
been in continuous traditional
coppice management since

1252! As the coppice shoots
regenerate, their dense, bushy
growth offers perfect cover
for the warblers that arrive to
spend the summer here. On
sunny days, the sheltered rides
attract basking and fluttering
butterflies, including the white
admiral, which loves feeding
from bramble flowers. Look
to the top of an oak tree and
you could glimpse a purple
hairstreak.

Down on the ground,
mammals including stoats,
yellow-necked mice and
badgers hunt, scamper
and snuffle through the
undergrowth. Hazel dormice
live here too, though you're
more likely to see the nibbled
hazelnuts they leave behind
than the mice themselves,
which live high in the tree
canopy.

CARLTON MARSHES

Opening hours: Visitor
centre open 10am–4pm,
seven days a week.
Access/conditions: Firm
wheelchair and pushchair-
friendly path around part of
the marsh, with easy access
gates. Part of the reserve
accessible for mobility
scooters.
How to get there: Buses stop
near the end of Burnt Hill
Lane on A146. By car, heading
out of Lowestoft on the A146
Beccles Road, Burnt Hill Lane is
on the right, with the reserve
signposted with a brown
sign. Train to Oulton Broad

South or North (then a 20- or 30-minute walk respectively).
Walking time: 1.5 hours.
30-minute visit: Take the all-weather trail around the first marsh.

Carlton Marshes is the Broads in miniature. Grazing marshes, fens, peaty pools, meadows, dykes, pools, scrub – this rich mosaic is an incredible hideaway for wildlife. An astounding 28 species of dragonfly have been spotted here, including the beautiful Norfolk hawker with its bright green eyes. In early summer the reserve comes alive with southern marsh orchids, marsh-marigolds and ragged robin as well as scarcer plants like bogbean, bog pimpernel and marsh cinquefoil. The flower-studded marshes are paradise for hungry hobbies and marsh harriers, while water voles live in dykes harbouring rare plants such as water soldier and frogbit. The open water of Sprat's and Round Water brims with life, including the insectivorous plant, bladderwort, which lives off the unsuspecting water fleas it traps in bladder-like sacs beneath the water.

Carlton Marshes is one of the best places in East Anglia to see (and hear!) grasshopper warblers, which reel from the reedbeds in competition with singing sedge and reed warblers. You may also spot bearded tits and Cetti's warblers in summer, while winter highlights include wigeon, teal and snipe.

LACKFORD LAKES

Bury St Edmunds, IP28 6HX; **OS Map** TL 801706; **Map Ref** H16

Opening hours: Café open 10am–4pm daily. Toilets and shop open until 5pm.
Access/conditions: Blue trail accessible for wheelchairs, with ramped access to four hides. Parts of the reserve accessible for mobility scooters. Fully accessible visitor centre.
How to get there: In the village of Lackford on the A1101.
Walking time: Around 1 hour.
30-minute visit: Choose from three different hides within a 10-minute walk from the visitor centre. Use the upstairs viewing gallery for panoramic views over the reserve.

Lackford Lakes never fails to fill you with wonder. A wildlife oasis throughout the year, it's the perfect place to get away from it all and enjoy watching a fantastic array of species.

Spring begins with an upswell of song from migrant warblers, including the unforgettable nightingale. Butterflies emerge to bask and feed in the sunshine, and are joined in summer by clouds of dragonflies and damselflies darting above the water like shimmering jewels. They have to compete with the swallows and martins, of course, which gorge on small flies hovering over the surface of the water. Great crested grebes, water rails and kingfishers nest on the lakesides.

As the season cools, a flush of red and gold marks the coming of autumn, when the lakes fill with a wonderful range of wildfowl. Shovelers, lapwings, goosanders, bitterns, goldeneyes – there is so much to see even as winter sets in. Pop into the café to warm up with a hot drink after your chilly wildlife walk.

About the Trust

Essex Wildlife Trust is committed to protecting wildlife and inspiring a lifelong love of nature. Supported by more than 1,900 volunteers and over 38,000 members, the Essex Wildlife Trust runs 11 Nature Discovery Centres, cares for 87 nature reserves and two nature parks, and manages 8,400 acres (3,400ha) of land for wildlife. From ancient woods and winding rivers to picturesque heaths and vulnerable wildlife corridors, the Trust safeguards Essex's precious and largely undiscovered natural heritage.

Essex Wildlife Trust
01621 862960
essexwt.org.uk

Danbury Ridge Nature Reserves

Danbury, CM3 4NZ
OS Map TL 787057;
Map Ref H25

A mosaic of woodlands, heathlands, commons, streams and bogs where lily-of-the-valley, greater butterfly-orchids and sanicle bloom. Dormice scamper through the canopy under cover of darkness and small copper butterflies fill summer days. Nightingales serenade the woodland.

Great Holland Pits

Great Holland, CO13 0EU
OS Map TM 204190;
Map Ref H22

Working gravel pit transformed into wildlife haven. Kingfishers, coots and little grebes make the most of the scars of pits, now ponds. Open grassland is painted by yellow archangel, moschatel and the bizarre-looking mousetail. Stop to admire the lovely views over Holland Brook from the high ground.

West Wood

Thaxted, CB10 2SA
OS Map TL 625331;
Map Ref H21

Admire rare and beautiful flowers, including oxlips and greater butterfly-orchids. Footpaths wind between hazel, ash and field maple trees; below goldcrests and buzzards. The warming days encourage speckled wood butterflies and countless dragonflies to emerge, while great crested newts start courting in the ponds.

Roding Valley Meadows

Chigwell, IG7 6DP
OS Map TQ 429942;
Map Ref H28

The largest remaining species-rich water meadow in Essex. In spring, devil's-bit scabious, knapweed and clover transform the grassland with blue, purple, red and white. Many butterflies and dragonflies soar over the river and climb through the grass, and in spring and summer, the calls of song thrushes, blackcaps and whitethroats ring out from the hedges.

BLUE HOUSE FARM

North Fambridge, CM3 6GU; **OS Map** TQ 856971; **Map Ref** H27

Access/conditions: Uneven mown grass paths with a few steep inclines. Stepped access onto the sea wall.

How to get there: Take B1018 towards Langford and continue to Heybridge Approach. Take second exit onto A414. Take third exit at next roundabout then second exit at next roundabout, onto B1018. Take third exit at next roundabout and drive on B1010/Fambridge Road for just over five miles, before turning left onto Blue House Farm Chase.

Walking time: 1–2 hours.

30-minute visit: Walk to the sea wall and see what you can spot.

This is a fantastic place to watch the change of the seasons and the wildlife it brings with it.

In winter, shuffling flocks of up to 2,000 dark-bellied brent geese graze on the marshes, joined by huge numbers of other wildfowl and wading birds including golden plovers, dunlin, wigeon and teal. Spring brings the 'plop' of water voles clambering in and out of the ditches, while lapwings perform their tumbling flight displays overhead. Don't forget to look out for passage migrants like ruffs and green sandpipers. A summer wander will treat you with close-up views of emperor dragonflies. If you're around during late afternoon, keep an eye out for short-eared owls gracefully hunting along the ditches.

THAMESIDE NATURE DISCOVERY PARK

Stanford-le-Hope, SS17 0RN; **OS Map** TQ 685810; **Map Ref** H30

Opening hours: Cottage car park open daily from 8.30am–4.30pm. Nature reserve open seven days a week from 9.30am–4pm.

Access/conditions: Footpaths accessible from Crown Green Cottage, Mucking Creek Sluice Gate and the main car park. These are gravel trails or mown paths.

How to get there: Nearest train station is Stanford-le-Hope, which is served by buses from Southend and Grays, then followed by a three-mile walk. By car, from A13, take A1013 from the west or A1014 from the east, towards

Stanford-le-Hope. Follow signs to Walton Hall Farm Museum, via Buckingham Hill Road, then left into Waltons Hall Road. Continue past the museum and take next right into Mucking Wharf Road. Carry on past the cottages onto the single-track road to the visitor centre.

Walking time: Reserve is on the 27-mile Thames Estuary path route, so your walk could take anything from 1 hour to a full day. See where your feet take you!

30-minute visit: Pop into the Nature Discovery Centre to browse the shop, grab a bite to eat and watch the birds on the estuary through floor-to-ceiling windows.

Thameside Nature Discovery Park is a birdwatching hotspot, a fantastic place for a family day out and an escape from the hustle and bustle. Start your visit at the Nature Discovery Centre for an unforgettable first impression: floor-to-ceiling windows and a fully accessible rooftop viewing deck offering breathtaking views over the Thames Estuary.

A landfill site given back to nature, the reserve is now vitally important for barn owls, short-eared owls, water voles, harvest mice, skylarks, cuckoos and shrill carder bees. In winter, internationally important numbers of ringed plovers and avocets and nationally important numbers of grey plovers, dunlin, black-tailed godwits and redshanks take up residence on the adjacent mudflats. In spring and summer, the grasslands support a treasure trove of butterflies, moths and bees.

TOLLESBURY WICK

Tollesbury, CM9 8SB; **OS Map** TL 970104; **Map Ref** H24

Access/conditions: Access from the marina along the sea wall. Footpath is exposed to the elements.

How to get there: Bus services to Tollesbury from Maldon, Colchester and Witham. By car, follow B1023 to Tollesbury then follow Woodrolfe Road towards the marina and Woodrolfe Green.

Walking time: 4 hours.

30-minute visit: Walk along the sea wall past the marina for stunning views of saltings on the left and the reserve on the right.

Worked for decades by traditional methods to help wildlife, Tollesbury Wick boasts a wonderful diversity of species. Clouded yellow butterflies flutter above the grassland in summer – succeeded by dark-bellied brent geese in winter – while majestic marsh harriers soar above, coming to roost at dusk. Walk along the sea wall from Tollesbury Marina to

fully appreciate the Essex coast. A permissive path leads to a bird hide at the lagoon where thousands of wildfowl and waders gather over winter to feed on the rich wet grassland, including large flocks of golden plovers, lapwings and wigeon.

Tollesbury Wick is also home to Essex Wildlife Trust's 'flying flock' of sheep, cattle and Exmoor ponies, who all help to manage this freshwater grazing marsh

in the most sustainable way possible. The rough pasture is perfect habitat for small mammals such as field voles and pygmy shrews, which makes this reserve the ideal hunting ground for numerous birds of prey.

Some of this reserve's most famous residents, though, are its badgers, which are taking on the role of the 'Time Team'. Their digging has unearthed archaeological finds dating back to the Iron Age.

FINGRINGHOE WICK NATURE DISCOVERY PARK

Fingringhoe, CO5 7DN; **OS Map** TM 041195; **Map Ref** H23

Opening hours: 9am–5pm, Tuesday–Sunday. Closed Mondays (except bank holidays), Christmas Day and Boxing Day.

Access/conditions: Various walking trails, including a designated dog trail. A wheelchair and all-terrain mobility scooter can be borrowed – contact 01206 729678 or fingrlnghoe@essexwt.org.uk in advance.

How to get there: At Fingringhoe, three miles from Colchester. Follow the brown nature reserve signs.

Walking time: At least 2 hours.

30-minute visit: Don't miss the vantage point overlooking the estuary.

When Essex Wildlife Trust bought Fingringhoe Wick – a former sand and gravel quarry – it looked more like a barren lunar landscape than a nature reserve. Now, you wouldn't think it was the same place, with grassland, gorse heathland, reedbeds, ponds, meadows and scrub providing homes for some very special wild creatures. Add stunning estuary views into the mix and it's little wonder that Fingringhoe holds a special place in the hearts of all who visit.

The list of wildlife is dizzying and includes 200 species of bird, 27 species of dragonfly and damselfly, 24 species of butterfly and 350 species of flowering plant, as well as badgers. Sitting on the west shore of the Colne Estuary means a wonderful range of overwintering birds arrive each year, spending the lean months feeding on the saltmarsh, foreshore and mudflats. Up to 700 avocets visit alongside dark-bellied brent geese, golden plovers, knot, lapwings, peregrine falcons, merlins and red-breasted mergansers. Spring sees adders emerge from hibernation and is the best time to hear Fingringhoe's famous nightingales in full song. They usually arrive in mid-April and there are regular nightingale walks to hear them. Come summer, the sea lavender on the saltmarsh looks spectacular, with turtle doves and slow worms adding to the wildlife bonanza.

East   117

HANNINGFIELD RESERVOIR NATURE DISCOVERY PARK

Downham, CM11 1WT; **OS Map** TQ 725971; **Map Ref** H26

Opening hours: 9am–5pm daily.
Access/conditions: Access the reserve through the Nature Discovery Centre.

Some walking trails are wheelchair-friendly.
How to get there: Bus between Wickford and Chelmsford; alight at

Downham village and walk down Crowsheath Lane. By car, off B1007 Billericay to Chelmsford into Downham Road and left onto Hawkswood Road. The entrance is just beyond the causeway opposite Crowsheath Lane.
Walking time: 3–4 hours.
30-minute visit: Don't miss the view from the Lyster Hide.

You will always be greeted with a warm welcome at Hanningfield Reservoir Nature Discovery Centre. Nestled among mature woodland and offering stunning views over the 870-acre (352ha) Hanningfield Reservoir, the Centre is a gateway to magical wild encounters.

Various paths around the reserve offer short strolls, serious rambles and everything in between, with sightings that change with the seasons. Spring brings a breathtaking show of bluebells, greater stitchwort and yellow archangel to the woods, while the sultry summer days erupt with thousands of swifts, swallows and martins feeding over the water during peak fly-hatches. Autumn and winter are great for birdwatching as important numbers of wildfowl use the reservoir to feed and roost. Gadwall, tufted ducks and pochards arrive in impressive groups.

If you're not sure where to see the best of the wildlife or which trail is for you, pop into the Nature Discovery Centre to pick up a trail guide and get advice from the passionate staff.

LANGDON NATURE DISCOVERY PARK

Basildon, SS16 6EJ; **OS Map** TQ 659874; **Map Ref** H29

Opening hours: 9am–5pm, Tuesday–Sunday; closed Mondays (except bank holidays), Christmas Day and Boxing Day; 9.30am–5.30pm, Sundays and bank holidays in summer.

Access/conditions: Good walking conditions all year-round. Some paths muddy in winter. Some steep slopes.

How to get there: Laindon station is on the Fenchurch Street to Southend line and is just under four miles from the reserve. Bus services run from Basildon. By car, it is east of the M25's J29, between the A127 and A13. Routes are signposted from the B148 turning off the A127/A13.

Walking time: Set aside a whole day to explore the entire reserve.

30-minute visit: Walk around the Dunton plotlands to see the range of old gardens and how nature is taking it all back.

Natural history meets social history at Langdon, where former plotland gardens lie alongside breathtaking wild space colonised by countless plants and animals. The reserve sits on some of the highest land in the county, captivating visitors with commanding views as well as excellent walks.

Though not necessarily rare, the wildlife at Langdon includes species that were once common in our countryside but are now threatened by intensive farming and development. These include secretive woodcock, purring turtle doves and operatic nightingales. Summer is the best time to see and hear them, while mixed flocks of finches and thrushes blow in with the nippy winter winds. Thirty butterfly species have been recorded, including white admiral, green hairstreak, marbled white and grizzled skipper. Then there are the orchids – green-winged and common spotted-orchids are just two of seven species that bloom between May and June. Badgers, foxes and weasels thrive in the meadows and all three species of woodpecker live in the woodland. The many ponds attract a wide range of dragonflies and damselflies, while in the darkness of an old well, cave spiders hunt unsuspecting prey.

EAST MIDLANDS

The East Midlands isn't easily defined, which makes it all the more fun to explore. Meadows erupt with orchids and cowslips each spring; open moors are blanketed by heather and patrolled by birds of prey; woodlands chime with songbirds; and glittering streams host dragonflies and damselflies. That's before you've even left the Peak District.

Incorporating Derbyshire, Leicestershire, Rutland, Northamptonshire, Nottinghamshire and Lincolnshire, the East Midlands is home to some of the most scenic wild places for outdoor adventures. The pretty villages, moorland plateaus and rolling green hills of the Peak District are perhaps the most famous but by no means the only place to explore. Further south lies Rutland Water, one of Europe's largest human-made lakes and undoubtedly one of the best places in the UK for birdwatching.

As you move towards the coast you'll find the stunning Lincolnshire Wolds. Woodlands, valleys and large open fields gently roll across this AONB, where there is no shortage of important wildlife refuges and picturesque walking routes. Keep your eyes peeled for brown hares snuggled into their forms and rare orchids nestled among the grass.

The East Midlands coastline is breathtakingly beautiful. Sand dunes dominate long, sandy beaches like those of Donna Nook National Nature Reserve, where wintering wildfowl are joined by hundreds of grey seals that return each year to give birth. The vast, unspoilt expanse of Gibraltar Point is unmissable, and is home to a huge diversity of wildlife right through the seasons.

Back inland and often overlooked, Nottinghamshire has a beautiful and varied landscape that's equally worth exploring. From the atmospheric woods of Sherwood Forest to the rolling hills of the Vale of Belvoir, not to mention the county's flagship nature reserve, Attenborough; there is no shortage of opportunities to stretch your legs and fill your heart with wonder.

NOT TO BE MISSED

- **Wye Valley Reserves, Derbyshire**
Three scenic Derbyshire Wildlife Trust nature reserves in a spectacular wooded valley that erupts with the colours of burnet moths, redstarts, dark green fritillaries and Jacob's ladder.

- **Attenborough, Nottingham**
An intricate network of flooded gravel pits and islands with something to enchant the whole family. Fantastic for winter wildfowl, migrant birds and dragonflies.

- **Gibraltar Point, Lincolnshire**
A spectacular stretch of unspoilt coastline with sweeping views out to sea and a dazzling diversity of life.

- **Prior's Coppice, Rutland**
A relic of the wildwood that once covered large parts of Leicestershire and Rutland. If you're lucky you may spot a grass snake!

- **Rutland Water, Rutland**
A haven for birds in every month of the year. Spot dancing grebes, hunting hobbies, sneaky cuckoos and even rarities like great northern divers.

Opposite: Gibraltar Point, Lincolnshire

DERBYSHIRE

About the Trust

Derbyshire Wildlife Trust is a small charity with an ambitious vision. It manages 48 nature reserves, nurtures six Living Landscapes that connect fragmented wild places, and is a leading organisation in badger vaccination. The charity also advises on local planning applications, runs 173 conservation projects and inspires people to immerse themselves in all things wild.

Derbyshire Wildlife Trust
01773 881188
derbyshirewildlifetrust.org.uk

Carr Vale
Bolsover, S44 6GA
OS Map SK 459702;
Map Ref L7

One of the best birdwatching spots in northern Derbyshire. Large flocks of wigeon and teal spend the winter by the water's edge, while finches and reed buntings feed in the surrounding vegetation. In summer, swallows and sand martins skim the water. Whitethroats and yellowhammers breed in the scrub.

Lea Wood
Cromford, DE4 5AE
OS Map SK 318562;
Map Ref L13

Visit in spring for wild daffodils and bluebells, and autumn for 96 types of fungi. Combine with a walk along Cromford Canal to look for

grass snakes, water voles and little grebes.

Erewash Meadows
Eastwood, NG16 5PR
OS Map SK 446495;
Map Ref L16

Traditionally managed wet grassland and marshland where ponds attract grass snakes and amphibians in summer. Lapwings perform their impressive aerial displays in spring and waders, wildfowl and hen harriers are winter highlights.

Gang Mine
Middleton by Wirksworth, DE4 4FT
OS Map SK 286555;
Map Ref L12

Part of a former lead mining area where spring sandwort, alpine pansies and alpine pennycress thrive. Wolf

spiders hunt in open areas and glow-worms illuminate summer nights.

Hilton Gravel Pits
Derby, DE65 5FW
OS Map SK 253313;
Map Ref L21

Brilliant for dragonflies and damselflies, including emperor and ruddy darter dragonflies, and emerald and red-eyed damselflies. Great crested and smooth newts breed here. Don't miss the fly agaric toadstools in the woodland in autumn. Enjoy a circular walk with good wheelchair and pushchair access when the paths are dry.

Ladybower Wood
Near Sheffield, S33 0AX
OS Map SK 205867;
Map Ref L2

Upland oak woodland

bursting with pied flycatchers, redstarts, wood warblers and tree pipits in late spring. You may spot the elusive purple hairstreak butterfly fluttering around the oak canopy in midsummer, or a mountain hare bedding down on the heather moorland.

Brockholes Wood
Crowden, SK13 1HZ
OS Map SK 071996;
Map Ref L1

A rare pocket of upland oak woodland with steep banks. Redstarts, willow warblers and tree pipits are summer must-sees; heather and bilberry thrive above the quarry.

THE AVENUE COUNTRY PARK AND WASHLANDS
Wingerworth, S42 6NG; **OS Map** SK 396670; **Map Ref** L8

Access/conditions: A range of trails including boardwalk. Access via squeeze stiles, which are just wide enough for mobility scooters. About 80 per cent of the reserve, including two viewing screens, is wheelchair accessible.
How to get there: From Chesterfield follow A61 south, past the Hunloke Arms. After 0.3 miles Mill Lane is the next road on the left. Reserve entrance is 0.5 miles down Mill Lane on the right. Regular public transport services stop on the A61 at Mill Lane, in Tupton on Queen Victoria Road, and in Grassmoor on North Wingfield Road.
Walking time: 2 hours.

30-minute visit: From the main entrance on Mill Lane, take the path to the left up the ramp for 100m to a lovely viewpoint. Return and turn left for 200m to visit the viewing screen by the reedbed and brook.

This wonderful wetland may be young, but its reedbed, marsh, ponds and grassland have attracted a spectacular array of wildlife since their creation in 2005. Though particularly important for great crested newts and water voles, these aren't the only star species. In spring, male skylarks ascend into the sky with a torrent of song as

they defend their territory and show off to females. Yellowhammers, another declining farmland bird, can be seen regularly and their characteristic call follows you around the grassland. Lapwings, tufted ducks and little grebes breed here, while the onset of winter brings wigeon, teal, snipe and, excitingly, bitterns. Look out for fieldfares and redwings feeding on windfall apples by the trails. The reserve is also great for insects. Dragonflies and damselflies perform aerial acrobatics over the ponds in summer as they snatch unfortunate flies and butterflies from mid-air.

DERBYSHIRE

WILLINGTON WETLANDS

Burton upon Trent, DE65 6YB; **OS Map** SK 291276; **Map Ref** L22

Access/conditions: No access onto the reserve itself, but three viewing platforms provide good views of the wildlife. Members can access the locked bird hide with a code (contact the Derbyshire Wildlife Trust in advance).
How to get there: The reserve lies on Meadow Lane, off the B5008 Willington to Repton road. There is a railway station in Willington – train services between Derby and Birmingham call here. A bus service from Derby runs hourly to Willington.
Walking time: 1 hour.

WILDLIFE FACT: CURLEW

The curlew is an iconic wading bird, its evocative call drifting hauntingly across wet grasslands, farmland and moors. The UK is an internationally important stronghold for curlews, but their numbers have halved here and are dropping in Europe too. A combination of intensive farming, an increase in predators, moorland drainage and afforestation, and climate change are thought to be pushing them towards the edge.

30-minute visit: Park on Meadow Lane and enjoy a short stroll to the first viewing platform, which provides good views.

This former gravel quarry teems with birds at any time of the year. Visit in winter to watch impressive flocks of wigeon, teal, pochards and shovelers diving, dabbling and paddling around the wetland. Spring is a great time to see curlews feeding in the wet grassland on the way to their northern breeding grounds. Summer walks reveal a whole new cast of characters – sand martins fill the sky, common terns fish over the lakes and reed warblers chatter from the reedbed. Such a huge variety of birds naturally attracts hungry predators: kestrels, hobbies, sparrowhawks and the occasional marsh harrier. But birds aren't the only hunters – several types of dragonfly and damselfly enjoy the wetland. You may even be lucky enough to spot a beaver, reintroduced to the area after 800 years of absence.

WOODSIDE FARM

Shipley, DE75 7JL; **OS Map** SK 449439; **Map Ref** L18

Access/conditions: Path conditions vary. Many suitable for wheelchairs but distance from parking and ground conditions can affect access.

How to get there: Park at Derbyshire County Council's Mapperley Reservoir car park or Shipley Country Park car park.

Walking time: There are a variety of walking options around the farm and the adjoining country park including the 10-mile, traffic-free Nutbrook Trail. You could easily spend a whole day exploring.

30-minute visit: Park at the Mapperley Reservoir car park and see how many birds you can spot along the footpath to Nutbrook Coffee Shop.

At 183 acres (74ha), Woodside Farm is the largest protected area in Derbyshire outside the Peak District National Park. It sits on the former Woodside Colliery, but where once the top sightings were railway sidings and coal mines, the nature reserve is now brilliant for birdwatching. Nuthatches, treecreepers and great spotted woodpeckers live in the woodland, barn owls hunt over the hay meadows and skylarks sing above the grassland. Dragonflies and damselflies rule the wetland areas and the grasslands offer a flower-rich buffet to common blue, gatekeeper, comma and meadow brown butterflies. Look out for the pretty pink heads of bee orchids in June and July – you may even spot a brown hare hunkered down in a cosy hollow.

Woodside Farm is a hub for Derbyshire Wildlife Trust's grazing animals. The Trust's vision for the site is to highlight how conservation and farming can go hand in hand, with cattle acting as architects of the sweeping grassland and the farm producing locally reared, ethically raised beef for sale.

WYE VALLEY RESERVES

Buxton, SK17 8SN; **OS Map** SK 140731; **Map Ref** L6

Access/conditions: The Monsal Trail connecting the reserves is accessible for all and allows people to see the adjacent reserves. The reserves themselves have some steep climbs and steps.
How to get there: All three reserves can be accessed from the car park at Miller's Dale.
Walking time: Spend anywhere from 1 hour to a whole day exploring.
30-minute visit: Enjoy the short circular route from Miller's Dale west along the Monsal Trail.

Three Derbyshire Wildlife Trust nature reserves make up this scenic retreat, stretching for almost four miles along the Wye Valley. Spectacular limestone crags await at Chee Dale, lovely wooded slopes usher you into Miller's Dale Quarry and breathtaking views over the River Wye reward those taking the steep climb up to Priestcliffe Lees. Whether you visit for the walks, the wildlife or both, you'll leave full of wonder.

Starting your adventure at Miller's Dale sets the tone for the whole walk. On hot July days the scent of fragrant orchids fills the air on the quarry floor. From early summer the entire reserve blooms with a multi-coloured carpet of cowslips, early purple orchids, harebells and wild strawberries visited by common blue butterflies and six-spot burnet moths. Kestrels sometimes nest on the crevice-strewn quarry faces.

Priestcliffe Lees is also a botanical paradise, with yellow mountain pansies and leadwort growing on the old lead spoil heaps. Dark green fritillary butterflies live here, and redstarts, blackcaps and willow warblers take up residence in the ash woodland for summer. At Chee Dale, in late June, look out for the spectacular bright blue spires of Jacob's ladder, as well as grass-of-Parnassus. As you walk beside the river you may be lucky enough to see a dipper 'bobbing' on the rocks as it searches for food.

NOTTINGHAMSHIRE

About the Trust

Nottinghamshire Wildlife Trust's vision is for a wilder Nottinghamshire, in which the fragmented landscape is reconnected and wildlife has the chance to thrive. By caring for numerous nature reserves, restoring habitats and giving everyone the chance to experience wildlife, the charity is shaping a future where wildlife thrives because of people, and people thrive because of wildlife.

Nottinghamshire Wildlife Trust
01159 588242
nottinghamshirewildlife.org

Bentinck Banks

Ashfield, NG17 9LJ
OS Map SK 562489;
Map Ref L15

Old railway lines now blanketed by grassland. Greater knapweed, burnet saxifrage, St John's wort and cowslips grow alongside orchids. Bullfinches and yellowhammers sing from the scrub. Park at Portland Park and use the railway crossing.

Bunny Old Wood (West)

Bunny, NG11 6QQ
OS Map SJ 200614;
Map Ref L23

An ancient woodland, rich in both history and wildlife. Bunny Old Wood is referred to in the Domesday Book and was used as a camp by Henry VII. Great and lesser spotted woodpeckers are among 50 bird species recorded.

Eaton Wood & Gamston Woods

Retford, DN22 0RB
OS Map SK 727772;
Map Ref L5

Two ancient woodlands meet in a wonderful mix of ashes, oaks, birches, field maples and hazel coppice. Primroses, wood anemones, bluebells and wood avens bloom, and 24 species of butterfly include purple hairstreaks. Please don't park on the roadside verges as these are rich in wildflowers.

Duke's Wood Nature Reserve

Eakring, NG22 8PA
OS Map SK 675603;
Map Ref L10

Once the location of the UK's first on-shore oilfield. Now, the reserve couldn't be more peaceful, with an oak, ash and hazel woodland meeting grassland dotted with primroses, bluebells, broad-

leaved helleborine and more lovely flowers. Rare species include dyer's greenweed and white-letter hairstreak butterflies.

Farndon Willow Holt & Water Meadows

Farndon, NG24 3SP
OS Map SK 767521;
Map Ref L14

Willow woodland, marsh, traditionally managed water meadows and an important collection of willows established in the 1950s by renowned local botanists, Mr and Mrs Howitt. Wildflowers include meadow crane's-bill, comfrey, angelica and meadowsweet.

Ploughman Wood

Near Lambley, NG4 4QE
OS Map SK 640468;
Map Ref L17

One of the few remaining ancient woodlands in

Nottinghamshire. Piles of dead wood offer refuge and food to beetles, bats, bracket fungi and hole-nesting birds. There is a magical bluebell display during spring, and the scent of honeysuckle drifts through the trees in summer.

Treswell Wood Nature Reserve

Retford, DN22 0ED
OS Map SK 762789;
Map Ref L4

Wood anemones, bluebells and primroses bloom in spring. Marsh-marigolds, yellow irises and water crowfoot grow around ponds where great crested and smooth newts live alongside 12 species of water beetle. Stoats and foxes are regularly seen in the woodland, where woodcock, jays, garden warblers and spotted flycatchers have all been recorded. Rarer residents include speckled bush crickets and hazel dormice.

SKYLARKS

Holme Pierrepont, NG12 2LU; **OS Map** SK 622389; **Map Ref** L19

Access/conditions:
Some accessible trails for wheelchairs/pushchairs. Cafés and toilets at Holme Pierrepont Country Park a short walk/drive away.
How to get there: Bus from Nottingham stops close to the junction of Regatta Way and Adbolton Lane, then a one-mile walk. By car, from A52 turn into Regatta Way following signs for the National Water Sports Centre. Follow the road around two large right-hand bends, at which point the road becomes Adbolton Lane, where you can park. Additional small car park at main entrance to the south of the road, and a layby on the northern side.
Walking time: 3 hours.
30-minute visit: From Adbolton Lane, walk the Mallard Trail through the wood.

Skylarks is thought to be the first nature reserve laid out specifically for wheelchair users. There are routes and walks for all, including a two-mile footpath linking viewing screens and boardwalks at some of the best parts of the reserve, to give visitors wonderful views across lakes, woodlands, ponds, reedbeds, meadows, scrapes and islands.

Great crested grebes drift gracefully across the water, kingfishers hunt from perches around the lake edges and reed warblers breed deep within the reedbed, sometimes becoming host parents for chicks of the visiting cuckoos. Lapwings can be seen year-round, with the largest numbers arriving in winter. In summer they're joined by little ringed plovers, which nest on the safety of the scrapes, and shy snipe, which you can hear 'drumming' in spring. This strange sound isn't made vocally but by air rushing past the males' tail feathers during mating displays,

BESTHORPE NATURE RESERVE

Besthorpe, NG23 7HL; **OS Map** SK 818640; **Map Ref** L9

Access/conditions: Track around the reserve is wheelchair/pushchair-friendly with new RADAR kissing gates. Disabled-friendly raised viewing screen overlooking Mons Pool. Some boardwalks.
How to get there: Trains run from Nottingham to Collingham and Besthorpe. By car, from A1133 Newark to Gainsborough Road, take the southern of two turns into Besthorpe village.
Walking time: 2–3 hours.
30-minute visit: Visit the hide overlooking Mons Pool to see the heronry.

Besthorpe Nature Reserve proves that even the most booming industrial site can bounce back. Its new lease of life spans two distinct areas north and south of Trent Lane: open water with islands, reedbeds and shingle to the north, and wildflower meadows to the south.

Immerse yourself in the lives of Besthorpe's birds in one of the hides around Mons Pool, where you could spot a kingfisher diving, little egrets stalking underwater prey, or reed and sedge warblers calling from discreet reed-perches. Little-ringed plovers breed on the islands and, excitingly, you can see one of the largest and most important heronries in Nottinghamshire raising their noisy young. In winter, Mons Pool fills with pochards, teal, shovelers, tufted ducks and wigeon, which come to eke out the lean months. The meadows brim with common cudweed, kidney vetch, orchids, great burnet and Yorkshire fog in summer, providing breeding and feeding opportunities for brown argus and Adonis blue butterflies, as well as stunning emperor moths.

RAINWORTH HEATH

Rainworth, NG21 0HR; **OS Map** SK 594591; **Map Ref** L11

Access/conditions: Limited wheelchair access but no stiles.
How to get there: Off the A617 in Rainworth. There is no parking. Visitors can access the reserve via a gate on the private road leading from Rainworth village to Rufford Colliery at SK 593591. Please don't park on this road.
Walking time: Allow at least a couple of hours to stroll around the reserve and watch the amazing wildlife.

Rainworth Heath is one of the last remaining areas of heathland in Nottinghamshire, and once you step onto the reserve it's easy to see why it is such a treasured fragment.

The wet heath is peppered with peaty pools fringed with sopping-wet sphagnum mosses. In spring, the fluffy heads of cotton-grass bob in the breeze, and at the height of summer, the bright pink flowers of cross-leaved heath add splashes of colour among the purple moor-grass and common sedge. On the dry heath, adders and common lizards bask on the warm, sun-soaked ground around patches of bell heather and in gaps under gorse bushes. You may spot a green woodpecker bouncing along the ground in search of ants, or a cunningly camouflaged common heath moth resting on the vegetation. Excitingly, turtle doves visit Rainworth Heath, alongside woodlarks, tree pipits and garden warblers.

To turn the reserve into an even more incredible home for wildlife, Nottinghamshire Wildlife Trust is re-establishing the heather, controlling bracken and scrub, and grazing with Hebridean sheep.

IDLE VALLEY

Retford, DN22 8RQ; **OS Map** SK 689829; **Map Ref** L3

Opening hours: Visitor centre open 10am–4pm daily.
Access/conditions: Four designated walking routes. Many trails suitable for wheelchairs/pushchairs. £3 donation for parking.
How to get there: From A1/Blyth Road, turn onto Old London Road and then right onto A638/Great North Road. Turn left after almost two miles and continue to the reserve.
Walking time: Give yourself a whole day to explore the reserve in full.
30-minute visit: Take the Lakeside Walk around Bellmoor Lake and pop into the Idle Valley Rural Learning Centre and Café.

With more than 1,000 acres (450ha) of lakes, wetland, grassland and scrub, Idle Valley is a truly wild escape – for both people and wildlife!

The reserve bursts into life with the onset of spring. Skylarks take to the skies in a flurry of song, orange-tip butterflies dance around cuckooflowers and the characteristic ditty of yellowhammers follows you around the grassland. This is where you're most likely to see hares hunkered down in their hollows on the ground, and, as the season melts into summer, bee orchids and common twayblades growing among the grasses. Bumper

moths and common blue and small skipper butterflies fill the air when the sun comes out, then as evening draws in, you could hear the sweet serenade of a nightingale drifting from the nearby scrub.

In autumn you might see kingfishers and tree sparrows more often as they fill up on food in preparation for the leaner months. As winter arrives, the lakes fill with little grebes, gadwall and other overwintering ducks who'll vacate again once a new spring rolls around, and redshanks and little ringed plovers move in to raise their young.

ATTENBOROUGH NATURE RESERVE

Attenborough, NG9 6DY; **OS Map** SK 516340; **Map Ref** L20

Opening hours: Car park open 9am–8pm daily. Visitor centre open 9.30am–4pm daily.
Access/conditions: Many trails around the reserve, including wheelchair/pushchair-friendly trails. £3 donation for parking.
How to get there: Attenborough train station is a five-minute walk from the reserve. Trent Barton bus service runs regularly between Nottingham Broadmarsh and Derby bus station (stop: Chilwell Retail Park/West Point Shopping Centre). By car, the reserve is off the A6005 between Beeston and Long Eaton. Turn onto Barton Lane at traffic lights at Chilwell Retail Park, head over the railway crossing, and the car park is at the bottom.
Walking time: Allow a whole morning or afternoon to explore the reserve, browse the shop and refuel with a bite to eat in the café overlooking the lakes.
30-minute visit: Explore the ponds around the car park, stroll around the wildlife area behind the Nature Centre or visit the Kingfisher Hide towards the River Trent.

Opened by Sir David Attenborough (though not named after him) in 1966, Attenborough Nature Reserve sits just a few miles from Nottingham city centre and offers a lifeline to the natural world.

Whether you're a seasoned birdwatcher or family wanting to get closer to nature, Attenborough has something to delight everyone. You can watch sand martins flying to and from their nest holes in a specially created bank, listen to sedge warblers throwing their scratchy song out from the reeds, and marvel at the aerial acrobatics of dragonflies hunting over the lakes. In spring, brown argus and orange-tip butterflies take to the air, enchanting visitors as they hunt for nectar.

Attenborough is paradise for bird lovers. In winter, the reserve becomes home to an important chunk of Nottinghamshire's shovelers and diving ducks, as well as teal, goosanders and even sea ducks. In spring and autumn, many birds pass through on migration and bitterns are regularly spotted skulking about in the reeds.

With a brilliant visitor centre, family activities and lakeside café on offer too, Attenborough is a memorable day out that will help the whole family connect with the natural world.

LEICESTERSHIRE AND RUTLAND

About the Trust

Leicestershire and Rutland Wildlife Trust cares for 35 nature reserves covering more than 3,048 acres (1,233ha). From woodland to meadows, wetland to heaths, the Trust is dedicated to restoring, recreating and reconnecting fragmented habitats to help wildlife recover and enrich the lives of all who visit.

Leicestershire and Rutland Wildlife Trust
01162 629968
lrwt.org.uk

Charley Woods
Copt Oak, LE67 4UY
OS Map SK 472137;
Map Ref L27

A mosaic of woodlands in the Charnwood Forest. Spring bluebell walks are essential, but it is worth visiting all year round, as the diverse mixture of trees and standing dead wood brings nuthatches, treecreepers, great spotted woodpeckers, green woodpeckers and jays.

Cribbs Meadow
Sewstern, LE15 7RQ
OS Map SK 899188;
Map Ref L28

Adder's-tongue ferns and cowslips bloom in spring and you can see agrimony, great burnet and yellow rattle in summer. Keep your eyes peeled for green-winged orchids, common spotted-orchids and water avens.

Dimminsdale
Ashby-de-la-Zouch, LE65 1RT
OS Map SK 376219;
Map Ref L24

See a spectacular snowdrop display in late winter. In March you may be lucky enough to see hares boxing in the fields. Deer and birds live in the mixed woodland and green woodpeckers *yaffle* across the grassland as they feast on nutritious ants.

Great Merrible Wood
Stockerston, LE16 8DG
OS Map SP 834962;
Map Ref L33

A haven for mammals including badgers, deer and foxes. Tits, finches, woodpeckers and treecreepers potter about in the trees and violet helleborine grows below. This reserve supposedly has the most varied fungi of any Leicestershire wood.

Holwell
Holwell, LE14 4SZ
OS Map SK 741234;
Map Ref L26

A hidden gem in the heart of Leicestershire. Dramatic rock faces and slopes make perfect sun-traps for butterflies including dingy skippers, green hairstreaks and Essex skippers. Willow warblers, blackcaps, lesser whitethroats and spotted flycatchers nest here in spring.

Loughborough Big Meadow SSSI
Loughborough, LE11 1NF
OS Map SK 539215;
Map Ref L25

One of the few Lammas meadows left in England. A kaleidoscope of great burnet, meadow saxifrage, yellow rattle, pepper saxifrage and narrow-leaved water dropwort. Listen for sedge warblers, whitethroats and reed buntings in summer.

Narborough Bog SSSI
Narborough, LE19 2AZ
OS Map SP 547978;
Map Ref L32

A wildlife refuge in suburbia where you can see jewel-blue kingfishers and all three species of woodpecker. Sunny days draw common blue, meadow brown and small heath butterflies to the wet meadows.

LAUNDE WOODS

Launde, LE7 9XB; **OS Map** SK 788035; **Map Ref** L31

Access/conditions: Ground can be rough and uneven.
How to get there: From the Tilton to Oakham road take any of several roads signposted to Launde. Continue through Launde park with the Abbey on your left, stopping at the top of the hill where a public footpath is signposted to the right and a bridleway to the left. Launde Big Wood can be seen in the distance to the west, while Park Wood, to the east, is partially hidden by a tall hedge. Walk along the public rights of way and enter the woods through the gates at their entrance.
Walking time: 2 hours.

Stepping into Launde Woods, which combines two of the most ancient woodlands in Leicestershire, is like stepping back in time. Oak, ash, hazel and field maple dominate Big Wood to the west, while Park Wood to the east was once a Forestry Commission plantation. The atmosphere is awe-inspiring, with amazing displays of wood anemones, bluebells and early purple orchids in spring. You may also spot the rarer greater butterfly-orchid or nettle-leaved bellflower. Soprano pipistrelle and brown long-eared bats have been found roosting at the reserve, nuthatches sing sweetly during spring, and white-letter hairstreak butterflies make the most of the dappled glades.

A large part of Park Wood was planted with conifers in the past. These have now been removed and the woodland restored with oak, ash and field maple. Narrow rides have been widened, glades created, and hazel coppiced to benefit plants like sweet woodruff and primroses.

LEA MEADOWS

Markfield, LE67 9PL; **OS Map** SK 509114; **Map Ref** L30

Access/conditions: A hand-gate leads into the meadows. Stick to paths so as not to damage this sensitive area.
How to get there: Lea Meadows can be walked to from Newtown Linford. From Leicester, drive through Newtown Linford village and take the left-hand fork down Ulverscroft Lane. Carry on for just over a mile. Entrance on the left by a public foot-path sign.
Walking time: 1 hour.

30-minute visit: Walk along the stream separating the two meadows to get a feel for the reserve.

A meeting of meadows, woodland and meandering stream, which makes for a peaceful, wild experience – you may even see a kingfisher.

More than 240 species of plant have been recorded, and summer brings a riot of colour in the form of betony, harebells, devil's-bit scabious and pignut, which attracts chimney sweeper moths. In wetter areas, hundreds of common and heath spotted-orchids flower alongside marsh speedwell and opposite-leaved golden-saxifrage. Drier parts are colonised by bitter-vetch, great burnet and pepper-saxifrage. The glittering stream is a haven for brook lamprey, which are rare in Leicestershire. They share the sparkling water with bullhead, minnows, three-spined sticklebacks and brown trout.

With so much action below the surface you'd be forgiven for forgetting to look up, but do scan the riverside alder trees in winter for flocks of siskins and redpolls.

COSSINGTON MEADOWS

Cossington, LE7 4UZ; **OS Map** SK 597130; **Map Ref** L29

Access/conditions: Plenty of paths. These can be muddy in wet weather.
How to get there: Head west out of Cossington on Syston Road towards Rothley. The reserve is on your right, north of the road.
Walking time: 1.5–2 hours.

30-minute visit: A brisk circular walk could result in seeing little grebes, lapwings and reed buntings.

Cossington Meadows is one of Leicestershire and Rutland Wildlife Trust's best reserves for birdwatching, with something exciting to see throughout the year. The deep pools attract ducks including gadwall, tufted ducks, wigeon and teal in the winter months, when you can occasionally see short-eared owls hunting – an unforgettable wildlife experience.

In summer, a fantastic diversity of wading birds arrives to take advantage of the mud left behind by receding winter floodwaters. Green sandpipers, greenshanks, oystercatchers, redshanks and little ringed plovers probe for tasty morsels – the redshanks and plovers even nest here. Grey herons, grey wagtails and kingfishers are reserve regulars, while rarities including velvet scoter and glossy ibis have been recorded in recent years.

Birds aren't the only creatures that thrive at Cossington Meadows. Grass snakes, frogs and toads all make their home here, and insects fly in their droves during summer. You could spot migrant hawker and black-tailed skimmer dragonflies plus small copper, common blue and brimstone butterflies.

PRIOR'S COPPICE SSSI

Braunston, LE15 8DB; **OS Map** SK 832049; **Map Ref** K15

Access/conditions: Access is through a kissing gate. The rides can be wet all year-round.

How to get there: The nearest approach by public transport is Oakham, 3.5 miles away. From Braunston, take the road towards Leighfield and follow signs for Leighfield Lodge. After 800m you'll see the reserve car park on the right.

Walking time: 1 hour.

30-minute visit: A short walk along the woodland rides and paths can reveal a surprising variety of wildlife.

A relic of the wildwood that once covered large parts of Leicestershire and Rutland. A walk here brings you close to some lovely birds, mammals, flowers and trees, and possibly even a grass snake!

The numbers are impressive: 71 species of bird including more than 40 breeding species. Nuthatches, blackcaps and garden warblers are often joined in spring by rarer visitors such as pied flycatchers and redstarts, filling the woods with a multi-layered melody. More than 200 species of moth have been recorded, along with orange-tip, brimstone, white-letter hairstreak and purple hairstreak butterflies. Speckled bush crickets have been spotted here too – an interesting and very local insect. The 230-strong list of flowering plants features a rainbow-bright line-up of wood anemones, early purple orchids, wood sorrel, wood forget-me-nots, broad-leaved helleborines, ragged robin and common spotted-orchids.

One of the joys of a walk around Prior's Coppice is reading the trees like a history book. Signs of traditional management lie everywhere, with some coppice stools dating back several hundred years.

RUTLAND WATER

Anglian Water Birdwatching Centre: LE15 8BT **Lyndon:** LE15 8RN; **OS Map** SK 878075; **Map Ref** K14

Anglian Water Birdwatching Centre: 🅿 🚻 ♿ ℹ️ 🍴 🛒 ⛱️ ♻️ 🥾 👨‍👩‍👧 🐑

Lyndon Visitor Centre: 🅿 🚻 ℹ️ 🍴 🛒 ⛱️ ♻️ 👨‍👩‍👧

Opening hours: Anglian Water Birdwatching Centre open year-round except Christmas Eve and Christmas Day (9am–5pm summer, 9am–4pm winter); Lyndon Visitor Centre open from mid-March to early September (9am–5pm summer, 10am–3pm autumn).

Access/conditions: Adults £6; concessions £5; children £3.50; families £16. Many of the hides and trails are wheelchair and pushchair-friendly. Electric buggies are available for hire – phone ahead to book (Anglian Water Birdwatching Centre: 01572 770651; Lyndon: 01572 737378).

How to get there: Anglian Water Birdwatching Centre is near Egleton village, 1.3 miles south-east of Oakham. Take A606 Oakham to Stanford road or A6003 Oakham to Uppingham road. There is a track from the village to the reserve car park. Lyndon Visitor Centre is located off Lyndon Road on the south shore of Rutland Water.

Walking time: More than 30 hides and four miles of walking trails to explore. Pack your lunch to spend the whole day connecting with nature.

30-minute visit: Call into the visitor centres to check the best places to visit on the day.

Rutland may be the smallest county in England, but it boasts one of the best nature reserves in the entire country. Rutland Water dedicates 1,000 acres (404ha) of land for wildlife and is an absolute haven for birds in every month of the year.

Spring is magical, as sand martins whizz over the water, great crested grebes perform their elaborate courtship dances and ospreys – breeding here for 20 years now – fish on Manton Bay in sight of the Waderscrape Hide at Lyndon.

Hobbies patrol the lagoons in April and chiffchaffs fill the air with their staccato song. A stop by the Anglian Water Birdwatching Centre could reward you with the sweet song of the nightingale or plaintive call of the cuckoo. Summer is a great time to watch the ospreys tending to their young on the camera feed that beams into both visitor centres. Big flocks of godwits, green sandpipers and even spoonbills drop into the reserve at this time too. Autumn sees fiery trees reflected in the water and numbers of waders, wildfowl and divers building. By the time winter arrives there can be as many as 25,000 ducks, geese and swans on the reserve. Scaup, common scoters and pochards are joined by great northern divers, Slavonian grebes and smews.

LINCOLNSHIRE

About the Trust

From the Humber to the Wash, Lincolnshire Wildlife Trust has been protecting the county's wildlife and inspiring people to care for nature since 1948. From saltmarshes and mudflats to woods, heaths and meadows, the charity safeguards almost 100 nature reserves and helps to protect 65 Roadside Nature Reserves, several Marine Protected Areas and more than 1,000 Local Wildlife Sites.

Lincolnshire Wildlife Trust
01507 526667
lincstrust.org.uk

Crowle Moor

Crowle, DN17 4BL
OS Map SE 759145;
Map Ref K2

One of the richest lowland peatlands in the north of England. Higher, drier areas carry heather, bracken and birch scrub; wetter parts have reedbeds, cotton-grass, sphagnum moss and willow carr. Rarer plants include bog rosemary, dune helleborine and greater yellow rattle, and the large heath butterfly lives here. Long-eared owls, nightjars and woodcock breed, and if you're lucky you may spot an adder or grass snake.

Fiskerton Fen

Fiskerton, LN3 4HU
OS Map TF 085720;
Map Ref K8

A fenland with open water and reedbeds. By expanding

the reedbed, the Lincolnshire Wildlife Trust has encouraged some of our rarest species to move in. The near-extinct great water parsnip has been reintroduced and yellowhammers, corn buntings, linnets and tree sparrows sing from the scrub. Marsh harriers and bitterns have been seen.

Wolds Edge Woods

Louth, LN11 8LU
OS Map TF 369832;
Map Ref K5

This string of ancient woodlands on the eastern edge of the Lincolnshire Wolds includes Legbourne, Muckton, Swinn, Rigsby and Hoplands Woods nature reserves. A rich array of wildflowers – including bluebells and wood anemones – grow on the woodland floor and can be explored using the waymarked routes.

Moor Farm and Kirkby Moor

Woodhall Spa, LN10 6YU
OS Map TF 226635;
Map Ref K11

These two adjacent reserves are the perfect place to get away from it all. More than 240 species of plant, 100 species of bird, 24 species of butterfly and 250 species of moth have been recorded in the mosaic of bog, heath and woodland, including common centaury, meadow crane's-bill and snipe. The breathtaking heathland of Kirkby Moor is home to cuckoos, adders, woodlarks and green woodpeckers.

Red Hill

Louth, LN11 9UE
OS Map TF 264806;
Map Ref K6

Chalk grassland, wonderful wildflowers – Red Hill has

it all. Felwort, yellow-wort, basil thyme, kidney vetch and pyramidal and bee orchids attract six-spot burnet moths and marbled white butterflies. Meadow pipits breed here, and if you tread gently, you may spot a grass snake or common lizard sunning itself.

Scotton Common
Scunthorpe, DN21 3PY
OS Map SK 873985;
Map Ref K3

Step into a heathland wonderland of heathers and purple moor-grass. Emperor moths thrive, the sandy banks attract solitary bees and tree pipits and woodlarks breed. Keep your eyes peeled for shy adders and common lizards.

Deeping Lakes
Deeping St James, PE6 8RJ
OS Map TF 187083;
Map Ref K13

Wildfowl and waterbirds flock to these flooded gravel pits. Common terns, great crested grebes, teal, gadwall and dunlin are just a handful of the species you could see from the wheelchair-accessible bird hide. Early marsh orchids grow in small wildflower meadows around the main lake and, in summer, the air fills with four-spotted chaser, emperor and brown hawker dragonflies.

DONNA NOOK

Louth, LN11 7PD; **OS Map** TF 422998; **Map Ref** K4

Opening hours: Seal viewing area, main car park and facilities open October–December, dawn–dusk.
Access/conditions: There is disabled ramp access from Stonebridge car park. Access from the main car park is over

an unsurfaced dune.
How to get there: Several access points off the main A10131 coast road. Park in the main car park (cost subject to change) or at the Stonebridge car park.
Walking time: Between

October and December, the beach is closed to visitors as the seals are breeding, but you can watch them from the special viewing area where you can spend as long as you like.

The beach at Donna Nook is famous for the grey seals who arrive to give birth in late autumn. More than 2,000 pups are born here each year and visitors can watch them growing up from a viewing area at the foot of the sand dunes. This reduces disturbance to the seals, which may look slow but are powerful predators with very sharp teeth!

Winter is also a great time to be on the lookout for birds foraging on the mudflats: snow buntings, Lapland buntings, shorelarks and twite gather around impressive flocks of dunlin and knot. In summer, Sandwich terns arrive to breed and reed buntings sing from stands of sea buckthorn.

LINCOLNSHIRE COASTAL COUNTRY PARK

Chapel St Leonards; **OS Map** TF 562732; **Map Ref** K7

Opening hours: A number of non-Wildlife Trust-owned cafés, visitor centres and viewing points are found throughout the Country Park, including the North Sea Observatory and Seascape Café in Chapel St Leonards. Check the Lincolnshire County Council website for full details and opening hours.

Access/conditions: Level footpaths.

How to get there: By car, there are multiple car parks between Sandilands and Chapel St Leonards, from where the Coastal Country Park can be explored.

Walking time: You could spend a whole day here. **30 minute visit.** Park at Anderby Creek and view Lincolnshire's big sky from the Cloud Bar before heading to the Round and Round Hide for expansive views over the coast, and inland over the Trust's Anderby Marsh nature reserve.

Lincolnshire Coastal Country Park encompasses an area of tranquil countryside, sandy beaches and Lincolnshire's famous big skies. The freshwater grazing marshes attract flocks of whooper swans and pink-footed geese in winter, while the mosaic of nature reserves plays host to visiting redwings and fieldfares. In summer, marsh harriers and barn owls breed and the reedbeds fill with warbler song.

There are a number of car parks and wonderful vantage points. The best views are from the Round and Round Hide and Cloud Bar at Anderby, and the North Sea Observatory at Chapel St Leonards. As well as grey and common seals, there is the chance of seeing a harbour porpoise as you gaze out to sea.

WHISBY NATURE PARK

Thorpe-on-the-Hill, LN6 9BW; **OS Map** SK 911661; **Map Ref** K9

Opening hours: Visitor centre open 9.30am–4.30pm, Monday–Sunday (November–February); 9.30am–4.30pm, Monday–Friday, and 9.30am–5pm, Saturday–Sunday (March–October).

Access/conditions: Level footpaths, the majority hard-surfaced. Can be muddy in places. Several wheelchair-accessible routes.

How to get there: Bus from Lincoln to Pennells Garden Centre, then a 20-minute walk. By car, the reserve is clearly marked with brown tourist signs from the A46. Parking costs £2 (March–October); £1 (November–February).

Walking time: Six waymarked trails offer plenty of opportunity for discovery. You can walk them all in around 3 hours.

30-minute visit: Stop by the bird feeding station, then visit one of the hides overlooking Grebe Lake.

Whisby Nature Park is a beautiful wetland retreat near Lincoln, full of wildlife, walks and trails the whole family will love.

Once barren and lifeless, this amazing place now abounds with banded demoiselles, southern marsh-orchids, goldcrests and sedge warblers where once it was quarried for sand and gravel. Swallows and sand martins swoop over the water in spring and summer, little terns breed here, and in winter, starlings form breathtaking murmurations over the misty lakes.

Whisby Nature Park has become synonymous with nightingales, and spring is the best time to be serenaded by their sweet melody. You may also be lucky enough to see or hear a cuckoo – a 'brood parasite', which lays its eggs in the nests of Whisby's reed and sedge warblers.

SNIPE DALES

Lusby, PE23 4JB; **OS Map** TF 319683; **Map Ref** K10

Access/conditions: Paths are seasonally wet and muddy, and steep in places. Wheelchair users may gain access to the marsh area by car (contact warden in advance). Dogs on leads permitted in the Country Park – not on the nature reserve.
How to get there: Signs from A158 (Skegness to Lincoln) and B1195 (Horncastle to Spilsby). There are car parks both at the Country Park and nature reserve.
Walking time: 3.5 hours.
30-minute visit: Walk from the Country Park car park to the Meridian Stone – a block of Spilsby Sandstone that marks the line of the Greenwich Meridian.

Nestled on the southern edge of the Wolds, Snipe Dales is a nature reserve and Country Park cradled by steep-sided valleys and fretted by streams. There are wonderful wide-open views, and as you stroll around the reserve you can marvel at one of the few surviving semi-natural wet valley systems in the county. The Country Park is the place for woodland wanders, with the culmination of the two habitats nurturing a fantastic range of wildlife.

In spring, the woods of the Country Park come alive with nesting willow warblers, blackcaps and coal tits alongside a host of other birds, including

goldcrests, treecreepers and sparrowhawks. Siskins and bramblings join them in winter, foraging for seeds in the trees. The Peasam Hill area of the nature reserve brims with common spotted-orchids, ragged robin, meadowsweet and cuckooflowers. The Central Flushes are the best place to watch dragonflies and damselflies darting after prey, while Furze Hill, as well as harbouring an old watermill, is a butterfly hotspot, with peacocks, painted ladies and holly blues fluttering around thistles and brambles. Whitethroats, linnets and finches feed and breed in this area too.

FAR INGS

Barton-upon-Humber, DN18 5RG; **OS Map** TA 011229; **Map Ref** K1

Opening hours: Check Lincolnshire Wildlife Trust website for up-to-date information.

Access/conditions: Many paths and two bird hides are wheelchair accessible.

How to get there: A 10- to 15-minute walk along the Humber bank from Barton-on-Humber and the bus and train stations. By car, leave A15 at A1077 turn-off. Take first exit from the roundabout, then first right (look for the brown tourist signs). Turn right at the bottom of the hill, then the reserve entrance is on the left.

Walking time: Allow a whole morning or afternoon.

30-minute visit: From the visitor centre, walk along the Humber bank to the hide overlooking the Pursuits Pit.

Get back to nature at this chain of flooded clay pits and sweeping reedbeds. In spring and autumn you can see migration in action as pipits, finches, swallows, martins, swifts, larks, starlings, waders and wildfowl all move along the estuary, feeding, breeding or sometimes just passing through. Late summer sees the biggest build-up of hirundines as swallows and martins use the reedbeds to roost. In autumn and winter,

head to the Humber bank to watch redshanks, wigeon, black-tailed godwits, skeins of pink-footed geese and more arriving to eke out the colder months. Bitterns call the reserve home all year round, so keep a sharp ear out for their 'booming' call and see if you can spot one from the double-decker hide at Ness End Farm.

Far Ings' pits fill with ducks like teal during winter, and the mix of freshwater and saltwater habitats means there are plenty of microscopic invertebrates for fish to eat, which in turn become prey for hungry herons and kingfishers.

GIBRALTAR POINT

Skegness, PE24 4SU; **OS Map** TF 556581; **Map Ref** K12

Opening hours: Check Lincolnshire Wildlife Trust website for up-to-date information.

Access/conditions: Most paths are level and well-surfaced, sometimes muddy. Some hides accessible for wheelchairs. No dogs on the beach and foreshore from 1 April–1 September.

How to get there: The reserve is about three miles south of Skegness and well signposted with brown tourist signs. Parking £2 for 2 hours or £5 all day.

Walking time: 2–3 hours.

30-minute visit: From the Beach Car Park head to the Mill Hill viewpoint, the highest point on the reserve and a good place to watch the bird migration.

A spectacular stretch of unspoilt coastline where sandy, muddy seashores, sand dunes, saltmarshes and fresh water coalesce in an unforgettable wild retreat. The sweeping views out to sea are incredible and the sheer diversity of life is dazzling.

In spring, the first of the migrants stop off to refuel or establish territories, and it isn't unusual to spot rare birds on the reserve or flying overhead. In summer, little terns fish in the shallows and skylarks are in full song above saltmarshes hazy with purple sprays of sea lavender.

In autumn, huge whirling flocks of knot, sanderling, grey plovers and redshanks can be seen on the high tides. In winter, wildfowl including brent geese, shelducks, wigeon and teal gather on the shore, foraging alongside shorelarks and snow buntings. Winter is also the best time to see birds of prey, with hen harriers, merlins and owls arriving to hunt.

Gibraltar Point has an important bird observatory where an army of dedicated volunteers ring birds and monitors the movements, condition and population of the birds that visit the reserve – all essential for conservation.

WEST MIDLANDS

The industrial history of the West Midlands is woven into the fabric of its natural landscape. The region's canals, once loaded with coal-laden barges, now teem with wildlife including water voles, kingfishers and herons. Colourful wildflowers wave gently on banks once bustling with busy labourers, and reservoirs built to supply the canals are now wonderful wetland habitats supporting impressive bird populations, especially during the winter months.

Nature has reclaimed the landscape of the West Midlands, and this is largely due to the incredible conservation work that has repaired the damage of heavy industry and paved the way for wildlife to return. The rare polecat has recolonised Herefordshire, while cleaner water means that even in urban centres otters have taken up residence in rivers and canals.

It's hard to imagine that much of the West Midlands used to be blanketed by forest. Luckily, some beautiful pockets of ancient woodland remain, transporting you back to a time before mining dominated the land. Dark and damp, these atmospheric woods are filled with weird, wonderful and often-rare fungi. Staffordshire's ancient woods are fantastic places to wander beneath monolithic oak and beech trees.

To the south of the Black Country, mining gave way to farming and transformed the landscape into the mosaic of fields, hedgerows and wooded hills you can see today. From the Black Mountains in the west to the Malvern Hills in the east, down to the sweeping Wye Valley, wildlife finds refuge in habitats that are sadly becoming rarer and rarer in the UK. Hedgerows form havens for songbirds and dormice, while unimproved hay meadows nurture beautiful wildflowers like the green-winged orchid.

Excitingly, the sandy soils of Staffordshire are fantastic places to spot reptiles, and support a wonderful range of mammals: badgers, hedgehogs, stoats, weasels and hares.

NOT TO BE MISSED

- **Brook Vessons and The Hollies, Shropshire**
Admire the biggest birch, holly and crab apple trees in Shropshire and stroll between 400-year-old holly trees wizened and creaking with age.

- **The Roaches, Staffordshire**
A magnificent 975-acre (394ha) landscape of soaring rock faces, wide-open moors, precious blanket bog and heather-covered hills.

- **The Doward Reserves, Herefordshire**
Six interconnected Herefordshire Wildlife Trust reserves where you could spot hawfinches, lesser spotted woodpeckers, white admiral butterflies and magpie inkcaps.

- **The Devil's Spittleful and Rifle Range, Worcestershire**
A glorious heathland, home to green tiger beetles, common lizards and emperor moths; redstarts, green woodpeckers and cuckoos

- **Moseley Bog, Birmingham**
The childhood playground of J. R. R. Tolkien, where fungi fill the woods in autumn and Bronze Age burnt mounds allude to a fascinating social history.

Opposite: Stiperstones Ridge, Shropshire

SHROPSHIRE

About the Trust

Shropshire has landscapes of great beauty and diversity. From the hills and valleys to the south, to the ancient watery wilderness of the meres and mosses to the north, there is so much to discover. Shropshire Wildlife Trust looks after 40 nature reserves, including ancient woods, flower-rich meadows, wetland bird havens and heathland, and is linking these up with other wild areas to help wildlife move beyond the boundaries of nature reserves.

**Shropshire Wildlife Trust
01743 284280
shropshirewildlifetrust.org.uk**

Clunton Coppice

Clunton, SY7 0HU
OS Map SO 338806;
Map Ref N24

A wonderful oak wood that shines at any time of year, but especially in spring when the trees ring with birdsong from wood warblers and pied flycatchers. Clunton is the site of the first proven record of a pine marten in England for at least 50 years. Nearly 20 individuals have now been recorded in the area.

Granville Country Park

Telford, TF2 7QG
OS Map SJ 719125;
Map Ref N15

The spirit of renewal fills the air at this former mining site. Pit mounds of waste have been transformed into flower-rich grassland dotted with orchids and ox-eye daisies, and bird's-foot trefoil feeds dingy skipper and green hairstreak butterflies. Footpaths are easy and the steep pit mounds can be avoided.

Harton Hollow

On Wenlock Edge, SY7 9JS
OS Map SO 481878;
Map Ref N22

Walk in these woods and you tread on an ancient barrier reef. Plants such as herb-paris and sweet woodruff grow here, thriving on the limestone that formed from the fossilised remains of ancient shelled creatures.

Llynclys Common

Oswestry, SY10 8LW
OS Map SJ 273238;
Map Ref N12

Llynclys Common has everything: woods, meadows, old quarries, sunny glades, a pond and big skies. Woodpeckers raid anthills, foxes sunbathe and butterflies bask on their favourite flowers. More than 300 plants have been recorded here including fairy flax, wild thyme, devil's-bit scabious, salad burnet and numerous orchids.

Melverley Meadows

Whitchurch, SY13 4EA
OS Map SJ 581405;
Map Ref N7

A wonderful series of hay meadows where traditional management means that dense hedges crowned with mature oaks enclose fields humming with insects. Ponds provide refuge for dragonflies and newts, while ragged robin, common spotted-orchids and pignut thrive among the grass. Visit in June to see the meadows in full bloom.

HOPE VALLEY

Minsterley, SY5 0JA; **OS Map** SJ 350017; **Map Ref** N18

Access/conditions: Well-marked footpaths throughout the woods. Flight of more than 100 steps on the southern side.

How to get there: Buses run through the valley from Bishop's Castle to Shrewsbury, Monday–Saturday. The valley is within walking distance via the Stiperstones NNR's network of public footpaths.

Walking time: The walk up the hill, along the western edge to the viewpoint and back to the car park takes around 45 minutes.

30-minute visit: Walk up through the woodland as far as you can.

This ancient woodland is recovering from a drastic attempt to transform it into a conifer forest in the 1960s. Luckily, the old oaks clung on despite the shady firs, sending out new shoots, which grew

back into sturdy branches when Shropshire Wildlife Trust felled the conifers 20 years later. Today, light once again bathes this long strip of woodland, where the top end of the loop-walk from the car park affords stunning views over the Stiperstones – a rugged, rocky ridge formed some 480 million years ago.

Hope Valley is an exhilarating walk at any time of year, with bluebells, yellow archangel and early purple orchids in spring, breeding buzzards and pied flycatchers in summer, and marauding siskins in the streamside alders in winter. There are hazel dormice in the woods but they are very secretive, crossing the road via touching branches in the treetops.

RHOS FIDDLE

Newcastle-on-Clun, SY7 8QT; **OS Map** SO 206857; **Map Ref** N23

Access/conditions: Rough, tussocky terrain. Boggy in wet weather.

How to get there: Take the Crossways Road out of Newcastle-on-Clun, fork left at Caldy Bank and carry on for 2.25 miles. Park on the grass on the left just before the second cattle grid, being sympathetic to the needs of local farmers and other road users.

Walking time: 1 hour.

30-minute visit: Walk from the information board along the track running towards the centre of the reserve and

back to get a real feeling of wilderness.

Rhos Fiddle is a hidden gem on the border between England and Wales – a heathland hilltop with big skies and the distinction of being one of the quietest places in Shropshire. It is a true ancient wilderness, surviving amid vivid green agricultural pastures. The boggy pools and surrounding wet heath attract wading birds like snipe, with the mournful cry of the curlew a stirring soundtrack during spring and summer walks. Skylarks take refuge here in vast numbers, filling the skies with their song as they rise and fall in dramatic display flights. Sphagnum mosses, cotton-grass and bog asphodel thrive in the wetter areas of the reserve, where black darter dragonflies hunt for unsuspecting midges and moths. From April–June, seize the opportunity to see scarce yellow mountain pansies growing in the unimproved grassland on the south-western slopes.

BROOK VESSONS AND THE HOLLIES

Snailbeach, SY5 0NS; **OS Map** SJ 382008; **Map Ref** N19

Access/conditions: Some uneven ground, steep hills and stiles.
How to get there: From Shrewsbury follow A488 through Minsterley, turn left to Snailbeach and you'll find the car park at the brow of the hill. Walk up the road above left, past the old lead mine buildings and up a steep hill. At the top, take a track to your left, which leads to Lordshill Baptish Church. Go through the gate, following the right fork of the track, and The Hollies is on your left, with Brook Vessons at the far end of The Hollies.
Walking time: 3 hours.
30-minute visit: Head straight for The Hollies from Snailbeach car park, stroll among the ancient trees and then return to the car.

This meeting of two atmospheric nature reserves is unforgettable. Start your stroll at The Hollies, where it won't take long for you to fall under the spell of this scattered grove of ancient holly trees, some approaching 400 years of age. Wizened and creaking, their trunks are dry as driftwood and riddled with beetle burrows. Their power of renewal is astonishing; one has a hole in its trunk, a window with a view; another is split in two at its base. Some have rowans rooted inside

them, a literal fall-out from redwings and fieldfares that have eaten rowan berries and let their droppings fall inside the holly trees. To explore Brook Vessons, walk to the top of The Hollies and keep to the brow of the hill before passing over a stile to your east. Ruined lead miners' cottages, gnarled ancient trees and tangled woods lend this place an awe-inspiring, almost ominous beauty that verges on the plain strange. A cluster of giant trees towering just 100m from one another boasts not just the biggest birch in Shropshire but some of the broadest rowans in Britain, the biggest holly in Shropshire and the county's biggest crab apple tree. The very cute hazel dormouse breeds here too.

WILDLIFE FACT: HAZEL DORMOUSE

The loss of ancient woodland and hedgerows across the UK means that hazel dormice are now seriously endangered. They hibernate during winter after feasting on nuts, seeds and berries to build up fat reserves. In spring and summer their diet switches to the blossoming flowers of trees like hawthorn and oak, and insects like caterpillars.

WHIXALL MOSS

Whitchurch, SY13 2RT; **OS Map** SJ 493354; **Map Ref** N8

Access/conditions: There are a number of marked walking trails. Can be very boggy after wet weather.
How to get there: You can arrive by car, canal boat, bike or on foot. There are car parks at Morris's Bridge and several other entrances to the Mosses. You can moor your canal boat near Morris's Bridge and walk to Whixall Moss, or you can walk from nearby Whixall Marina.
Walking time: The excellent footpath network means there are walks of all lengths. To explore the whole of Whixall Moss, including the bird hide on Charles Sinker Fields, pack your lunch and set aside a full day.
30-minute visit: Take the lane from Morris's Bridge to

Charles Sinker Fields and visit the bird hide.

Whixall Moss is a magical place where you can reconnect with nature in a truly wild setting. As one of the largest raised peat bogs

in Britain, the Moss offers a tranquil escape where the peace is broken only by tinkling birdsong, the peeping of wading birds or the shrieks of passing birds of prey.

Start your walk at Morris's Bridge, where you'll find one

of several car parks and a lane that leads to Charles Sinker Fields, a birdwatching hotspot. Settle into the bird hide and keep your eyes peeled for lapwings, teal, common sandpipers and curlews. Wood sandpiper and spoonbill are two of the more unusual birds spotted here – you never know what might turn up. On the reserve itself there is no end to the wonderful wildlife you might encounter. Raft spiders skim across bog pools brimming with rare mosses while carnivorous round-leaved sundew plants slowly devour insects at the water's edge. Specialist

bog insects like white-faced darter dragonflies and large heath butterflies skim above the cotton-grass, while hen harriers, hobbies and, in

winter, short-eared owls soar overhead. Don't miss a trip up the viewing platform where an awe-inspiring panorama awaits.

PONTESFORD AND EARL'S HILLS

Pontesford, SY5 0UH; **OS Map** SJ 409048; **Map Ref** N17

Access/conditions: Good network of paths around the reserve. The tracks leading from the main car park are steep.

How to get there: Buses from Shrewsbury to Bishop's Castle, Monday–Saturday. The reserve is eight miles south-west of Shrewsbury on the A488. If travelling by car, turn left at Pontesford (brown sign on roadside) and park in the car park.

Walking time: 1 hour.

30-minute visit: Walk up to the Lower Camp on Pontesford Hill. A short circular walk is possible on the west side of the hill along the forestry track and back along the road.

Locals see the shape of a sleeping dragon in Earl's Hill, and fiery its beginnings certainly were. It roared forth from a volcano some 650 million years ago, and an Iron

Age hill fort was built at the summit around 600BC. Now, the hill entices visitors to its lofty heights with innumerable wild delights and spectacular views across the valley.

A woodland of hazel, oak and yew trees erupts with colour during spring as bluebells, wood anemones and primroses unfurl on the

forest floor. Nest boxes attract pied flycatchers, redstarts and tree pipits, and the rocks of a babbling brook make perfect perches for bobbing dippers. Summer brings a zesty sprinkling of yellow stonecrop to screes on the eastern flanks of the hill, while higher still, an enchanting meadowland awaits, speckled with the white of heath bedstraw, the russet of sheep's sorrel and the tiny purple flowers of wild thyme. The latter offers small blue and orange-tip butterflies a delectable nectar buffet, but they're not the only ones who visit the meadow for fine dining. Green woodpeckers are regulars, attracted by the anthills of yellow meadow ants.

THE ERCALL

Wellington, TF6 5AL; **OS Map** SJ 640096; **Map Ref** N16

Access/conditions: Gentle walks to the quarry floor. Steep climbs to explore the woods in full.

How to get there: Bus to Wellington, then walk down Ercall Lane. By car, from M54, leave at J7 onto B5061. Follow signs to The Wrekin and then the Buckatree Hotel. Turn left at The Wrekin towards the entrance and brown signs on the right.

Walking time: This 131-acre (53ha) reserve is linked to the council-owned Limekiln Woods and The Wrekin, so walks can vary from 1 hour to a full day.

30-minute visit: From the entrance head up the main footpath to the quarry, where you can see ripples in the rockface formed by waves that lapped the shores of an ancient ocean 500 million years ago.

The Ercall is less well known than The Wrekin, but it has its own grandeur. Ancient oak woodland, spectacular views and more than 500 million years of geological history are ripe for discovery. Picture volcanoes spewing thick, sticky lava over the barren landscape, clouds of ash pouring into the atmosphere and earthquakes shaking the land to form this internationally famous geological time capsule. Twenty million years later, the sea swept across the volcanic desert, leaving behind

beautiful white sands marked with ripples that you can still see today. Winter – when the vegetation is at its lowest – is the best time to admire this fossilised beach.

It isn't just the old rocks that make The Ercall a wonderful place to visit. In spring, the woods are awash with bluebells and the singing of birds just returned from Africa. In summer, bountiful bird's-foot trefoil makes this a stronghold for butterflies, including the dingy skipper: just one of a staggering 821 species of invertebrates recorded here. The Ercall is also an excellent place to look for autumn fungi.

WOOD LANE
Ellesmere, SY12 0HY; **OS Map** SJ 421331; **Map Ref** N9

Access/conditions: Access paths are mostly gravel but can be wet. An all-ability trail leads from the lower car park to the small hide and both hides are suitable for wheelchair access. Permit required to access the hides.
How to get there: Take A528 south from Ellesmere (towards Shrewsbury). Turn left at Spunhill crossroads, signposted to Colemere, and follow this narrow road to the car park entrance on the right-hand side of the road.
Walking time: A slow stroll takes about 30 minutes, excluding time spent in the hides (permit required – contact the Shropshire Wildlife Trust). Both hides are within a short walk (30m and 250m) of the lower car park.

You might be surprised to learn that Wood Lane nature reserve is one of the best birdwatching spots in Shropshire. Several large lagoons with islands are encircled by a working sand and gravel quarry, the reserve itself built on old workings since left to nature. But the busy backdrop doesn't impact on the birdlife – far from it. More than 180 species have been recorded at this wetland wonderland since the nature reserve was established in 1999.

Greenshanks, godwits and whimbrels drop in to feed on their spring and autumn migration journeys, probing the mud alongside little ringed plovers, lapwings and curlews. This great gathering of wading birds is testament to Shropshire Wildlife Trust's exacting management of Wood Lane. Pumps control the water levels so that optimum amounts of mud and water are available for the birds all year round. But waders aren't the only must-see – scores of nest boxes installed by the Trust are home to breeding tree sparrows. Yellowhammers and reed warblers also raise their families at Wood Lane, while around 500 pairs of sand martins nest in the mountainous heaps of sand rearing up in the background. Hobbies occasionally harass the sand martins during summer, ospreys pass through on migration, and in winter, huge flocks of wildfowl, like teal, amass.

STAFFORDSHIRE

About the Trust

With more than 15,000 members, a passionate team of staff and volunteers, and 43 beautiful nature reserves, Staffordshire Wildlife Trust is dedicated to protecting and enhancing the county's wildlife and wild places. With nature in critical condition, the charity is working with planners, developers and landowners, connecting with the local community and pioneering conservation projects to ensure a wilder future for Staffordshire and all who live there.

Staffordshire Wildlife Trust
01889 880100
staffs-wildlife.org.uk

Parrot's Drumble

Talke Pits, ST7 1UH
OS Map SJ 822525;
Map Ref N5

A hidden gem with a stunning bluebell display, plus moschatel, dog's mercury and wood anemones. Look out for great and lesser spotted woodpeckers.

Brankley Pastures

Barton-under-Needwood, DE13 8BN
OS Map SK 166211;
Map Ref N13

A special remnant of wood pasture with a family-friendly trail. Look out for flowers including harebells and tormentil. Search for fly agarics in autumn. Keep your eyes peeled for little

owls, pied flycatchers and countless insects.

Rod Wood

Cheddleton, ST13 7DU
OS Map SJ 997529;
Map Ref N4

Wildflower meadows brimming with orchids, hay-rattle, yellow rattle and eyebright. Boggy areas nurture ragged robin, marsh-marigolds, meadowsweet and water mint. Spot meadow brown, speckled wood and green hairstreak butterflies on sunny days.

Weag's Barn

Grindon, ST13 7TX
OS Map SK 099541;
Map Ref N3

Traditional management encourages lousewort,

eyebright, harebells and self-heal to grow. Woodland is being allowed to regenerate naturally. Enjoy spectacular views from the hill topped by the derelict Weag's Barn.

Black Brook

Leek, SK17 0TA
OS Map SK 022646;
Map Ref N1

Former conifer plantation restored to a moorland haven for rare birds. Spring walks are atmospheric, with bubbling curlew calls drifting across the moor. Summer brings flowering bilberry, cotton-grass and seas of purple heather that attract bilberry bumblebees and green hairstreak butterflies. Walk to the hill at Gib Torr Rocks for the best views.

CROXALL LAKES

Alrewas, WS13 8QX; **OS Map** SK 189139; **Map Ref** N14

Access/conditions: Fairly flat, smooth paths. Kissing gate RADAR key access only to main track. Other areas pedestrian kissing gates only.
How to get there: Follow A513 from Rugeley, passing through Kings Bromley and Alrewas. Continue along this road, passing over A38. After around a mile, pass over the River Tame – reserve entrance is the second track on the left.
Walking time: It's a 30-minute walk there and back, not including stops in the two bird hides.
30-minute visit: A very quick visit to the first hide.

Previously quarried for sand and gravel, Croxall Lakes is now a safe haven for a wide range of wintering and breeding birds, with two hides where you can settle down to watch the action. Winter brings crowds of dabbling wigeon and teal to the 26-acre (10.5ha) main lake, as well as the odd smew, which isn't commonly seen in Staffordshire. The second lake may be smaller, but it holds the main wildlife scrape, where large groups of lapwings, redshanks and oystercatchers breed during spring and summer. Their ceaseless calling lends Croxall Lakes a real feeling of remote wilderness.

As well as birds, water-dwelling mammals thrive here, with otters leaving tantalising clues along the river corridor and water voles occasionally being spotted. Harvest mice build their nests in the reedbed, where they can hide away from predators.

COTTON DELL

Near Oakamoor, ST10 3AG; **OS Map** SK 052446; **Map Ref** N6

Access conditions: Paths are often wet and muddy and can be very steep in places.
How to get there: From Cheadle take B5417 east to Oakamoor. As you descend into the village turn right before the bridge, then left onto the free Staffordshire County Council car park. From here, walk back to the main road and continue east over the bridge. Take the second turning on the left up

an unadopted road. Reserve entrance is 350m up this track. **Walking time:** 3 hours.

If you go down to the dell today, you'll be sure of a memorable wildlife walk. Cotton Brook flows through the heart of the reserve, with a scenic path following it through wooded valleys and flower-rich grasslands, past wildlife-rich ponds and scrub singing with birds. Bluebells, wood anemones and wood sorrel grow around ancient oaks and birches while holly, field maple and hazel trees make up the scrubby areas. Green tiger beetles shimmer in the sunshine as they scamper across bare sandy patches in cattle-grazed pastures that beam with wildflowers in summer. Bees, butterflies and other insects feed from beautiful pink carpets of scabious, knapweeds, orchids and betony. Don't forget to look out for life along the river as you walk alongside Cotton Brook – you could see a dipper plunge into the water to snatch unwary invertebrates from under the rocks.

DOXEY MARSHES

Stafford, ST16 1PU; **OS Maps** SJ 902251; **Map Ref** N11

Access/conditions: Flat surfaced paths cover most of the reserve. Access onto reserve via RADAR kissing gates (for disabled access). Main bird hide has combination lock – contact the Staffordshire Wildlife Trust for code.
How to get there: Walk from Sainsbury's car park in Stafford (around 30 minutes). You can also park in the car park at the end of Wootton Drive.
Walking time: 2 hours.
30-minute visit: Walk down to the viewing platform at Boundary Flash.

You'd be hard-pressed to find a better place to get away from it all. Doxey Marshes is a wetland oasis just a stone's throw from the centre of Stafford, but you'd never guess you were so close to the hustle and bustle. Spring is a great time to watch lapwings performing their tumbling display flight while uttering their evocative *pee-wit* calls. Two hides offer brilliant vantage points for birdwatching throughout the year: summer hobbies, autumn godwits and year-round little egrets from the

rectangular hide at Tillington Flash, and spring green sandpipers, autumn dunlin and year-round snipe from the octagonal hide overlooking the scrape. Winter brings wigeon, teal and wildfowl galore to every available patch of water, where the birds busy themselves feeding and resting after a long journey from continental Europe.

The spring migration is just as exciting, when rarities like cattle egrets have been known to drop in.

But it isn't all about the birds. Cuckooflowers and ragged robin brighten up Doxey Marshes in spring while shy otters, harvest mice and water shrews live secret lives among the water vegetation.

LOYNTON MOSS

Woodseaves, ST20 0NX; **OS Map** SJ 786241; **Map Ref** N10

Access/conditions: Generally flat apart from the ascent to Rue Hill. Paths can be uneven, wet and boggy. Pedestrian kissing gates on-site.
How to get there: Go through Woodseaves on A519 between Eccleshall and Newport. Cross the Shropshire Union Canal a mile towards Newport – car park entrance is around 200m past the canal on the right.
Walking time: 2 hours.

Discover a unique landscape formed by retreating ice sheets around 10,000 years ago, at the end of the last ice age. A mosaic of fen, oak woodland, reedbed, scrub and wet woodland creates a landscape teeming with life. Bluebells and greater stitchwort fill the dry woodland in spring, filling the air with a subtle fragrance. Skylarks send their song tumbling down from great heights and buzzards

soar overhead on broad wings. Willow warblers, reed warblers and reed buntings breed in the reedbed during spring.

Some of the most exciting residents of Loynton Moss are much smaller. The reserve is home to a number of rare insects, including three special moths with wonderful names: dentated pug, small yellow wave and round-winged muslin. Sunny days bring

butterflies aplenty, from butter-yellow brimstones and beautiful orange-tips to speckled woods and holly blues. Unusual wetland plants including marsh cinquefoil, cowbane and elongated sedge thrive deep among the wetland vegetation, while the grassland fills with yellow rattle, bird's-foot trefoil and knapweed in summer – much to the delight of bees!

THE ROACHES

Leek, ST13 8UA; **OS Map** SK 004621; **Map Ref** N2

Access/conditions: Pedestrian gates, steps, and rough and uneven terrain.
How to get there: There is a small car park at Gradbach, near the youth hostel, from where you can start your adventure (use postcode SK17 0SU). There is also layby parking near Upper Hulme at Rockhall.
Walking time: There are a number of public footpaths across the estate, so you can walk for as long as you like.

On 1 May 2013, Staffordshire Wildlife Trust began its 125-year lease of the Roaches, a magnificent 975-acre (395ha) landscape on the edge of the Peak District National Park. Whether you're an eager climber, an enthusiastic hiker or a keen naturalist, this awe-inspiring wild place has something for everyone. Soaring rock faces, wide-open moors, precious blanket bog and heather-covered hills make the Roaches one of the most photographed

landscapes in Staffordshire, and one of the best for watching wildlife.

For panoramic views and the chance of seeing nesting peregrine falcons in spring, climb the stone steps to the left of the stone cottage built into the hillside and walk along the rocky ridge. After about half a mile you'll reach Doxey Pool, which is allegedly haunted by a mermaid who lures travellers to a watery grave! Or you could explore the less visited northern

end of the estate, with its sheltered woodlands and the stunning rock chasm known as Lud's Church. Either way, you'll be sure of some unforgettable wild encounters. You could spot soaring buzzards, chuckling red grouse or shimmering green hairstreak butterflies. You may hear the mournful call of a curlew drifting across the moor or spot flocks of meadow pipits darting hurriedly overhead.

HIGHGATE COMMON

Swindon, DY7 5BS; **OS Map** SO 835895; **Map Ref** N21

Access/conditions: Network of paths crossing the reserve can be muddy and uneven. Toilets at Cory Community Centre are open when wardens are on-site.

How to get there: Park in the car park on Highgate Road, where there are also toilets. Car park locked at 4pm.

Walking time: Taking your time on the many paths could while away a couple of hours.

30-minute visit: From Moddlers car park (SO 837900), walk out into the middle of the common then retrace your steps.

Did you know that Highgate Common is rarer than rainforest? It's a small remnant of an ancient lowland heath that once stretched for more than 15 miles. Now, the UK has lost 80 per cent of its open heathland, with Highgate Common occupying just 326 acres (132ha) of its original range. Luckily, Staffordshire Wildlife Trust protects this precious remnant and all of the wildlife that lives there.

Around 140 different solitary bees and wasps thrive on the common, including some incredibly rare species. You can't miss the countless small holes they make in the sandy paths. But you won't just find bees and wasps here – in total, more than 5,000 different insects buzz, hum and dart around the dazzling heathland. Dragonflies, glow-worms, purple hairstreak and white admiral butterflies,

oil beetles and green tiger beetles are just a selection of the fascinating creatures you could spot. And that isn't all – grass snakes, common lizards and slow worms bask in the sunshine, and there is no shortage of birdlife. Spring is the best time to experience their complex chorus echoing over the common, with cuckoos, yellowhammers, tree pipits, skylarks and green woodpeckers vying for your attention.

BIRMINGHAM AND THE BLACK COUNTRY

About the Trust

Founded in 1980 following a successful campaign to save Moseley Bog, The Wildlife Trust for Birmingham and the Black Country was the first organisation in what became a major urban wildlife movement by the 1990s. Its vision is that by recognising the importance of the area's unique natural heritage, shaped by local history, it can restore the natural environment and connect more people to the natural world every year.

The Wildlife Trust for Birmingham and the Black Country
01215 230094
bbcwildlife.org.uk

Hill Hook Local Nature Reserve

Four Oaks, B74 4DT
OS Map SK 105003;
Map Ref N20

Nestled in Four Oaks, Sutton Coldfield, not far from Sutton Park, Hill Hook Local Nature Reserve is a hidden oasis of green bordered by residential streets. The reserve may be small, but size doesn't matter – grassland, scrub, open water, marsh and woodland form a wonderful home for a rich variety of wildlife. The reserve's focal point, the Mill Pool, attracts breeding frogs, common toads, dragonflies and damselflies and harbours interesting plants around its edges. Lesser spearwort, pink purslane and marsh cinquefoil can all be found. Bluebells,

yellow archangel and wood anemones grow in the woods where, in spring, the trees come alive with the sounds and sights of whitethroats, willow warblers and blackcaps. Summer is the best time to see butterflies and orchids in the meadow to the north of Hill Hook Road.

Portway Hill

Rowley Regis, B69 1NX
OS Map SO 974891;
Map Ref N25

High on the Rowley Hills looking over Sandwell, Birmingham and Dudley, Portway Hill is home to an astounding wealth of grassland wildflowers and butterflies. There is no finer place to appreciate the wild wonders you can find just

a stone's throw from the bustling cityscape. Ox-eye daisies and field scabious grow alongside rare beauties like the diminutive bee orchid. Hare's-foot clover – a really unusual-looking plant – also grows here. Downy hairs cover its pale pink flowers, giving it the look of a hare's fuzzy paw. The beautiful range of flowers in turn attracts a stunning array of butterflies. On summer walks you could spot everything from green hairstreaks and small skippers to small coppers and orange-tips. You may also see one of the few colonies of marbled white butterflies in Birmingham and the Black Country. If you can tear yourself away from the butterflies, look out for peregrine falcons, kestrels and the wingless Roesel's bush-cricket.

DEER'S LEAP WOOD

Smethwick, B16 0QG; **OS Map** SP 033870; **Map Ref** N26

Access/conditions: Walking trail throughout. Only some parts of the reserve are accessible by wheelchair.

How to get there: Bus runs from Birmingham city centre to Rotton Park/George Dixon School, then an eight-minute walk. By car, from M5, take J1 and follow A4252. Take A457 and Shenstone Road to Roebuck Road and park here, being considerate of residents.

Walking time: Exploring the whole reserve takes around 30 minutes. Why not sit a while and listen to the birdsong?

Sitting just 2.5 miles west of Birmingham city centre, Deer's Leap Wood is a peaceful retreat where you can forget about your day-to-day worries and immerse yourself in nature. The reserve packs a lot into its 4.5 acres (1.9ha): a woodland, pond, boundary brook and meadow areas. In fact, this mix of habitats and the wildlife it safeguards has been designated as a Site of Local Importance for Nature Conservation.

Deer's Leap Wood can be traced back to medieval times when both it and the surrounding area formed part of the Rotton Park estate. Now, the birch, oak and alder trees offer prime feeding and breeding spots for great spotted woodpeckers and other woodland birds, while fungi thrive on the woodland floor. The large pond attracts mallards and herons above and smooth newts below, while the damp banks offer perfect growing conditions for water mint, flag iris and the wonderfully scented meadowsweet. The upper meadow is a haven for grasshoppers, dragonflies and other insects. Keep your eyes peeled as you stroll past the brook – you could spot a grey wagtail.

MOSELEY BOG AND JOY'S WOOD

Moseley, B13 9JX; **OS Map** SP 093820; **Map Ref** N27

Access/conditions: There are multiple routes through the reserve, and entrances off Yardley Wood Road, Pensby Close and across the field from the car park on Windermere Road (near B13 9JP). Many routes are suitable for pushchairs and wheelchairs.

How to get there: About five miles south-east of Birmingham city centre. Bus to Cole Bank Road. From Moor Street, take the train to Hall Green station, then a 15-minute walk. By car, follow the brown signs to Sarehole Mill from the Stratford Road (A34).

Walking time: 1 hour.

30-minute visit: From the Yardley Wood Road entrance, head into Joy's Wood, following signs for Moseley Bog. Continue along the brook to emerge back into Joy's Wood.

Moseley Bog was saved from development in the 1980s following a huge public campaign and is now the Trust's flagship urban nature reserve. Wet woodland, wet meadows, fen and a pond sit alongside Bronze Age burnt mounds and the remains of Victorian greenhouses, marrying magical natural highlights with a rich social history.

In spring you can see bluebells unfurling around gnarled trees, goldfinches and willow warblers fill the air with song and the hammering of great spotted woodpeckers echoes all around. In summer, Moseley Bog is alive with insects. Butterflies abound and, after nightfall, moths take their place and may fall prey to foraging pipistrelle bats. In autumn, colourful fungi emerge from the leaf litter and add to the magnificent colour of the turning leaves. Winter transforms the reserve into a scene from a film as low-lying mists drift across the landscape – sometimes spooky, but always amazing. It's little wonder this mysterious landscape inspired *The Lord of the Rings* author, J. R. R. Tolkien, to create the 'old forest' in his books.

HEREFORDSHIRE

About the Trust

Supported by over 5,000 members and more than 250 volunteers, Herefordshire Wildlife Trust cares for 55 nature reserves, works with partners to create Living Landscapes and inspires people of all ages to discover and care for the wildlife. By acting as a wildlife champion, joining up disconnected wild places and bringing people closer to nature, the charity is forging a wilder future for Herefordshire.

**Herefordshire Wildlife Trust
01432 356872
herefordshirewt.org**

Common Hill SSSI

Fownhope, HR1 4QA
OS Map SO 591347;
Map Ref M29

A patchwork of small meadows and orchards. Plants include betony, cowslips and bird's-nest orchids; butterflies include marbled and wood whites.

The Sturts

Eardisley, HR3 6PA
OS Map SO 336475;
Map Ref M26

Three areas of species-rich grassland on the River Wye floodplain. The Sturts East nurtures ragged robin, devil's-bit scabious, pignut and rare aquatic beetles. The Sturts North is home to micro-habitats with their own interesting plant communities. The Sturts South is a great place to watch birds, including barn owls and yellowhammers.

Lea and Paget's Wood

Fownhope, HR1 4PS
OS Map SO 593345;
Map Ref M30

One of the most stunning ancient woods in the area. Spectacular drifts of bluebells put on a show in spring and you can spot herb-paris, wild liquorice and greater butterfly-orchids. Keep your eyes peeled for all three woodpeckers and silver-washed fritillaries. Dormice are secretive residents

Titley Pool

Titley, HR5 3RI
OS Map SO 323594;
Map Ref M16

Home to breeding great crested grebes. Shimmering clouds of dragonflies and damselflies hunt over the ponds in summer. Hungry herons and goosanders feed on perch, roach, eels and pike. Winter birds include teal, tufted ducks and pochards.

The Parks

Ewyas Harold, HR2 0HL
OS Map SO 369295;
Map Ref M31

A majestic sweep of grassland lying on the gentle slopes of Dulas Brook. The brook itself supports otters and a thriving population of white-clawed crayfish. The grassland of The Parks is a haven of wildflowers and fungi.

Merrivale Wood

Ross-on-Wye, HR9 5RU
OS Map SO 603229;
Map Ref M32

An ancient woodland haven for blackcaps and marsh tits. Goshawks have been spotted and, in summer, the open glades and woodland margins fill with butterflies.

BODENHAM LAKE

Bodenham, HR1 3JR; **OS Map** SO 528513; **Map Ref** M25

Access/conditions: Two easy access paths around part of the lake, both starting from the car park.

How to get there: Off the A417. Turn into Millcroft Road, passing the Englands Gate Inn, and continue until you reach the reserve car park, on the left.

Walking time: Around 3 hours.

30-minute visit: Follow the surfaced path from the car park to a picnic glade with views across the lake.

Bodenham Lake is one of the largest stretches of open water in Herefordshire, offering 50 acres (20ha) of sanctuary to more than 160 species of bird. Oystercatchers, little ringed plovers and lapwings breed on the sand and gravel islands, while buzzards live in the woods, announcing their presence with mewing calls as they soar above the trees. Herons lurk at the edge of the water and kingfishers zip by in brilliant flashes of blue. In summer, hobbies arrive to feed on the clouds of dragonflies and damselflies that emerge, themselves, to hunt unfortunate insects. Azure and common blue damselflies and black-tailed skimmer and brown hawker dragonflies are some of the most common species you'll see. Two bird hides look out onto reeds where reed and sedge warblers and reed buntings call throughout spring and summer. Snipe and water rails forage in the shallow areas in front of the Old Hide.

QUEENSWOOD COUNTRY PARK AND ARBORETUM

Leominster, HR6 0PY; **OS Map** SO 506514; **Map Ref** M24

Opening hours: Visitor centre open daily from 10am–4pm.

Access/conditions: There is a surfaced, waymarked, easy access trail for mobility scooters alongside more challenging trails and paths of different lengths. Parking up to £4 per day.

How to get there: Bus from Hereford and Leominster stops at the top of Dinmore Hill. By car, the reserve is signposted off the A49 at the top of Dinmore Hill.

Walking time: Allow at least 4 hours to explore the reserve and enjoy the visitor centre.

30-minute visit: Take a brisk walk along the Badger Trail.

Once part of the vast ancient oak wood that stretched to the Welsh borders and beyond, Queenswood Country Park and Arboretum is a peaceful place to get back to nature. As well as a tree collection with more than 1,200 rare and exotic trees from all over the world, you'll find rare plants and lots of wonderful wildlife.

Spring arrives with famous blossom displays, the hammering of all three species of woodpecker and the wonderful songs of chiffchaffs, blackcaps and willow, wood and garden warblers. As spring melts into summer, silver-washed fritillary and purple hairstreak butterflies take to the air in the oak woods, where the nationally scarce oak splendour beetle dines on dead wood and parasitic bird's-nest orchids grow under beech trees. In autumn, Queenswood is transformed by a riot of colour as the leaves turn and eventually drop, blanketing the forest floor with a fiery carpet.

BIRCHES FARM

Near Kington, HR5 3EY; **OS Map** SO 296538; **Map Ref** M23

Access/conditions: Surfaced path around visitor centre. No surfaced paths around the reserve itself making it unsuitable for those with limited mobility. Please keep to the mown path around the reserve.
How to get there: Leaving Hereford on A438, continue onto A4111 through Eardisley towards Kington, following the road up the hill. After a left-hand sign to Chickward, the road bends to the right and you'll see Birches Farm on your right.
Walking time: 2 hours.
30-minute visit: Stroll through the wildflowers in Great Meadow, or take a seat on the bench beside the pond and watch the wildlife go by.

Birches Farm offers a rare window into a landscape long forgotten. Centuries of protection from the deep plough, modern fertilisers and seed mixes has preserved a stunning array of wildflowers across this beautiful patchwork of fields and hedgerows, protected through traditional management. The Herefordshire Wildlife Trust grazes the reserve with cattle before cutting for hay in late summer. As a result, spring brings a show of cowslips, bluebells and cuckooflowers before the rush of orchids in May and June, when common spotted, early purple, twayblade and green-winged orchids flower in fantastic numbers. Devil's-bit scabious, bird's-foot trefoil, bugle, yellow rattle and knapweed grow across the reserve while dyer's greenweed thrives on the sloping northern fields. Delicate harebells flower in late summer before autumn crocuses steal the show. It goes without saying that these wonderful carpets of wildflowers and long grasses help to support countless other life, including skylarks and drinker moths.

The farm's hedgerows are just as important for wildlife, providing food for caterpillars and shelter for birds. Whitethroats and lesser whitethroats dart through the hedgerows during summer, while redwings and fieldfares feed on their berries in autumn and winter. Redstarts and willow warblers visit the farm too, and red kites regularly soar overhead. Hares are often seen bounding through the meadows and you may well spot signs of badgers.

THE DOWARD RESERVES

Great Doward, HR9 6DX; **OS Map** SO 548157; **Map Ref** M33

Access/conditions: No surfaced paths; many paths and tracks can be muddy. Gates at Leeping Stocks and Miners Rest. Gate at Woodside locked when grazing animals are on-site. Access at Lord's Quarry is restricted – use viewpoints along the fence.

How to get there: Reserve is nine miles from Ross-on-Wye. Take A40 from Ross, exit at Whitchurch and follow signs to Biblins and Doward Park Campsite. Park at Leeping Stocks, White Rocks or the Biblins Forestry England car park (near King Arthur's Cave).

Walking time: Allow a whole morning or afternoon to explore.

30-minute visit: Park at White Rocks and walk through the reserve.

The Doward Reserves lie at the heart of the Wye Valley, in the Doward Living Landscape, and include six separate Herefordshire Wildlife Trust nature reserves: King Arthur's Cave, White Rocks, Leeping Stocks, Miners Rest, Woodside and Lords Wood Quarry. They're all within easy walking distance of one another, so you can spend the whole morning or afternoon searching for hawfinches, lesser spotted woodpeckers, white admiral butterflies and other incredible wildlife.

King Arthur's Cave is a great place to start your adventure – take a torch to delve into the deceptively large cave. Keep following the main track to extend your walk beyond the reserve, into Forestry England woodland that links King Arthur's Cave with the Wye Valley Walk and other footpaths within the Trust's Lord's Wood reserve. Here, you may spot kestrels breeding on the cliff ledges in spring and countless fungi thriving on the woodland fringes in autumn, including magpie inkcaps.

White Rocks and Miners Rest are great places to spot butterflies, with marbled whites and ringlets at the former and grizzled skippers and pearl-bordered fritillaries at the latter. Leeping Stocks has magical bluebell displays in spring and Woodside marks a change in the landscape, from woodland to wildflower meadows where cowslips, adder's-tongue ferns and bitter vetch thrive.

WORCESTERSHIRE

About the Trust

Worcestershire Wildlife Trust is the leading local charity working towards a county rich in wildlife. The Trust manages 3,000 acres (1,214ha) of land and works with other organisations and landowners to protect and connect green spaces across the county. It also inspires local communities and young people to care for wildlife where they live.

**Worcestershire Wildlife Trust
01905 754919
worcswildlifetrust.co.uk**

The Christopher Cadbury Wetland (Upton Warren)

Upton Warren, B61 7ER
OS Map SO 935671;
Map Ref M9

Non-Worcestershire Wildlife Trust owned café open daily, 10am–3pm.

Little ringed plovers, avocets, turnstones and whimbrels on the Flashes pools. The Moors pools attract sedge warblers, hobbies and jack snipe. Greenfinches love the feeding stations. Wheelchair access to some hides (contact the Worcestershire Wildlife Trust). Non-Worcestershire Wildlife Trust members must purchase a £3 permit.

Droitwich Community Woods

Droitwich, WR9 0RQ
OS Map SO 880624;
Map Ref M14

A nature trail leads visitors through woodland, through meadows being transformed by restoration, and along the River Salwarpe. Butterflies flutter along woodland rides and the slow-moving margins of the river and canal help dragonflies to thrive.

Grafton Wood

Grafton Flyford, WR7 4PG
OS Map SO 971558;
Map Ref M22

Owned and managed with Butterfly Conservation, Grafton is the centre of the Midlands' only colony of brown hairstreak butterflies. The reserve is also home to the most northerly Bechstein's bat breeding roost in the UK.

Lower Smite Farm

Hindlip, WR3 8SZ
OS Map SO 880590;
Map Ref M17

A circular trail takes in an orchard, wetland, several ponds and arable fields where you could spot skylarks, whitethroats, greenfinches and up to 15 species of dragonfly. Information available at the offices: 9am–5pm, Monday–Friday. Wheelchair access limited to the area around the farmhouse and granary. Disabled toilet open during office hours.

Windmill Hill

Evesham, WR11 8QS
OS Map SP 072476;
Map Ref M27

Limestone grassland with lovely views of the Avon Valley. Bee orchids, wild liquorice, dog-violets and spiny restharrow grow; marbled white, brown argus and small heath butterflies flutter. There is limited roadside parking, some steep slopes and stiles.

Monkwood

Worcester, WR2 6NX
OS Map SO 804606;
Map Ref M15

Working with Butterfly Conservation, Worcestershire Wildlife Trust is restoring this special woodland to as natural a state as possible. Mature trees, coppicing, sunny glades and rides nurture 36 species of butterfly including white admirals and purple hairstreaks. Small pools are home to dragonflies and a variety of freshwater creatures.

PIPER'S HILL AND DODDERHILL COMMONS

Bromsgrove, B60 4AS; **OS Map** SO 958650; **Map Ref** M12

Access/conditions:
Some paths on difficult terrain. No wheelchair access.
How to get there: On B4091 heading south-east from Bromsgrove to Hanbury – about four miles from Bromsgrove and two miles from Hanbury.
Walking time: 45 minutes.
30-minute visit: Explore the paths at leisure.

These two old commons boast more than 240 veteran trees – some of the oldest in the county – with many being more than several hundred years old. These ancient beech, sweet chestnut and oak giants mean the reserve really comes to life in autumn, with spectacular colours sweeping through the wood and fungi waiting to catch your eye. Tits, nuthatches and woodpeckers love the old trees, taking advantage of the cracks and holes in the aged bark. Saproxylic species of beetle, which depend on the dead or dying wood, thrive here.

Don't miss the old fish pond at the edge of the wood. It's home to a great variety of freshwater invertebrates and attracts dragonflies like the broad-bodied chaser.

TIDDESLEY WOOD

Pershore, WR10 2AD; **OS Map** SO 929462; **Map Ref** M28

Access/conditions:
Woodland paths can be muddy. No entry to the old military firing range in the south-west corner.
How to get there: Take A44 from Pershore towards Worcester and turn left near the town boundary, just before the summit of the hill, into an unclassified road signposted for Besford and Croome.
Walking time: 1.5 hours.
30-minute visit: Follow the main central track through the wood.

Tiddesley is a wood of three lives: deer park, commercial forestry plantation, and now an outstandingly important ancient woodland being restored to its natural glory.

Bluebells, wood anemones, violets and cowslips carpet coppiced areas in spring, while in summer, white admiral and gatekeeper butterflies add yet more colour. Chiffchaffs provide a wonderful soundtrack to walks. Violet helleborines grow in the shadier areas, and herb-paris, greater butterfly-orchids and twayblades can be found where some light penetrates. White-legged damselflies hunt along the rides and mown paths.
The orchard near the main entrance is home to the rare noble chafer beetle – look out for them feeding on hogweed along woodland rides.

WILDLIFE FACT: ANCIENT WOODLAND

Ancient woodland is an irreplaceable habitat that has grown and adapted alongside our wildlife over hundreds of years. Yet what remains covers less than three per cent of the UK. Ancient woods are home to special communities of plants and animals not found elsewhere, and which rely on the specific conditions of these veteran woods for survival. Ancient woods can't simply be planted again – once what little we have left is gone, it's gone for good. Some indicators of ancient woods include bluebells, wood anemones and even certain species of slugs and snails.

THE DEVIL'S SPITTLEFUL AND RIFLE RANGE

Bewdley, DY12 1PU; **OS Map** SO 796744; **Map Ref** M8

Access/conditions:
Please keep to paths (these are sandy) and abide by the signs. There are kissing gates.
How to get there: Park at WCC Blackstone car park on the A456 between Stourport and Bewdley. A footpath runs from A456 Kidderminster to Bewdley Road via Sandy Lane. Bus from Worcester travels by the reserve.
Walking time: 1.5 hours.
30-minute visit: Climb to the top of the Devil's Spittleful rock on the west side of the main road into the reserve.

This important wildlife refuge is one of the largest areas of heathland left in Worcestershire. Sandy soil, bell heather and acid grassland dotted by gorse and silver birch nurture a fascinating and unusual set of plants and animals. In spring, glistening green tiger beetles speed across the sand and fly among the heather, and visitors should look for purple hairstreak butterflies as the seasons turn. There are some unmissable day-flying moths, including the stunning emperor moth with its shimmering eyespots and bright orange hindwings.

Keep your eyes and ears peeled for redstarts, cuckoos, lesser whitethroats, yellowhammers and green woodpeckers. In late summer and autumn you may spot common lizards basking in the sunshine. The heather is at its best in late July and August but there are many other plants to discover – heath dog-violets, early forget-me-nots and small cudweed flower from June–September. When autumn falls, seek out some of the 140 species of fungi, from oyster mushrooms to liberty caps.

IPSLEY ALDERS MARSH

Redditch, B98 0SE; **OS Map** SP 076677; **Map Ref** M10

Access/conditions: Follow the paths, boardwalk and circular trail waymarkers. The marshland is boggy year-round. All entrances have kissing gates.

How to get there: Take the A448 from Bromsgrove towards Warwick, then onto the A4189 signposted Warwick. Turn left onto Ipsley Alders Drive. Take the first right into Far Moor Lane. Follow the road and turn left into Furze Lane. Park in Furze Lane, respecting local access.

Walking time: 1 hour.

30-minute visit: From the entrance by Winyates Green Meeting Rooms, stroll along the boardwalk to get the maximum view of the marsh.

This important remnant marsh in the middle of Redditch sits on sedge peat, a rare habitat in the Midlands. Spring water rises below much of the reserve, ensuring that parts are waterlogged all year round. This is heaven for dragonflies like the impressive emperor, which rules the skies with azure beauty during summer.

Cattle grazing preserves the fantastic floral diversity here, with 170 species of plant attesting to Worcestershire Wildlife Trust's hard work. Hemp agrimony, common spotted-orchids, fen bedstraw, marsh woundwort and water mint grow alongside Worcestershire rarities like marsh stitchwort and blunt-flowered rush.

Though the flowers die back during winter there is still plenty to see. Snipe feed on the marsh and flocks of siskins and redpolls fill the alder trees. All three species of woodpecker breed on the reserve in the summer months, as well as reed buntings, grasshopper warblers and cuckoos.

WARWICKSHIRE

About the Trust

Warwickshire Wildlife Trust is the leading local independent conservation organisation whose mission is to bring people closer to nature and create a land rich in wildlife.

Warwickshire Wildlife Trust
024 7630 2912
warwickshirewildlifetrust.org.uk

Claybrookes Marsh

Coventry, CV3 2ED
OS Map SP 380769;
Map Ref M3

A refuge for 49 scarce insect species including bees, wasps and beetles. Bird's-foot trefoil and hare's-foot clover attract marbled white and small heath butterflies. Look out for common spotted-orchids, yellow loosestrife and St John's wort.

Draycote Meadows SSSI

Rugby, CV23 9RB
OS Map SP 448706;
Map Ref M7

Traditional hay meadows with cowslips, meadow vetchling, yellow rattle and adder's-tongue ferns. Green-winged orchids and rare moonwort also grow. Waxcap and meadow coral fungi are abundant. The hedgerows bustle with birds.

Hampton Wood and Meadow

Warwick, CV35 8AS
OS Map SP 254600;
Map Ref M20

Savour spring carpets of primroses, bluebells, wood anemones and lesser celandines. Admire yellow archangel. Spot white-letter hairstreak, white admiral and holly blue butterflies. Secretive woodcock spend the winter. Open to Wildlife Trust members only.

Leam Valley

Leamington Spa, CV32 4EW
OS Map SP 330658;
Map Ref M11

Shimmering banded demoiselles and magnificent emperor dragonflies zip along the River Leam, where kingfishers nest. Grass snakes swim among yellow water lilies and snakes-head fritillaries grow in the rich marsh. Butterflies are plentiful.

Rough Hill Wood

Redditch, B80 7EN
OS Map SP 052637;
Map Ref M13

Bluebells and wood anemones grow beneath sessile oak and small-leaved lime trees. Look out for cuckoos, chiffchaffs and all three types of woodpecker. Fungi thrive in autumn.

Ufton Fields

Southam, CV33 9PU
OS Map SP 378615;
Map Ref M19

This old limestone quarry is now home to 28 butterfly species, including marbled white, and 14 species of dragonfly and damselfly. Leeches and water scorpions lurk in the pools. Turtle doves take cover in the scrub and siskins busy themselves in the alder trees.

Welcombe Hills

Stratford-on-Avon, CV37 6XR
OS Map SP 205565;
Map Ref M21

You could see great spotted and green woodpeckers, sparrowhawks, little owls, treecreepers and breeding ravens. Brimstone butterflies flutter in the spring sunshine. Audio trail on Wildlife Trust website.

CLOWES WOOD AND NEW FALLINGS COPPICE

Solihull, B94 5JP; **OS Map** SP 101743; **Map Ref** M6

Access/conditions: Gently sloping, mostly accessible paths. Some areas prone to mud. Narrow bridges and steps.

How to get there: Train to Earlswood then walk or cycle 0.5 miles. From J3 of M42, turn onto A435 towards Birmingham. Take third exit at roundabout into Station Road, then first right into Forshaw Heath Road, then left into Wood Lane.

Walking time: 1.5–2 hours.

30-minute visit: Walk around the perimeter of New Fallings Coppice and Clowes Wood, up to the railway line, then turn back towards the car park.

Clowes Wood is a piece of history: Warwickshire Wildlife Trust's first nature reserve. It may be cut through by the Birmingham to Stratford railway, but wildlife thrives. Bluebells, wood sorrel and wood anemones blanket the woodland in spring, when the air is thick with the intoxicating scent of wild garlic. Lily-of-the-valley grows in the woods, while in summer, the wet meadow becomes a riot of colour thanks to heath spotted-orchids and marsh violets. This reserve is the perfect place for an autumn fungi hunt: look out for red cracking bolete and blusher mushrooms plus weird and wonderful slime moulds. Listen for chiffchaffs in spring and see if you can find the burnt stone pile dating back to the Bronze Age.

SNITTERFIELD BUSHES

Stratford-on-Avon, CV37 0JH; **OS Map** SP 200603; **Map Ref** M18

Access/conditions: Relatively flat; concrete access paths, some of which are suitable for wheelchairs and buggies. RADAR gate on north side. Parking for Wildlife Trust members only.

How to get there: Train to Bearley Halt then walk or cycle 0.75 miles. Follow signs to Snitterfield from the A46 Stratford bypass. Go through the village on the road to Bearley. The reserve lies on both sides of the road after one mile.

Walking time: 1.5 hours.

30-minute visit: Head into the northern part of the wood to see coppiced areas and rides rich in wildflowers.

Surrendering to an exquisite carpet of bluebells, primroses and early purple orchids during springtime, the woodland supports an impressive 250 species of plant including herb-paris, meadow saffron and bird's-nest orchids. Fragrant agrimony and columbine bloom in summer. Autumn brings a splendid selection of fungi including boletes, milkcaps and puffballs-galore under a blazing orange canopy. Sixty species of bird have been recorded at Snitterfield Bushes. Woodcock arrive for winter, while turtle doves and warblers are spring highlights. Watch colourful jays burying acorns in autumn, the forgotten seeds giving rise to oak saplings in the coming warmer months.

WHITACRE HEATH

Tamworth, B46 2EH; **OS Map** SP 209931; **Map Ref** M2

Access/conditions: Steep slope up from member's-only car park. Woodland paths can be uneven and include steps up to boardwalks and embankments.

How to get there: Train to Water Orton and bus to Lea Marston and walk or cycle 0.25 miles. From J9 of M42, take A4097 towards Marston then turn right into Haunch Lane, picking up the Birmingham Road through Lea Marston. The reserve lies on the right, 0.3 miles outside the village.

Walking time: 1.5 hours.

30-minute visit: Take a stroll along the Red Trail, which takes 30 minutes to 1 hour.

Part of the incredible Tame Valley Wetlands, which span from Coleshill to Tamworth, Whitacre Heath is a vital refuge for breeding water birds. Little grebes, water rails and teal feed and breed in and around the pools, while waders including lapwings, redshanks, curlews and snipe are regular visitors to the inviting wet grassland. There are wonderful areas of wet woodland dominated by alder and willow trees, where a number of different finches, tits, woodpeckers and thrushes thrive throughout the year. You'll also find a fantastic selection of fungi, mosses and liverworts in the woods, where the abundance of dead wood offers a veritable buffet for important beetle species. But the insect life doesn't end there. Brown argus and white-letter hairstreak butterflies flourish alongside impressive

emperor dragonflies and small but startling emerald damselflies. They patrol pools where frogs and toads also breed. You may even be lucky enough to spot the arch nemesis of these amphibians – the grass snake – as it basks in the spring sunshine between March and April.

WILDLIFE FACT: WOODPECKERS

We have three woodpecker species in the UK: the great spotted woodpecker is the most common, followed by the green woodpecker and then the rare lesser spotted woodpecker, which is largely confined to the south of England. Spring is the best time to try and spot woodpeckers, when they drum on tree trunks and leaf cover is thin enough to reveal the tops of the trees. Green woodpeckers are the easiest to see, flying down to the ground to feed on ants in heath and grassland. Two of the best places to see woodpeckers in Warwickshire are Ryton Wood and Whitacre Heath.

BRANDON MARSH

Coventry, CV3 3GW; **OS Map** SP 386761; **Map Ref** M4

Opening hours: Open all year. Visitor centre: 9.30am–4pm, Monday–Friday; 10am–4pm, Saturday and Sunday.

Access/conditions: Free entry for Wildlife Trust members with a valid membership card; adults £3.50; concessions £2.50; children £2 (under 4s free); families £9 (two adults and up to three children). Relatively flat and wheelchair-friendly, with some wheelchair-accessible paths. Some areas can be muddy.

How to get there: Train to Rugby and Coventry then bus links to Brandon Village and walk or cycle, or take the bus to Willenhall or Wolston and walk or cycle to the reserve. Three miles south-east of Coventry. The reserve is on Brandon Lane, which can be accessed off the A45 or through Brandon Village.

Walking time: More than two miles of paths to explore. Walks can take anything from 1 hour to a full afternoon.

30-minute visit: Explore the Geology Wall and mouse maze and check out the birds from the Wright hide.

This magnificent wetland is a jewel in Warwickshire Wildlife Trust's crown, recently extended by the acquisition of Brandon Reach to provide a vital wildlife corridor linking Piles Coppice to Claybrooks Marsh. There is something to see at any time of the year, with spring bringing pied flycatchers and even rarer visitors. Spring is also the best time to encounter amphibians, with great crested, palmate and smooth newts flourishing. In summer, butterflies boom

in the undisturbed grassland where foxes, stoats and wily weasels hunt for rabbits and small mammals. Autumn is prime fungi-hunting time, with a mind-boggling 600 species recorded at the reserve. Field bird's-nest fungus emerges in the sensory garden, waxcaps pepper the short grass and jelly babies hide in the woods. Winter is fantastic for water birds like teal, pochards, shovelers and grebes, as well as bitterns and siskins.

ALVECOTE POOLS

Tamworth, B78 1AS; **OS Map** SK 244048; **Map Ref** M1

Access/conditions: Flat, with wheelchair access adjacent to the canal. Kissing gates. Muddy in winter.

How to get there: Train to Tamworth, then bus to Alvecote and walk or cycle. Between Polesworth and Tamworth in north Warwickshire. Access to

the site off Robeys Lane, where there is limited parking. Additional car park at nearby Pooley Heritage Centre (charge applies).

Walking time: Up to 2 hours.

30-minute visit: Head up the spoil heap to see the amazing views over Warwickshire and Staffordshire.

This impressive mosaic of pools, wetland, marsh, woodland and grassland makes Alvecote Pools a patchwork oasis for countless marsh-loving plants, amphibians and wetland birds. Common frogs and toads along with smooth and great crested newts all relish the damp areas, which of course makes them favoured hunting grounds for grass snakes. In summer the rare, insect-eating plant, wavy bladderwort, lurks below the water's surface – Alvecote Pools is the only place you can find it in Warwickshire. Summer is also a great time to see the vibrant purple spikes of southern marsh-orchids, dozens of different dragonflies and hundreds of species of beetle. The arrival of autumn is heralded by the appearance of that classic fairy toadstool, fly agaric, in the woods. Winter brings brilliant bird-spotting

opportunities with great crested grebes, pochards, shelducks and little ringed plovers congregating on the pools. Keep your eyes peeled

for the turquoise flash of a hunting kingfisher or the spectacle of a great white egret spearing fish with its long, sharp beak.

RYTON WOOD

Coventry, CV8 3EP; **OS Map** SP 386728; **Map Ref** M5

Access/conditions: Extensive network of paths – please stick to these to avoid getting lost. Relatively flat with some muddy stretches. Car park for Wildlife Trust members only, but access and parking is also available through Ryton Pools Country Park.
How to get there: Take the train to Coventry, then bus to Bubbenhall and walk. One mile south of Ryton-on-Dunsmore.
Walking time: 1–2 hours.
30-minute visit: Wander around the waymarked trails.

This ancient wood is the largest surviving area of semi-natural woodland left in Warwickshire. To prove it, it harbours an important population of rare small-leaved lime trees – the most common tree in the UK 5,000 years ago and an indicator of ancient woodland. Spring is heralded by a joyful riot of

colour: carpets of primroses, wood anemones and yellow pimpernel. Bluebells take your breath away in the clear, sunny glades and the bright, grassy rides are perfect for common spotted-orchids, barren strawberry and broad-leaved helleborines. Honeysuckle – the county flower of Warwickshire – scrambles through the low-growing hazel trees and fills the air with a sweet

perfume. Such abundant plant life is wonderful for insects and Ryton Woods is a great place to look for white admiral, purple hairstreak and silver-washed fritillary butterflies. The wood links with Ryton Pools Country Park, Wappenbury and Old Nun Wood, and Bubbenhall Wood and Meadow to form a vital living landscape, with opportunities for lovely long walks.

One visit is all it takes to discover that it's far from grim up north. There is wonderful wildness to be found even in its old mill towns, which themselves add a fascinating layer of history to landscapes bursting with biodiversity. Craggy mountains and limestone pavement, peat bogs and open moorland, wildflower meadows and windswept coasts – the North of England has it all.

The most well-known of these backdrops is the world-famous Lake District. Red squirrels thrive in the dense forests of Penrith, Keswick and Grasmere, while white-clawed crayfish cling on in Cumbria's sparkling waters. The exposed hills of the Lakes are a haven for not only hardy hikers, but peregrine falcons and red deer, while Ennerdale Water is home to England's only migratory population of Arctic charr. Of the UK's natterjack toad population, 50 per cent can be found on the Cumbrian coast – the UK's stronghold.

But there is much more to the North than the Lake District. Nature lovers can experience everything from rolling wildflower meadows in Cheshire to noisy congregations of wading birds in Lancashire and Merseyside. In fact, the nutrient-rich mud of Lancashire's Ribble Estuary supports more than 270,000 curlews, redshanks, knot, black-tailed godwits and more each year – one of Britain's most important gatherings of wildfowl and waders.

Further inland, the rolling coastline gives way to the upland fells and heather-clad moors of the Forest of Bowland: domain of the increasingly rare and unceasingly persecuted hen harrier. Yorkshire, too, boasts upland beauty before giving way, once more, to the sea. On this parallel coastline, masses of squawking seabirds raise a family on the sheer faces of Flamborough Cliffs. Then there is Spurn Point – a small but iconic spit of land battered by wild and unruly winds, yet brimming with wading birds, wildfowl and winter rarities.

To the north-east you'll find the bleak, wind-ravaged heathland of Northumberland National Park, home to Hadrian's Wall and the UK's very first National Trail, the Pennine Way. Precious populations of black grouse lek in these windblown hills, while elsewhere in the county,

streams wind through bluebell-laden wooded valleys and upland hay meadows hum with insects. The Rivers Wear, Tyne and Tees attract water voles and dragonflies, while at Kielder Water – the largest human-made lake in Northern Europe – visitors can delight in sightings of magnificent ospreys and secretive adders.

NOT TO BE MISSED

Hutton Roof Crags, Cumbria
A limestone wonderland filled with orchids, including dark-red helleborine and fly orchid, and rare butterflies like high brown and pearl-bordered fritillary.

Blacka Moor, Sheffield
Woodland gives way to sweeping open moorland that brims with bilberry and heathers – the perfect place to get away from it all.

Flamborough Cliffs, Yorkshire
Tens of thousands of fulmars, gulls, kittiwakes, guillemots, razorbills and puffins breed here every year.

Brockholes, Lancashire
A former sand and gravel quarry with ancient woodland and flower-rich grassland where dragonflies, solitary bees, butterflies, birds and brown hares thrive.

Hatchmere Nature Reserve, Cheshire
Home to Cheshire's first pair of beavers, released after 400 years of local extinction.

Opposite: Flamborough Cliffs, Yorkshire

NORTHUMBERLAND

About the Trust

Northumberland Wildlife Trust has been saving wildlife and wild places and helping people to get closer to nature since 1971. The Trust looks after more than 60 nature reserves in Newcastle, North Tyneside and Northumberland and works with more than 600 volunteers to do even more for wildlife, from fundraising to tree planting.

Northumberland Wildlife Trust
01912 846884
nwt.org.uk

Annstead Dunes

Seahouses, NE67 5BT
OS Map NU 225307;
Map Ref R2

Sloping sand dunes are being revitalised by Northumberland Wildlife Trust's grazing Exmoor ponies. Look out for bloody crane's-bill, lady's bedstraw, bird's-foot trefoil and restharrow. Narrow-bordered five-spot burnet and cinnabar moths feed from the flowers and common lizards bask on the warm sand. Watch redshanks, curlews, sanderlings and ringed plovers feeding on the beach.

Big Waters

Seaton Burn, NE13 7EG
OS Map NZ 227733;
Map Ref R6

Open water and reedbeds fringed by wet woodland where willow tits and tree sparrows shelter. Great crested grebes, tufted ducks and herons spend their days on the water, occasionally joined by water rails and bitterns.

Swallows amass on migration in autumn, and winters are busy with crowds of wildfowl. Wildlife Trust members can access the two locked hides for £10 (contact the Trust in advance).

Ford Moss

Ford, TD15 2QA
OS Map NT 970375;
Map Ref R1

Lowland raised peat bog with stunning views over the Till Valley and the Cheviots. Heather dominates the drier areas, but wetter zones brim with peatland treasures. Sphagnum mosses, sundews, cranberry, cross-leaved heath and cotton-grasses thrive. Large heath butterflies still breed on the reserve, while other wildlife highlights include common lizards, adders, red grouse and woodcock.

Juliet's Wood

Slaley, NE47 0BH
OS Map NY 977587;
Map Ref R10

Lose yourself among towering oaks. Rowan, birch and wild cherry trees grow alongside hazels and hollies; a diverse mix that supports a wealth of wildlife. Birds include barn and tawny owls, wood warblers, pied flycatchers and treecreepers. Mammals include roe deer, badgers, stoats and weasels. Dog's mercury lines the woodland edge.

Holywell Pond

Holywell, NE25 0LB
OS Map NZ 319751;
Map Ref R7

Sitting near the coast, this pretty pond offers welcome respite for wigeons, greenshanks and green sandpipers in winter. Little grebes, pochards and sedge warblers breed here in spring. Common spotted and northern marsh orchids grow in the grassland. The public hide is always open; the member's-only hide can be accessed for £10 by contacting the Northumberland Wildlife Trust.

BRIARWOOD BANKS

Plankey Mill, NE47 7BP; **OS Map** NY 791620; **Map Ref** R9

Access/conditions: Park at National Trust pay and display car park at Allen Banks then enter via footpath on west bank of River Allen. Paths can be uneven, steep and muddy.
How to get there: Bus runs from Newcastle to Carlisle via Bardon Mill, then a 40-minute walk. By car, the National Trust car park is signposted off the A69 east of Haydon Bridge.
Walking time: 1.5 hours.

Semi-natural ancient woodland is pretty rare in Northumberland, but this reserve is one of the best-remaining patches in the county. Wild garlic, woodruff and dog's mercury fill the air with multi-layered scent and rare plants await eager botanists. Keep your eyes peeled for bird's-nest orchids, wood fescue and herb-paris.

Briarwood Banks may soon be home to hazel dormice too. It sits next to their most northerly haunt, so Northumberland Wildlife Trust is removing non-native tree species to restore the wood to prime dormouse habitat, hoping they'll scamper over through the tree canopy. Happily, red squirrels still live here, alongside roe deer, pied flycatchers and great spotted woodpeckers.

WHITELEE MOOR

Carter Bar; **OS Map** NT 700040; **Map Ref** R3

Access/conditions: Remote and wild – visitors should have hill-walking experience if attempting long walks. Path is rough and mostly unmarked.
How to get there: On the A68 (Newcastle to Jedburgh) at the crossing of the Scottish border. Park at the tourist car park on the border at Castle Bar, or by the track at the reserve's south-western corner.
Walking time: A leisurely visit takes 2 hours, but you could spend all day adventuring.
30-minute visit: Enter at Carter Bar and admire the

views along the footpath as long as time allows.

The perfect place to get away from it all, Whitelee Moor is windswept, rugged and home to incredible wildlife. Sphagnum mosses, cloudberry, bog asphodel and cotton-grasses grow on blanket bog surrounded by heather moorland, grassland and fen. The River Rede passes through the reserve, bringing otters on the hunt, while palmate newts breed in small pools along the burn. This is also the best area to watch for adders and common lizards. The lower slopes are blanketed by heather and home to birds including red grouse, merlins, peregrine falcons and hen harriers. The beautiful northern eggar moth flutters above the vegetation in the afternoon sunshine alongside ringlet and small heath butterflies. Skylarks, stonechats and meadow pipits fill the air across the reserve with their songs and calls, while dunlin and golden plovers breed on the high ground.

HAUXLEY

Low Hauxley, NE65 0JR; **OS Map** NU 285023; **Map Ref** R4

Opening hours: From 10am daily (check Trust website for up-to-date opening hours).
Access/conditions: Mostly wide, level paths. There is an accessible 1km route to two accessible hides.
How to get there: Buses run from Newcastle to Alnwick via Amble, then a 50-minute walk.

By car, from A1068 just south of Amble, follow directions to Hauxley. After High Hauxley village, turn right onto a track from where the reserve is signposted. £2 parking all day.
Walking time: 2 hours.
30-minute visit: Visit the main Reception Hide to see some of the birds on the ponds.

Hauxley is a wild retreat for families, birdwatchers and everyone in-between. Right next to the beach, it offers fantastic views across the length of Druridge Bay, and its former life as a coal mine left behind ponds and pools now brimming with birds.

Six hides offer peaceful places to sit; look out for tree sparrows, reed buntings and curlews – or just soak up the views. Hauxley is on the migration route for many birds undertaking epic journeys in spring and autumn, making these seasons the best for birding. Reserve staff often record 140 species in a year, including some rarities! As well as birds you could spot stoats and otters, while red squirrels are a regular sight.

Visit during summer to admire fabulous flowers including viper's bugloss, bloody crane's-bill and northern marsh orchids, which draw in common blue and wall brown butterflies. To spot dragonflies, head to Hauxley's smaller ponds, where common hawkers and common darters zip deftly after prey.

EAST CHEVINGTON

Druridge Bay, NE61 5BX; **OS Map** NZ 270990; **Map Ref** R5

Access/conditions: Level, well-surfaced paths. Park in Druridge Bay Country Park (charge applies) and follow the coastal footpath south to the reserve.

How to get there: Take A1 towards Newcastle upon Tyne. At Causey Park, take A1068 to Druridge Country Park, where you can park. On-site parking down the small unclassified road opposite the Red Row turning.

Walking time: 3 hours.

30-minute visit: Walk the coastal cycle route for views over the reedbeds and grasslands.

East Chevington is one of the best birdwatching spots in Northumberland, with something to see at any time of year. Terns, water rails and snipe use the ponds and margins, while spring and autumn see a fantastic cast of migratory birds pass through. In spring, skylarks, stonechats and grasshopper warblers breed in the grassy areas and sing along the coastal path. Reed warblers, reed buntings, marsh harriers and bearded tits raise their families in the sprawling reeds. In autumn, noisy skeins of pink-footed geese honk overhead, and in winter, prehistoric-looking bitterns arrive to spend the season hunting along the reed-edge.

The thriving grassland at East Chevington blooms with dyer's greenweed; bloody, meadow and cut-leaved crane's-bill; bird's-foot trefoil and five species of orchid: common spotted, northern marsh, marsh helleborine, bee and lesser butterfly. These rich pickings attract 21 species of butterfly, while hares hunker down among the cover of the vegetation. Barn and short-eared owls are often seen quartering the grassland.

East Chevington's pools are occupied by newts, frogs and toads; water shrews scamper along the reserve margins; and harvest mice build their intricate nests among the grasses.

CUMBRIA

Brown Robin

Grange-over-Sands, LA11 6EN
OS Map SD 411791;
Map Ref Q8

Limestone woodland where elusive hawfinches feed on cherry and hornbeam seeds. In spring, the woodland floor comes alive with bluebells, wood anemones, wild garlic and primroses. Coppicing has been reintroduced to part of the wood, encouraging the growth of woodland flowers. Cattle graze a wonderful grassland where an absence of fertiliser ensures that waxcap fungi and wildflowers flourish. Keep your eyes peeled for yellow meadow ants and the green woodpeckers that feed on them.

Staveley Woodlands

Staveley, LA8 9QT
OS Map SD 482984/SD 477984 (Craggy Wood);
Map Ref Q5

A number of woodlands come together to form Staveley Woodlands nature reserve. The most recent, Craggy Wood, was bought with help from local campaigners in 2020 and there are plans to link Dorothy Farrer's to Craggy Wood via a woodland corridor. A spring bluebell walk is essential, but also look out for early purple orchids and the scarcer herb-paris, otherwise known as 'true lover's knot'. Summer is the best time to see birds, with pied flycatchers, spotted flycatchers and redstarts flitting through the canopy.

Drumburgh Moss

Near Drumburgh village, CA7 5DR
OS Map NY 255586;
Map Ref Q1

Extensive restoration work of this raised bog by Cumbria Wildlife Trust has healed much of the scars wrought by drainage and peat extraction. By raising the water level, bog vegetation including carnivorous sundews and peat-forming sphagnum mosses have returned. Spring brings the bobbing white heads of cotton-grass, displaying skylarks and flowering bog rosemary, heather and cranberry. Summer is a wonderful time to see adders basking in the sunshine and autumn brings short-eared owls on the hunt. Head up the viewing platform for fantastic views across the mire to the hills beyond.

Humphrey Head

Grange over Sands, LA11 7LY
OS Map SD 388746;
Map Ref Q9

The geographical position, proximity to the sea and limestone rock of Humphrey Head has resulted in a special array of plants waiting to be discovered. Common and hoary rock-rose, limestone bedstraw, green-winged orchid and wild thyme grow on the cliff top, while further down, bloody crane's-bill and the rare spiked speedwell await. Yew, hazel and Lancastrian whitebeam trees cling on by sending their roots into cracks in the rock – true survivors. Peregrine falcons spook redshanks, curlews and snipe on the saltmarsh.

CLINTS QUARRY

Egremont, CA22 2SZ; **OS Map** NY 008124; **Map Ref** Q3

Access/conditions: Direct access from the public road. Circular path has some steep sections with steps and can be muddy.
How to get there: Buses run from Whitehaven to Egremont, which is one mile from the reserve. By car, from Egremont take A5086 towards Cleator, then first left signed for Moor Row. Parking is in a layby on the right just after the junction, or 100m further on, opposite the reserve entrance.
Walking time: 1.5 hours. Virtual tour on Cumbria Wildlife Trust website.

30-minute visit: Walk into the quarry to experience the grassland, woodland and quarry face, and return by the same path.

Industry may have given birth to Clints Quarry, but nature has nurtured it. Now works have ceased, the damp conditions between the spoil heaps encourage northern marsh orchids and common spotted-orchids to grow. The drier slopes of the heaps themselves are blanketed by wild strawberries, ox-eye daisies, carline thistles, and the beautiful pink heads of pyramidal orchids and bee orchids. This abundance of wildflowers and grasses is great news for butterfly lovers. Common blues, orange-tips, gatekeepers, ringlets and meadow browns flutter on sunny days, as well as five-spot burnet moths that shimmer in the sunshine.

Typical of old quarries, there are plenty of ponds to discover. Palmate newts, sticklebacks and pond snails swim beneath the surface while dragonflies dart above. There is also a peaceful woodland where you can see treecreepers and long-tailed tits.

HUTTON ROOF CRAGS

Burton-in-Kendal, LA6 1NX; **OS Map** SD 543799; **Map Ref** Q7

Access/conditions: The whole area is open access land with a number of public footpaths and informal paths. These can be narrow, muddy and cross uneven, rocky terrain.

How to get there: Bus leaves hourly from Kendal to Burton-in-Kendal. By car, from J36 of M6 take A65 then A6070 towards Burton. At Clawthorpe Hall Business Centre take the left turn signed for Clawthorpe. Park on the roadside where the bridleway is signed for Burton (SD 543783), then follow the bridleway across the field and into the wood until you reach the reserve.

Walking time: Allow 1.5 hours for the trail marked by red posts and 3 hours to walk from Clawthorpe Road to Hutton Roof village.

30-minute visit: Park in Hutton Roof village and follow the public footpath onto the common. The Rakes, a steeply angled limestone pavement, can be seen from here.

Hutton Roof Crags contains some of the best areas of limestone pavement in Britain. Specialist plants flower between the fissures in the stone, in the grassland and in woodland areas where coppicing and cattle grazing nurtures staggering floral diversity. The thin limestone soil is perfect for dark-red helleborines, a rare and beautiful orchid that entices passers-by with a sweet vanilla scent. Juniper thrives, blooming with small yellow flowers, which give way to its famous blue-black berries. Spring is the time to look for weird and wonderful fly orchids, while summer brings lily-of-the-valley and angular Solomon's-seal. Summer also sparks a butterfly bonanza. Brimstones and green hairstreaks are followed by some of the UK's rarest butterflies: pearl-bordered, high brown and small pearl-bordered fritillaries. Dark green fritillaries and graylings are high-summer specials.

There are stunning views from Hutton Roof Crags all year round, as well as constantly changing birdlife. Spring and summer bring willow warblers, skylarks and woodcock, while autumn heralds an influx of winter thrushes accompanied by gregarious gangs of long-tailed tits.

FOULSHAW MOSS

Witherslack, LA11 6SN; **OS Map** SD 458837; **Map Ref** Q6

Access/conditions: Various routes along an easy, accessible boardwalk. No access off the boardwalk as the boggy ground is very soft with lots of deep water.

How to get there: Buses run from Kendal, Grange, Ulverston and Barrow to Witherslack. By car, from Kendal take A590 towards Barrow in Furness. At the end of the dual carriageway at Gilpin Bridge, continue for 0.6 miles before turning onto a track immediately before a signed parking layby. Follow this track to the car park.

Walking time: 40 minutes. Virtual tour on Cumbria Wildlife Trust website.

30-minute visit: Walk from the car park to the viewing platform to admire the panorama. Stop by the bird screen to watch redpolls, siskins and tree sparrows feeding.

Drainage and tree planting in the 1950s and 1960s destroyed much of this precious peat bog. Now, this incredible wild place is thriving thanks to Cumbria Wildlife Trust's ambitious 15-year restoration programme. Bog plants like cranberry are flourishing, and insect-eating sundews lie in wait along the periphery of the wooden boardwalk that criss-crosses the reserve, ensnaring insects with the sticky droplets on their many filaments. Dragonflies, including the rare white-faced darter, pull impressive aerial manoeuvres above the bog pools, while on the ground, a kaleidoscopic array of pink, wine-red, orange, yellow and green sphagnum mosses form a living carpet of colour. Wetland birds like snipe and water rails take refuge among the mossy hummocks and pools, while birds of prey like hobbies, sparrowhawks and peregrine falcons take advantage of the abundant prey. Most excitingly, a pair of ospreys breeds here in summer.

One of the main attractions of Foulshaw Moss is undoubtedly its reptiles. Slow worms are secretive, but you have a good chance of seeing adders soaking up the sunshine among dead bracken during spring. Common lizards bask on the boardwalk throughout summer.

A trip up the viewing platform is essential to truly appreciate the scale of Foulshaw Moss. It's also a great vantage point for red deer and hen harrier-watching in autumn and winter.

SMARDALE

Kirkby Stephen, CA17 4HG; **OS Map** NY 742083; **Map Ref** Q4

Access/conditions: The tracks from Smardale car park to Smardale Gill viaduct (1.5 miles) and Newbiggin-on-Lune (3.5 miles) are level and suitable for wheelchairs and pushchairs. The Waitby Link track (0.5 miles) is level and Waitby Greenriggs (1.5 miles) is uneven with some steps.

How to get there: The nearest railway station is Kirkby Stephen West. Buses run from Kendal, Sedbergh and Brough to Kirkby Stephen. By car, from the A685 between Ravenstonedale and Kirkby Stephen, take the Smardale turning. Cross over the railway and turn left at the T-junction. Bear right over the disused railway and turn immediately right. Car park is 200m on your right.

Walking time: The 3.5-mile length takes 2 hours. The circular trail, which leaves the reserve just beyond the cottages, crossing County Bridge and then returns at the viaduct, takes 2.5 hours from Smardale car park. The 1.5-mile walk to Waitby Greenriggs takes 1 hour. Virtual tour on Cumbria Wildlife Trust website.

30-minute visit: Walk from the Smardale car park as far as the Settle-Carlisle viaduct and back.

Smardale nature reserve encompasses three wildlife refuges that collectively make up five miles of the disused Tebay-Darlington railway line. Woodland, which is thought to have been growing since medieval times, contrasts with species-rich limestone grassland to create a true wildlife haven. Must-see flowers include fragrant orchids, bird's-eye primroses and bloody crane's-bills, but the main attraction is Smardale's butterflies. One particular butterfly, in fact: the Scotch argus. Smardale is one of only two sites in England where it can be seen. It flies alongside dark green fritillaries, northern brown arguses and dingy skippers in summer. Summer also brings exciting migrant birds like redstarts and pied flycatchers, while green woodpeckers, ravens and sparrowhawks are resident all year round. Winter is a great time to spot red squirrels racing between the trees, particularly at the Waitby Link portion of the reserve. As well as providing a continuous corridor for wildlife, this fascinating geological time tunnel showcases unusual rock formations.

SOUTH WALNEY

Barrow-in-Furness, LA14 3YQ; **OS Map** SD 225620; **Map Ref** Q10

Access/conditions: Free entry for Wildlife Trust members; non-members £3; children £1. Four hides have step-free entrances. Off-road mobility tramper available for hire (suggested £5 donation) – call 01539 816300 to book in advance.

How to get there: By car, from Barrow-in-Furness follow signs for Walney Island. Cross Jubilee Bridge onto the Island and follow a brown sign left at traffic lights. Follow this road for 0.6 miles then turn left down Carr Lane. Pass Biggar Village and follow the road to South End Caravan Park. Follow the road for a further 0.6 miles until you reach the reserve.

Walking time: Choose from the three-mile red trail and two-mile blue trail. Virtual tour on Cumbria Wildlife Trust website.

30-minute visit: In winter, head to the Bank Hide overlooking Gate Pool to watch wigeon, teal and eider ducks. In spring and summer, wander at your leisure while the reserve is awash with colour.

With stunning views across Morecambe Bay, this coastal reserve is full of interest and a fantastic place for birdwatching. It's also home to the only grey seal colony in Cumbria. They can be seen from the hides, playing in the water at high tide.

Almost 250 species of bird are known to breed at South Walney, including gulls, waders and terns. Visit in spring to watch (and hear!) the comical courtship of eider ducks. South Walney is one of the southernmost places in Europe to see them breeding, with females almost invisible as they sit, camouflaged, on their nests. Spring and autumn bring migrant birds – wheatears, willow warblers and Sandwich terns – then curlews, spotted redshanks and greenshanks that enjoy the central pools with teal, wigeon and goldeneyes. There are plenty of beautiful flowers too. Henbanes, hound's-tongue and yellow-horned poppies bloom on the shingle, while pyramidal orchids, viper's-bugloss and wild pansies brighten up the dunes.

EYCOTT HILL

Near Berrier, CA11 0XD; **OS Map** NY 394301; **Map Ref** Q2

Access/conditions: No surfaced paths. Uneven and wet ground.

How to get there: Regular bus service between Penrith and Keswick. Nearest bus stop is 1.5 miles from the reserve, at the Sportsman's Inn. By car, from J40 of M6 follow A66 towards Keswick. Turn right after seven miles, signposted for Hutton Roof, then take the next left, signposted for Hutton Roof, Berrier and Whitbarrow. Follow this road for 1.6 miles, then the reserve and car park will be on the left.

Walking time: Public Rights of Way give access from Berrier and Mungrisdale, and waymarking posts lead to the summit from both sides of the reserve. Both routes take around 1 hour. Virtual tour on

Cumbria Wildlife Trust website.

30-minute visit: Take the short waymarked route to the viewpoint.

A peaceful upland shaped by volcanic activity 460 million years ago, with ancient lava

WILDLIFE FACT: CLIMATE HEROES

Upland bogs like those on Eycott Hill are true heroes in the fight to slow climate breakdown and adapt to the changes we already face. When healthy and wet, sphagnum mosses thrive and form the peaty soil that locks up carbon for millennia. They also filter water and soak it up like a sponge, reducing the risk of flooding on lower ground.

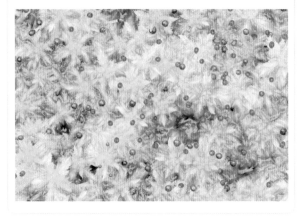

flows still visible across the reserve. Montane flowers including mountain pansy and mountain everlasting grow on the rocky outcrops, while boggy areas are colonised by 18 species of sphagnum moss, fluffy cotton-grass and the beautiful grass-of-Parnassus – not a grass at all, but a delicate white flower also known as the 'bog star'. A newly created hay meadow at the reserve entrance erupts with dazzling colour in summer, attracting butterflies including small pearl-bordered fritillaries. Golden-ringed dragonflies hunt over boggy areas while reptiles take cover in dry-stone walls. Some wonderful species of bird breed here, and it's hoped that the ongoing restoration of the reserve, including hedgerow planting, will help their numbers grow further. Listen for the frantic singing of skylarks as they ascend into the big skies, and the haunting cries of curlews. The abundance of owl pellets on the ground is evidence of short-eared owls feeding here, so keep your eyes peeled.

DURHAM

About the Trust

Across County Durham, Darlington, Gateshead, South Tyneside and Sunderland, Durham Wildlife Trust is working hard to protect wildlife for future generations. Managing 37 nature reserves and two visitor centres, and supported by more than 8,000 members and 250 volunteers, the Durham Wildlife Trust safeguards local nature from the Tees to the Tyne.

Durham Wildlife Trust
0191 584 3112
durhamwt.com

Baal Hill Wood

Wolsingham, DL13 3HE
OS Map NZ 075384;
Map Ref R14

A peaceful remnant of ancient woodland home to an impressive 400-year-old oak tree. Visit in spring to see beautiful carpets of bluebells and wild garlic in flower, and birds like wood warblers, redstarts and pied flycatchers in the trees.

Blackhall Rocks

Blackhall Colliery, TS27 4DG
OS Map NZ 474389;
Map Ref R15

A former coastal colliery, home to Durham brown argus butterflies and rare cistus forester moths. Bloody crane's-bill, grass-of-Parnassus and bird's-eye primrose are just some of the plants found here. Offshore, a rocky reef and kelp forest support cuttlefish, squat lobsters and sea slugs.

The Whinnies

Middleton-St-George, DL2 1UL
OS Map NZ 351137;
Map Ref R24

This former ironworks now nurtures fairy flax, bird's-foot trefoil and fragrant orchids; dingy skipper, common blue and small copper butterflies; yellowhammers, tree sparrows and curlews. Visit in summer to see dragonflies and damselflies darting over the ponds.

Malton

Lanchester, DH7 0TP
OS Map NZ 180460;
Map Ref R13

Malton more than makes up for its small size with its sheer diversity of life. Oak woodland, mature hedgerows, ponds, meadows and scrub offer homes to tawny owls, green and great spotted woodpeckers, and the unusual bulrush wainscot moth. Great crested newts breed in the ponds.

Raisby Hill Grassland

Coxhoe, DH6 4LP
OS Map NZ 333354;
Map Ref R16

A beautiful limestone grassland with a dazzling array of plants – fairy flax, devil's-bit scabious, burnet saxifrage and columbine; dark red helleborine, fragrant and pyramidal orchids. An abundance of common rock-rose supports a small colony of northern brown argus butterflies, and wych elms offer vital food to the larvae of white-letter hairstreaks. In spring, brown hares box on the spoil screes.

Shibdon Pond and Meadow
Blaydon, NE21 5LU
OS Map NZ 192628;
Map Ref R8

Good numbers of wildfowl and waders make this one of the best wetlands in Tyneside. Lapwings, golden plovers, snipe and teal feed and shelter alongside water rails, redshank and sandpipers. Kingfishers are a common sight, and in summer, swifts, swallows and martins feed across the water.

BISHOP MIDDLEHAM QUARRY
Bishop Middleham, DL17 9BB; **OS Map** NZ 331326; **Map Ref** R17

Access/conditions: Difficult terrain and steep cliff faces – please stick to footpaths.
How to get there: The reserve is 1km north of Bishop Middleham Village on the minor road to the A177. Park in the layby opposite the reserve entrance.
Walking time: The circular route takes around 1 hour but can take longer depending on how often you stop to admire the flowers.
30-minute visit: Walk to the limestone flora on the quarry floor.

One of the most important disused quarries in the country, never mind the county! Unusual plants like moonwort, autumn gentian and fairy flax thrive in the limestone soils alongside pyramidal, common spotted, fragrant and bee orchids. But there is one plant that is even more special than the rest: the rare dark red helleborine, which is thriving here. Of course, this spectacular flower-show attracts some very important butterflies including dingy skippers, small heaths and one of the county's largest colonies of the rare Durham brown argus, which is best seen in June and July. But don't forget the moths – six-spot burnet, wood tiger and hummingbird hawk-moths can all be seen here.

HAWTHORN DENE
Hawthorn Village, SR7 8SH; **OS Map** NZ 427458; **Map Ref** R12

Access/conditions: Mixed terrain with a surfaced pathway around the top. Muddy at times.
How to get there: From the junction with B1432, 1km south of Cold Hesledon, head east until the end of the surfaced road, and park in laybys adjacent to modern bungalow. Follow the track through the gate for around 350m before turning right onto the nature trail into the wood.
Walking time: 2 hours.
30-minute visit: Take the shorter walk that misses out the eastern grassland.

Hawthorn Dene is a steep-sided ravine that cuts through the magnesian limestone of the Durham Coast, blanketed by elm, ash and yew trees. Snowdrops, wild garlic and bluebells decorate the woodland floor from spring, and rarer flowers such as bird's-nest orchids and herb-paris can also be found. Jays, treecreepers and great spotted woodpeckers are at home in the trees while roe deer sneak

around the trunks below.

But Hawthorn Dene offers so much more than woodland. The remains of an old railway platform and impressive railway viaduct will capture your imagination, and the nearby coastal path offers the opportunity for longer walks towards Seaham, Beacon Hill and the Durham Heritage Coast.

HANNAH'S MEADOW

Hunderthwaite, DL12 9UP; **OS Map** NY 934187; **Map Ref** R22

Access/conditions: Mixed terrain with pathways and boardwalks. Not suitable for mobility scooters but raised walkways provide limited access for wheelchairs and pushchairs.

How to get there: Follow B6277 from Barnard Castle to Romaldkirk then follow the Balderhead Road via Hunderthwaite. Limited roadside parking at reserve entrance.

Walking time: 40 minutes.

An upland hay meadow and grazing pasture, where decades of traditional management have left their mark in the form of wonderful wildflowers and fantastic wildlife. The meadows were previously owned by Hannah Hauxwell for more than 50 years. Living alone at Low Birk Hatt Farm without the luxury of electricity or running water, Hannah managed the land using traditional methods, avoiding artificial fertilisers and re-seeding.

Visit in June and early July to see the meadows at their finest, with ragged robin,

wood crane's-bill, marsh-marigolds, yellow rattle, adder's-tongue ferns and globeflowers. Keep an eye out for rarer species like frog orchids and moonwort too.

As if that wasn't enough, your walk is guaranteed to be accompanied by a stunning avian soundtrack. Curlews bubble and lapwings *pee-wit* as they fly above this

incredible upland landscape. Redshanks hide away in the grass and meadow pipits make their home in the rushes and sedges.

LOW BARNS

Witton-le-Wear, DL14 0AG; **OS Map** NZ 160315; **Map Ref** R18

Opening hours: Visitor centre open 10am–4pm.
Access/conditions: Good access with smooth, wide pathways suitable for all mobilities.
How to get there: From A68 follow brown signs through Witton-le-Wear, turning right at the Victoria pub. Once over the level crossing, the reserve is 0.5 miles along the road

on the right. From A689 the reserve is 0.75 miles west of High Grange. Parking is free for members; non-members are encouraged to leave a £2.50 donation.
Walking time: 45 minutes for the nature trail.

Bordered by the River Wear, this beautiful wetland offers a peaceful escape for the

whole family. However, Low Barns wasn't always a haven for wildlife. It started life as farmland before being mined for sand and gravel until 1964, when it was given to Durham Wildlife Trust.

The Trust has done a fantastic job of transforming the site into the thriving nature reserve it is today. Lakes, streams, ponds,

reedbeds and grassland interconnect to help wildlife move through the landscape, with more space to feed, breed and shelter. Damselflies and dragonflies, including the striking southern hawker, hunt over ponds where common frogs and smooth newts breed. Kingfishers are regularly spotted fishing near the bird hides and flycatchers breed in the woods.

Foxes, otters, roe deer and stoats are some of Low Barns' more secretive residents, but step lightly and, with some patience, you may catch a glimpse of them. The reserve's butterflies are much showier: dingy skippers and small coppers flit from flower to flower in the summer sunshine.

RAINTON MEADOWS

Houghton-le-Spring, DH4 6PU; **OS Map** NZ 323485; **Map Ref** R11

Opening hours: Visitor centre open 10am–4pm.
Access/conditions: Mixed terrain with three nature trails and a number of accessible paths linking lakeside viewing areas.
How to get there: Sunderland/Durham buses stop at Rainton Bridge Business Park a short walk from the reserve. By car, follow brown signs for Rainton Meadows from A690, or leave A1(M) at Chester-le-Street and head west on A183, then A1052, and B1284 takes you past the site entrance.
Walking time: 2 hours.
30-minute visit: Take the route along the lower slopes and lakeshore.

More than 200 species of bird have been recorded at this former opencast coal mine in Sunderland. In just 20 years this fledgling wetland has come alive with redshanks, oystercatchers and lapwings; warblers, finches and farmland birds. Little ringed plovers are some of the more unusual visitors to Rainton Meadows, while all five of the UK's owl species can be seen at different times of the year. Stoats and weasels bound through the grassland, brown hares hide among the vegetation and roe deer are seen regularly. There are insects aplenty, with dragonflies and damselflies hunting over the wetlands and butterflies dancing across the grasslands.

In winter, a four-legged conservation team of sheep and Exmoor ponies arrives to keep the grassland in check, preparing it for a new season of wildflower growth.

Don't miss stopping at the Meadows Coffee Shop to round off your visit with a delicious scone or slice of cake.

TEES VALLEY

Cattersty Gill

Skinningrove, TS12 2QX
OS Map NZ 705204;
Map Ref P3

An important refuge for migrant birds, which stop to refuel in this secluded valley perched high on the cliffs. Past rarities have included dusky warbler and red-flanked bluetail. Once used as a tip for slag waste, the reserve is now a haven for wildflowers, which thrive on the lime-rich soil. The colour and scent of kidney vetch, pyramidal and common spotted-orchids, centaury and yellow-wort fill the grassland each spring and summer.

Gravel Hole

Stockton-on-Tees, TS20 1UY
OS Map NZ 447231;
Map Ref R19

A disused sand and gravel quarry where lime-loving plants flourish. As well as orchids, the rich flora includes cowslips, kidney vetch and field scabious. Notable butterflies include dingy skipper, common blue and small heath. Beetles, bees, moths and other insects add yet more colour, while dense hedgerows offer refuge for whitethroats, thrushes and occasionally winter waxwings.

Hardwick Dene

Stockton-on-Tees, TS19 8QA
OS Map NZ 419205;
Map Ref R20

A secret valley saved from development. Scrubland offers a safe haven for nesting birds in spring then transforms into a berry buffet for fieldfares, redwings and blackbirds in winter. A wildflower meadow beams with common spotted-orchids, devil's-bit scabious, betony and ragged robin. The dene is a stronghold for the white-letter hairstreak butterfly, named for the white 'W' shape on the underside of its hindwings.

Margrove Ponds

Saltburn-by-the-Sea, TS12 3BT
OS Map NZ 654162;
Map Ref P6

An impressive total of more than 150 bird species have been recorded here, including a number of scarce and rare birds. The main pond attracts teal, tufted ducks and little grebes; snipe feed in the damp grassland to the left of the track; and reed warblers hide in the reed swamp. In good weather conditions you may spot raptors including sparrowhawks, buzzards and kestrels soaring above the hillsides visible from the pond.

BOWESFIELD

Stockton-on-Tees, TS18 3EX; **OS Map** NZ 440160; **Map Ref** R23

Access/conditions: Access through the Bowesfield development or by following the Teesdale Way north (downstream) from Preston Park.

How to get there: At the roundabout of Concorde Way, Myton Way and Bowesfield Lane in Bowesfield Farm Estate, turn onto the new Bowesfield Farm Development. The nature reserve is on the floodplain below the development.

Walking time: 1 hour.

30-minute visit: Take a brisk walk around the surfaced paths, which connect a series of pools and reedbeds for views of the ducks and wading birds.

What was once agricultural land has been restored to a floodplain by Tees Valley Wildlife Trust. Extensive pools, ditches and reedbeds form a wildlife corridor along the river, and young trees are being planted on the edge of the floodplain to form a rich broadleaved woodland.

Visit early in the day and you may be rewarded with a sighting of an otter, fox or roe deer, but the tiny harvest mice that live in the rough grassland are much harder to see. A network of surfaced paths and bridges connects three large, reed-fringed pools where reed warblers and reed buntings breed during spring

and an occasional Cetti's warbler might be heard. In autumn, ducks and wading birds increase as they arrive to pass the winter months. As many as 2,000 have been counted on the reserve, including teal, curlews, gadwall, shovelers, ruffs and golden plovers.

PORTRACK MARSH

Stockton-on-Tees, TS18 2PN; **OS Map** NZ 465194; **Map Ref** R21

Access/conditions: Major paths are surfaced and suitable for wheelchair and pushchair access. The unsurfaced pathway on the north edge has some steps. The reserve can be muddy in winter.

How to get there: From the A66, follow signs for Tees Barrage, head straight over

the roundabout and right into Whitewater Way. Follow the road to the Talpore. Portrack Marsh is a short walk from Stockton and Middlesbrough.

Walking time: 2 hours.

30-minute visit: Walk along the riverside footpath to the information board, then follow the footpaths to the riverside and pond-dipping platform.

Portrack Marsh is the last remaining wetland on the lower Tees. Its large pools are a magnet for birds during the winter months, with redshanks and lapwings feeding on the riverbank or taking refuge on the marsh at high tide. Shovelers, pochards, tufted ducks and teal are occasionally joined by goldeneyes or scaups. Kingfishers, grey wagtails and bullfinches offer a touch of colour to brighten up the short, dull days and incredible starling murmurations swirl over the reeds. Spring is equally full of life. Grasshopper warblers, wheatears and whinchats arrive with sand martins and common terns.

But don't discount the other wildlife. Grey and common seals can be seen on the Tees, gorging themselves on salmon and sea trout, and otters have been spotted moving between the river and the reserve.

COATHAM MARSH

Redcar, TS10 5BW; **OS Map** NZ 586248; **Map Ref** P1

Access/conditions: Paths are mostly surfaced. The section along the Fleet towards Kirkleatham Lane is prone to flooding in winter. The path between the car park and the footbridge is suitable for wheelchair access.
How to get there: Off the A1085 (Redcar to Middlesbrough). At crossroads with Kirkleatham Lane, turn left and head up to next mini roundabout. Turn left onto Tod Point Road and continue over the railway bridge. The reserve is on the left.
Walking time: 1.5 hours.

30-minute visit: Follow the footpath through the meadow and head towards the viewpoint on Middle Marsh.

Coatham Marsh offers a sanctuary to wetland birds against an unflinchingly

industrial backdrop. The dramatic, redundant Redcar blast furnace lurks in the background, and the two lakes on the southern side of the reserve are actually human-made relics of historic soil extraction for steelworks. These are fringed with dense reedbeds, which provide nesting places for reed, sedge and grasshopper warblers. Old slag heaps are now decorated by swathes of marsh orchids and clusters of bee orchids as well as yellow rattle, eyebright and knapweed. Foxes and stoats potter between the heaps, and an abundance of small mammals attracts ghostly barn owls on the hunt for their dinner.

Winter is a fantastic time to see huge flocks of ducks and wading birds taking advantage of the nutritious feeding grounds. Pochards, redshanks and wigeon overwinter alongside black-tailed godwits and snipe. With the reserve sitting so close to the coast, they are sometimes joined by rare visitors like spoonbills and the peculiar stone curlew.

MAZE PARK

Thornaby, TS5 4AB; **OS Map** NZ 464191; **Map Ref** P4

Access/conditions: Major footpaths are surfaced and suitable for wheelchairs and pushchairs. Damper areas have boardwalks.

How to get there: From A66, follow signs for Tees Barrage. The right at the first roundabout leads to the entrance. Maze Park is a short walk from Stockton and Middlesbrough and incorporates part of the Sustrans National Cycle Route.

Walking time: 40 minutes

Maze Park is a green oasis right at the centre of Teesside, with brilliant views across the area from the top of its many mounds – a clue to its industrial past. Tees Valley Wildlife Trust bought the land in 1998, and now, these lime-rich slag mounds have been managed to encourage a wonderful array of wildflowers. Yellow-wort and black medick grow alongside common centaury and bird's-foot trefoil, nurturing more than 12 species of butterfly including the increasingly scarce grayling and dingy skipper. You may also spot grey partridges and skylarks hiding among the grass.

A small colony of sand martins nests in the steep riverbanks, which are also the best place to watch a true autumn spectacle: the annual salmon run. You may even spot common and grey seals preying on the preoccupied fish.

As well as planting 15 acres (6ha) of woodland, Tees Valley Wildlife Trust has built a network of surfaced paths and boardwalks so visitors can enjoy as much of Maze Park as possible. The tallest mound offers the best panorama, and there is seating around the reserve so you can stop to take in the peace and quiet.

SALTBURN GILL

Near Redcar, TS12 1NY; **OS Map** NZ 674208; **Map Ref** P2

Access/conditions: The paths are muddy in winter and care should be taken when climbing the steep steps. The site is not really suitable for disabled access.

How to get there: From Redcar, take A174 to Saltburn. Follow the road down Saltburn Bank onto the seafront, cross over the bridge, take the first right and park in the public car park. Walk towards the Northumbrian Water pumping station and take the signposted public footpath to the entrance.

Walking time: 1 hour.

30-minute visit: Follow the footpath up to Lum Hole (where the bridleway and footpath cross), then retrace your steps back to the car park.

This 52-acre (21ha) woodland has remained largely undisturbed since the time of the great forests. A dense canopy of oak, ash, hazel and holly trees shelters a winding path, which runs the entire length of the secluded valley.

Spring and early summer are by far the best times to visit, when the woodland flowers put on a show. The vibrant yellow lesser celandines bloom first and are shortly followed by carpets of wild garlic and bluebells. Other plants to look out for include dog's mercury, woodruff, bugle, moschatel and wood avens. Even after the summer flowers have died back and the golden autumn leaves have fallen from the trees, Saltburn Gill is worth visiting to spot fungi, or ferns with strange-sounding names like hart's tongue, hard-shield, broad-buckler and male fern.

The birds, too, offer something new with each season. Saltburn Gill's spring soundtrack is a rich mix of chiffchaffs, willow warblers, robins, wrens and spotted

flycatchers that won't fail to make your heart soar. Though the migratory species leave during autumn and the birdsong dies down, it's a great time to look out for mixed tit flocks roving through the trees as they search out the last insects before winter.

LAZENBY BANK

Lazenby, TS14 6QZ; **OS Map** NZ 585191; **Map Ref** P5

Access/conditions: A network of woodland tracks provides circular walks. These can be rough and muddy. The Dave's Wood area of the reserve lies largely on flat ground.
How to get there: Park in the layby on the A174 (westbound), close to Greystones roundabout. Walk up the old trackway named Sandy Lane, which leads you to the woodland.
Walking time: 2 hours.
30-minute visit: Explore Dave's Wood, the first plot you'll come to when visiting Lazenby Bank.

The skyline to the south of Middlesbrough is dominated by a long, green, wooded slope stretching all the way from Wilton Castle to the rocky outcrop at Eston Nab. This is Lazenby Bank, a beautiful and varied woodland offering a quiet sanctuary for wildlife and visitors.

Parts of Lazenby Bank are ancient woodland – a rare and irreplaceable habitat – where complex communities of trees, plants, fungi, micro-organisms and insects have evolved alongside one another in perfect harmony. Spring walks will be brightened by swathes of bluebells and pretty patches of wood anemones. Autumn strolls often reveal the unmistakeable white-spotted red caps of the fly agaric toadstool. Mushrooms often mean molluscs, which feed on their tender caps, and Lazenby Bank is home to two special ones: the ash-black slug (the largest land slug species in the world), and the handsome English chrysalis snail.

The reserve is also a great place to take in some local history. The remains of its mining past are scattered throughout the woodland: cobbled tramways, a keystone dating from 1871, and the shell of a fan house.

LANCASHIRE, MANCHESTER AND NORTH MERSEYSIDE

About the Trust

The Wildlife Trust for Lancashire, Manchester & North Merseyside was formed in 1962 by a group of people, just like you, who knew they needed to take action to protect wildlife. Now, the Trust is the largest wildlife conservation organisation in the region – caring for 42 nature reserves, helping local communities bring wildlife back to their towns and cities, reintroducing locally extinct species and pioneering peatland restoration.

The Wildlife Trust for Lancashire, Manchester & North Merseyside

01772 324129
lancswt.org.uk

Longworth Clough

Bolton, BL7 9PU
OS Map SD 695102;
Map Ref O5

An industrial relic redesigned by nature and transformed into a peaceful oasis, nestled in the West Pennine Moors. Small skipper, green-veined white and meadow brown butterflies flit and flutter in a landscape brimming with yellow irises, bog asphodel and sneezewort. Tormentil and heath bedstraw grow on the grassy slopes and dippers feed in Eagley Brook. Woodcock, tawny owls and wood warblers live in the woodland.

Moston Fairway

Moston, M40 3NT
OS Map SD 884016;
Map Ref O8

You'd never guess that the cotton-grasses and orchids of Moston Fairway were just a mile from Manchester city centre. This urban wilderness combines urban marsh, woodland, grassland, boggy fen and mossland habitats into an area no bigger than a football pitch. Reed buntings, linnets and kestrels are regular visitors, while smooth newts breed here each year. Look out for brown hawker and broad-bodied chaser dragonflies in summer.

Salthill Quarry

Clitheroe, BB7 1QL
OS Map SD 755426;
Map Ref O2

Rock-faces and footpaths scattered with fossilised sea lilies reveal Salthill Quarry's hidden pre-history at the bottom of the ocean. Now, bee orchids, harebells, bird's-foot trefoil and lady's bedstraw colour the landscape. August and September bring the beautiful pink blooms of autumn gentian. Don't miss a ramble through the woodland, which fills with warbler song in spring.

Cadishead & Little Woolden Moss

Irlam, M44 5LR
OS Map SJ 698951;
Map Ref O10

Sphagnum moss, common lizards and dragonflies are reclaiming these peatlands, once extracted for peat. The Trust's ongoing restoration work means these adjacent reserves are now once again home to fluffy cotton-grasses and carnivorous sundews; merlins and short-eared owls; lapwings and skylarks. During summer, the rare bog bush cricket calls among the heather.

Warton Crag
Carnforth, LA5 9RB
OS Map SD 494730;
Map Ref O1

Limestone cliffs decorated with wildflowers including common rock-rose, pignut and early purple orchids. Coppicing means that violets thrive, and with them pearl-bordered and small pearl-bordered fritillary butterflies, which lay their eggs almost exclusively on this plant. Look out for an incredible range of lichens and don't miss the panoramic views over Morecambe Bay.

WIGAN FLASHES
Wigan, WN3 5UF; **OS Map** SD 585030; **Map Ref** O7

Access/conditions: Wheelchair access is possible, but some wheelchairs may have difficulty fitting through the gates (contact the Lancashire Wildlife Trust in advance). Picnic area at Ochre Flash.
How to get there: By car, leave M6 at J25 and head north on A49. Turn right onto Poolstock Lane (B5238). Reserve entrances on Carr Lane near Hawkley Hall School, off Poolstock Lane and on Warrington Road (A573).
Walking time: A network of paths means walks can vary from 1 hour to a whole day. You could also extend your walk onto the Leeds and Liverpool Canal.
30-minute visit: Explore the self-guided nature trail around Ochre Flash.

As you feel the quietude and birdsong wash over you, it's hard to believe that Wigan Flashes started life as a casualty of industry. The 'flashes' themselves are lakes formed as a result of mining subsidence and now form part of a stunning mosaic of open water, reedbed, fen, rough grassland, wet woodland and scrub habitats where wildlife

thrives. In spring and summer, sedge warblers, common terns and water rails breed across the reserve. In winter, the flashes swell with ducks, great crested grebes and herons.

If you're lucky you may even spot an elusive bittern skulking through the reeds.

Wigan Flashes sits at the heart of a network of willow tit habitats, supporting 10 per cent of the UK's population of this endangered bird. But it isn't all about the birds – the reserve is home to unusual flowers including marsh helleborine and yellow bird's-nest.

LUNT MEADOWS

Maghull, L29 8YA; **OS Map** SD 355021; **Map Ref** O6

This spectacular wetland nature reserve, nestled along the meandering River Alt, was transformed from intensively farmed arable land to a flood storage reservoir and birder's paradise. Spring and summer see the water burst into life as breeding lapwings, redshanks, dunlin and oystercatchers jostle for position with herons, egrets and sometimes breeding avocets. There are birds of prey aplenty, with marsh harriers, peregrine falcons, sparrowhawks and barn owls all regularly hunting over the reserve. Winter brings short-eared owls, who return each year to quarter the grassland. If you can tear your eyes away from the birds, see how many different dragonfly species you can spot, and check the watery channels beside the paths for our good friend the water vole, or Ratty as he was known in *The Wind in the Willows*.

Access/conditions: Paths are unsurfaced and can be rough underfoot. Narrow kissing gates are unsuitable for wheelchairs, but work is underway to improve access. **How to get there:** Bus from Waterloo Interchange. By car from A578/Broom's Cross Road north of Aintree, take B5422 to Sefton and follow signs to Lunt. After a mile you'll see the reserve entrance on the right. **Walking time:** 1 hour. **30-minute visit:** From the car park, turn right onto the footpath towards Showricks Bridge to see the remains of a Mesolithic settlement.

BROCKHOLES

Preston, PR5 0AG; **OS Map** SD 588306; **Map Ref** O3

Opening hours: Visitor centre open 10am–5pm, April–August; 10am–4pm, September–March; closed Christmas Eve and Christmas Day. **Access/conditions:** A selection of walking trails suitable for pushchairs, wheelchairs and those with limited mobility. Kissing gates are accessible for smaller wheelchairs – larger wheelchairs and mobility scooters can use the vehicle access gates with a key (contact the Trust in advance). **How to get there:** Buses stop at the Tickled Trout pub, then a 10-minute walk. By car, from J31 of the M6, turn right at the roundabout, signed A59/

Blackburn. Stay in the left-hand lane and just before the traffic lights, take the first exit, signed 'Brockholes Nature Reserve'. Parking £5 all day.

Walking time: Exploring each trail, watching the wildlife and relaxing in the Kestrel Kitchen café will take a whole morning or afternoon.

30-minute visit: Stroll around the shortest trail on the reserve map, where you could spot a kestrel and lots of dragonflies and damselflies.

Whether you're a seasoned birdwatcher, outdoorsy couple or really wild family, you'll fall in love with Brockholes. Lancashire Wildlife Trust has transformed this former sand and gravel quarry into a haven for both wildlife and people. Children can learn about the wonders of nature in the welcome centre and along the nature trails, and the reserve gives back to the local community through Forest School and green well-being projects.

The grassland brims with orchids and yellow rattle, the woodland shines bright with bluebells, and tranquil lakes support huge numbers of birds. Spring sees a baby boom as lapwings, oystercatchers and common terns breed on Meadow Lake and Number One Pit. In May, whimbrel roost in large numbers, while throughout spring and summer, swifts, sand martins and hobbies create fantastic aerial displays. As the sun shines, the reserve literally buzzes with insects: brown hawker dragonflies, countless solitary bees and white-letter hairstreak butterflies are just a few of the star species. In autumn, the lakes fill with overwintering waders and wildfowl. In winter, bitterns arrive. But Brockholes isn't just about the birds: keep your eyes peeled for brown hares, roe deer and weasels.

Don't miss a stroll onto the UK's only floating Visitor Village – an eco-friendly hub that floats on Meadow Lake and hosts a welcome centre, gift shop and the Kestrel Kitchen café.

MERE SANDS WOOD

Rufford, L40 1TG; **OS Map** SD 447157; **Map Ref** O4

P wc & i 🛒 🍴 ♿ 🚶

Opening hours: Check Lancashire Wildlife Trust website for up-to-date information.
Access/conditions: The majority of paths are suitable for wheelchairs and prams. Hides and visitor centre are fully accessible. Two motorised buggies available for loan from the visitor centre (call the Trust in advance).
How to get there: Off the A59 in Rufford along Holmeswood Road. Leave Holmeswood Road at the brown nature reserve sign.
Walking time: 1–2 hours.
30-minute visit: From the visitor centre, take the left-hand path and see what you can spot from the first bird hide.

Mere Sands Wood is a true wildlife haven. Spring and summer see new life bloom in the form of marsh orchids and broad buckler ferns while the air buzzes with dragonflies and birdsong. Watch bullfinches, tree sparrows, long-tailed tits and sparrowhawks in the woodland and keep a sharp ear out for cuckoos – a regular spring visitor. Take a seat in one of the lakeside hides in spring and you may even see great crested grebes performing their elaborate courtship ritual. Autumn and winter mark the arrival of overwintering birds like charming teal, handsome pintails and comical shovelers, and it's a great time to spot kingfishers hunting from vantage points near the hides.

But Mere Sands Wood isn't just a birder's paradise – roe deer, stoats and foxes creep through the woods. Floral highlights include yellow bartsia, yellow-wort and lesser centaury, plus a fantastic array of orchids including marsh helleborines and common spotted.

YORKSHIRE

About the Trust

Wherever you are in Yorkshire, you're never more than 20 miles from a Yorkshire Wildlife Trust nature reserve. The Trust cares for more than 100 special wild places and works to create new wild areas and wildlife corridors, connecting the landscape so wildlife can thrive. It is also involved in hundreds of conservation projects, and inspires both adults and children to care for nature.

Yorkshire Wildlife Trust
01904 659570
ywt.org.uk

Askham Bog
York, YO23 2UB
OS Map SE 574479;
Map Ref P13

Described by Sir David Attenborough as a 'cathedral of nature conservation', Askham Bog is a remarkable survivor of Yorkshire's ancient fenlands, carved by a retreating glacier 15,000 years ago. Marsh orchids, marsh violets and meadow thistles grow at the edges of the bog, while rare gingerbread sedge can be found in Far Wood. Bird lovers will relish the chance to see woodcock, willow tits and grasshopper warblers, plus lesser redpolls and siskins in winter. Spectacular emperor dragonflies hunt overhead on warm days.

Stirley
Huddersfield, HD4 6FA
OS Map SE 145137;
Map Ref P17

Yorkshire Wildlife Trust is restoring this once intensive farm with help from dedicated volunteers and a herd of traditional cattle. Hedges are being planted, ponds created, nest boxes erected and the grassland cut for hay in summer, increasing the diversity of not just plants but insects too. Look out for little owls in spring and enjoy the fluttering flight of orange-tip butterflies. The grassland really comes to life in summer, with kestrels hovering high above, meadow brown butterflies feeding from the flowers and swallows swooping overhead.

Garbutt Wood
Thirsk, YO7 2EH
OS Map SE 506835;
Map Ref P7

The views across the Vale of Mowbray are a compelling reason to visit this beautiful nature reserve. As if that wasn't enough, you're also in for some wonderful wild encounters. Dilberry and heathers thrive above the cliff, while lichens, mosses and ferns populate the boulder-strewn scree. In spring, look out for tree pipits, redstarts and blackcaps in the trees. Plants include ragged robin, common spotted-orchids, meadowsweet and wood sorrel, while fungal highlights include fly agarics and milkcaps.

Filey Dams
Filey, YO14 0DP
OS Map TA 106807;
Map Ref P8

A magnet for migratory birds and a haven for plants, small mammals and amphibians. The main hide is wheelchair accessible and takes in a small copse with tree sparrow nest boxes. From here, head along the boardwalk to a quiet pool where dragonflies skim the water and water voles munch noisily on water forget-me-nots. The East Pool hide is a great place to watch little grebes, greenshanks and wood sandpipers in autumn. There is no shortage of moths, which in turn feed hungry Daubenton's and Nathusius's pipistrelle bats.

Strensall Common
Strensall, YO32 5YB
OS Map SE 647615;
Map Ref P12

A fabulous heathland where pink cross-leaved heath and beautiful blue marsh gentian intermingle with the purple spikes of heather. Common lizards bask on silver birch stumps and southern hawker dragonflies patrol sunny spots. Green and purple hairstreak butterflies live alongside a nationally important population of dark-bordered beauty moths. Keep your eyes and ears alert for woodlarks, green woodpeckers and, in spring, cuckoos!

Southerscales
Chapel-le-Dale, LA6 3AR
OS Map SD 742769;
Map Ref P9

A vast expanse of limestone pavement perched high on the side of Ingleborough. Off the pavement lies a wonderland of rare and delicate limestone grassland and bog plants. Frog orchids, bird's-eye primroses, baneberry, green spleenwort and mountain everlasting all wait to be discovered. Round-leaved sundew thrives on the insects it catches in its sticky fingers. But plants aren't the only draw – you could spot emperor moths, black darter dragonflies and wheatears.

Sprotbrough Flash
Sprotborough, DN5 7NB
OS Map SE 537015;
Map Ref P18

One of the richest wild places in South Yorkshire.

A lake, grassland and ancient woodland make for a peaceful retreat where you can breathe in the scent of bluebells and while away hours watching the birds. Spot sedge warblers, reed buntings and tufted ducks at the lake; look for all three species of woodpecker in the wood, and see if you can spot the small-leaved lime trees. Brown hares bound and grass snakes bask in the grassland; great crested grebes dance on the lake in spring, and ravens nest nearby.

Ripon City Wetlands
Ripon, HG4 3LR
OS Map SE 330685;
Map Ref P10

Once a working quarry, now a safe refuge for bitterns, avocets, little ringed plovers, kingfishers and otters. Wander along the marked trail and settle down to watch the wildlife at one of two viewing places, which could reveal teal, gadwall and shovelers in winter or sedge warblers and reed warblers in spring. Flocks of sand martins fly overhead and clouds of damselflies emerge in summer – perfect fodder for hungry hobbies.

NORTH CAVE WETLANDS
North Cave, HU15 2LY; **OS Map** SE 886328; **Map Ref** P15

Opening hours: The little Butty Bus is open 8am–2.30pm, Tuesday–Sunday, for hot and cold food and drinks.
Access/conditions: Part of the circular footpath is surfaced and accessible for wheelchairs. Three hides are wheelchair accessible.
How to get there: From the west, leave M62 at J38 onto northbound B1230. Follow this to North Cave village. Turn left at the crossroads and follow the road around in a sharp left-hand bend. Soon after, turn left onto Dryham Lane.
Walking time: 1.5 hours.
30-minute visit: Visit any of the hides and see how many birds you can spot.

A true 21st century nature reserve created in the

footprint of a former quarry. From spring avocets and common terns to summer dragonflies and winter wildfowl, there is something to see all through the year.

The best places to spot butterflies, dragonflies and damselflies are the grassy banks beside the perimeter path – watch out for speedy emperor dragonflies and even water voles. See if you can spot the small colony of brown argus butterflies fluttering around the meadow between Main Lake and Carp Lake, which is opened in the summer months.

Spring welcomes little ringed plovers, oystercatchers and one of the UK's largest sand martin colonies back to breed. Summer is the time to spot grass snakes and stoats, while autumn sees a great shift, with summer-visiting birds making way for overwintering species like teal and wigeon. You may even spot some rare passage birds!

WHELDRAKE INGS

York, YO19 6AX; **OS Map** SE 694444; **Map Ref** P14

Access/conditions: Only accessible on foot along newly surfaced loose stone track. Paths level but muddy after wet weather. The reserve floods in winter.
How to get there: Bus to Sutton upon Derwent or to Holme-on-Spalding-Moor. By car from Wheldrake, follow Carr Lane towards Thorganby. Half a mile after a sharp right turn there's a track on the left to the reserve.
Walking time: 2 hours.
30-minute visit: Visit the first hide to watch the wildfowl, or simply enjoy the flowers.

Wheldrake Ings has been a haven for wildlife for centuries. Sitting on a natural floodplain, it sees winter floodwaters that host flocks of thousands of overwintering

waders and wildfowl such as whooper swans, wigeon and pintails. As the waters recede in spring, a time of vibrant growth begins, with marsh-marigolds and cuckooflowers adding colour to the fields. Tucked within the growing grassland, waders including lapwings, redshanks and curlews raise their young. Late June sees the meadows at their best, filled with the crimson heads of great burnet and cream sprays of meadowsweet. Other star species include spotted crakes, water rails, willow tits, peregrine falcons and hobbies. You may even spot an osprey or black tern on migration.

WILDLIFE FACT: FLOWER-RICH MEADOWS

Flower-rich meadows – including floodplain meadows like those at Wheldrake Ings – are now incredibly rare in the UK. We've lost around 98 per cent of flower-rich meadows in the last century alone due to land drainage, changes in agriculture and urban development. The precious meadows that remain harbour rare plants including dyer's greenweed and green-winged orchids. The plants in turn nurture countless insects, which themselves support rich populations of threatened birds.

FLAMBOROUGH CLIFFS

Bridlington, YO15 1BJ; **OS Map** TA 238719; **Map Ref** P11

Access/conditions: Accessed by the coast path that runs through the reserve. Clifftop terrain is hilly with some steep slopes.
How to get there: Bus runs from Bridlington to North Landing (Flamborough). By car, from Bridlington take B1255, following signs for Flamborough. Once in the village, follow signs for North Landing or Thornwick Bay (non-Yorkshire Wildlife Trust car parks with a charge).
Walking time: The coast path runs east (1km to Breil Nook, 15 minutes) and west (2km to North Cliff, 30 minutes) through the reserve from North Landing car park, but there is always the option to walk further and extend your

adventure along the path.
30-minute visit: Walk to the first cove from the car park – Newcombe Hope – to watch the thousands of seabirds on the opposite cliffs in summer.

Flamborough Head has one of the most important seabird colonies in Europe, and in summer the cliffs seem to shift and ripple as tens of thousands of breeding

fulmars, gulls, kittiwakes, guillemots, razorbills and puffins jostle for position, creating an incredible cacophony of noise. But it isn't only the cliffs themselves that are fantastic places to watch wildlife. The clifftop grassland hosts nesting skylarks and meadow pipits, and the chalk grassland in Holmes Gut blooms with bird's-foot trefoil, common spotted-orchids and pyramidal orchids that attract small skipper butterflies and burnet companion moths.

Though the seabirds steal the show, don't discount the much shyer songbirds that wait to cast their spell. In Holmes, linnets with their crimson patches and brilliantly bright yellowhammers nest in the gorse scrub, while Thornwick's two reedbeds offer safe nesting places for reed warblers, sedge warblers and reed buntings.

The seabirds have departed by autumn, but there is still so much to see. Short-eared owls hunt in the clifftop fields and the berry-laden wooded areas offer sanctuary to hungry redwings, fieldfares and bramblings. Even more migratory birds await out at sea, where you could spot skuas, divers and grebes bobbing on the swell.

POTTERIC CARR

Doncaster, DN4 8DB; **OS Map** SE 599003; **Map Ref** P19

Opening hours: Visitor centre open 9.30am–4pm. Car park locked at 5pm.
Access/conditions: A number of wheelchair and pushchair-friendly routes. Visitor centre and toilets are accessible.
How to get there: Bus (park and ride) from Doncaster train station – disembark at B&Q on White Rose Way, cross White Rose Way and follow signs for Potteric Carr (five-minute walk). By car, the reserve is half a mile from J3 of M18, just south of Doncaster.
Walking time: You could easily spend a whole day exploring the various trails and watching the incredible wildlife. Don't forget to pop into the café to refuel before heading off in another direction!
30-minute visit: Stroll around the lake in front of the visitor centre then browse the shop for treats.

Potteric Carr is a wild oasis for the whole family, with events and trails for all. It is a remnant of the vast fenland that once stretched all the way across the Humber basin to the coast. Around each corner you'll discover a mosaic of habitats, from reedbeds swaying gently under big open skies to winding woodland trails and networks of ponds teeming with life.

Spring brings an influx of migrant birds: chiffchaffs, willow warblers and whitethroats fill the trees; reed and sedge warblers chatter in the reedbeds; and the sky brims with swooping swallows, swifts and martins. You may even be lucky enough to hear a cuckoo or booming bittern, or spot a grass snake on the hunt.

In summer, the meadows are full of butterflies. Brimstones, large whites, orange-tips, small coppers, common blues and peacocks all busy themselves feeding from the colourful wildflowers. Banded demoiselle, large red and blue-tailed damselflies and four-spotted chaser, broad-bodied chaser and black-tailed skimmer dragonflies pull dazzling aerial manoeuvres over the ponds and pools. Bearded tits breed in the reedbeds – listen out for their characteristic *ping* call.

Autumn is the time to see spectacular starling murmurations swirling and diving over the reeds, often chased by hungry sparrowhawks! Settle into a hide to watch marsh harriers soaring overhead or kingfishers hunting from nearby tree branches before warming up with a hot drink in the visitor centre.

SPURN

YORKSHIRE

Opening hours: Spurn Lighthouse usually open Friday, Saturday and Sunday (ask in café). Discovery Centre open 9am–5pm daily. Café open 10am–4pm daily. Lighthouse entry: adults £4; concessions £3; children £2; family £10.

Access/conditions: Soft sand at the washover – not suitable for wheelchairs. Wheelchair-accessible routes around the north end of the reserve. Discovery Centre is wheelchair accessible. Access dependent on tide times and weather (check the Trust website). Some dog-free areas – please follow dog-friendly walking routes.

How to get there: From Hull take A1033 east towards Withernsea. At Patrington take B1445 towards Eastington village. At Eastington, follow the signs towards Spurn Point. Parking is £5 all day for non-Yorkshire

Wildlife Trust members.
Walking time: 4 hours.
30-minute visit: Walk from the Blue Bell car park down to the seaward coast, to the Warren and then down the roadway back to the car park.

Spurn is Yorkshire's very own Land's End – an iconic and constantly moving peninsula, which curves between the North Sea and the Humber Estuary. Big skies and ever-changing wildlife make this evocative landscape ripe for adventure. Utterly wild and with an extensive human history echoed in the peninsula's derelict buildings and hidden structures, no two days at Spurn Point are ever the same.

The reserve is famous for bird migration, with waders and wildfowl dropping by on their spring and autumn passage and plenty of rarities blowing in on storm winds. Whimbrels

and ring ouzels are real spring highlights, while autumn brings woodcock, wrynecks, yellow-browed warblers and great grey shrikes. In winter, shelducks and Brent geese flock to the mudflats to feed while curlews, grey plovers and knot roost on the saltmarsh at high tide, occasionally spooked by merlins and peregrine falcons. But this is just the beginning. Beach mudflats, saltmarsh, dunes, grassland, open water, saline lagoons and sea buckthorn scrub all mix to provide homes for a fantastic array of wildlife. The beautiful plants include sea lavender, sea aster, sea rocket and sea holly, which add splashes of purple across the reserve. Bright pink pyramidal orchids bloom in the grassland, where you could also spot roe deer and foxes early in the morning. Don't forget to look out to sea – it isn't unusual to catch sight of a passing harbour porpoise or grey seal.

SHEFFIELD AND ROTHERHAM

About the Trust

Sheffield & Rotherham Wildlife Trust is dedicated to bringing people closer to the natural wonders on their doorstep – proving that you don't have to travel far to have magical wild encounters. As well as running innovative education programmes and events, the Sheffield & Rotherham Wildlife Trust safeguards 15 nature reserves and campaigns for nature on a national scale.

Sheffield & Rotherham Wildlife Trust
01142 634335
wildsheffield.com

Carbrook Ravine
Sheffield, S13 8ES
OS Map SK 393860;
Map Ref P25

A peaceful retreat nestled among the urban landscape. Woodland, wetland and wildflower meadows are home to bluebells, song thrushes and skylarks. Owls and sparrowhawks hunt small mammals in the vast grassland and the golden male fern grows in the wet woodland.

Carr House Meadows
Wharncliffe Side, S35 0DX
OS Map SK 282954;
Map Ref P22

Fall in love with these flower-rich meadows as you meander through yellow rattle, orchids and swathes of red and white clover. Butterflies, beetles and spiders thrive in the rich foliage, while bullfinches,

blackcaps and goldfinches are just a few of the breeding birds.

Centenary Riverside
Rotherham, S60 1DS
OS Map SK 421921;
Map Ref P23

A former steelworks transformed into a refuge for dragonflies, damselflies and 23 different species of butterfly. Sand martins dart over the ponds in summer and reed warblers nest among the reeds. Designed as a floodplain, the reserve protects residential Rotherham from potential floodwaters.

Kilnhurst Ings
Kilnhurst, S64 5TA
OS Map SK 465975;
Map Ref P20

A post-industrial washland reclaimed by dragonflies

and birds. Watch snipe, linnets and lesser redpolls in winter, and great spotted woodpeckers all year round. In summer the grassland fills with butterflies including small coppers, common blues and gatekeepers.

Moss Valley Woodlands
Sheffield, S8 8DZ
OS Map SK 363809;
Map Ref P29

Beautiful ancient woodlands carpeted with bluebells, sweet woodruff and wood anemones in early spring and summer. Majestic beech and oak trees tower overhead, and woodpeckers pluck insects from the standing dead trees. Listen for the distinctive song of yellowhammers and linnets. Countless footpaths and bridleways link the reserve to walks in the wider valley.

Salmon Pastures

Sheffield, S9 3QB
OS Map SK 371881;
Map Ref P24

This tiny but important wildlife haven is a great place to spot gatekeeper and orange-tip butterflies; mistle thrushes, goldfinches and long-tailed tits; kingfishers, grey wagtails and occasionally dippers. Home to 22 species of hoverfly, Salmon Pastures is a vital part of Sheffield's green corridor.

WYMING BROOK AND FOX HAGG

Sheffield, S10 4QX; **OS Map** SK 269859/283865; **Map Ref** P26

Access/conditions: The reserves have footpaths and bridleways, some unsurfaced paths and small bridges. Some parts of Fox Hagg are very steep.

How to get there: Buses stop on Redmires Road or on Manchester Road. By car, drive out of Sheffield along Redmires Road or enter via Manchester Road.

Walking time: 4 hours.

30-minute visit: Take the shortest circular route around Fox Hagg.

These neighbouring reserves offer magnificent views over Sheffield's Rivelin Valley. Green and luxuriant in summer, white and bleak in winter, the hillsides sweep down towards the reservoirs in the valley's centre.

Wyming Brook is home to some really special wildlife including common lutestring and northern spinach moths, and pine seed-eating crossbills. Dippers forage for aquatic insects along the fast-flowing streams, and in late spring, migrant species such as spotted flycatchers, wood warblers and pied flycatchers arrive for their summer holidays.

Fox Hagg is a patch of heathland and woodland filled with bilberry, bracken and heather. Keep your eyes peeled for linnets, bullfinches and goldcrests flitting between the scattered birch and woodland edge. Scrub is cut on a five-year cycle and bracken is controlled to allow the heather to thrive.

WOODHOUSE WASHLANDS

Sheffield, S13 9XD; **OS Map** SK 438852; **Map Ref** P27

Access/conditions: The Trans-Pennine Trail running along an edge of the reserve allows easy access for wheelchairs in good weather (muddy when wet). Reserve closed when flood defence system in operation.

How to get there: Bus or train from Sheffield to Woodhouse station – both stop five minutes from reserve. By car, from Sheffield city centre, take A57 then first exit from the roundabout onto Mosborough Parkway. Take first exit at next roundabout onto Coisley Hill (B6064). Continue to Market Street then turn left onto Station Road to continue on B6064 until Furnace Lane. **Walking time:** 2 hours.

Sitting on the boundary between Sheffield and Rotherham, Woodhouse Washlands is a picturesque mosaic of grassland, scrub and floodplain grazing marsh. There is a fantastic array of different birds, especially during summer when the sky fills with spectacular numbers of swifts, swallows and martins all feeding on clouds of insects. Summer is also the time to watch hobbies hunting dragonflies and swallows, and to hear grasshopper warblers reeling away in the vegetation. Skylarks breed here, filling the sky with song. In winter, redwings feed in the hawthorn hedges.

Woodhouse Washlands

is part of a flood alleviation scheme that hasn't just transformed the marshland itself. Running alongside the reserve, the River Rother – once one of the most polluted rivers in Europe – is now home to thriving communities of fish, invertebrates and birds. Look out for kingfishers flitting past and, in winter, ducks including goosanders.

BLACKA MOOR

Totley, Sheffield S17 3BJ; **OS Map** SK 287806; **Map Ref** P28

Access/conditions: Can be wet and boggy. Steep uphill climbs on many routes.
How to get there: Buses stop opposite the nature reserve on Hathersage Road (A625). By car, drive along A625 towards Hathersage for the Stony Ridge car park, or park at the Piper Lane layby on the A625. There is another car park at Strawberry Lee Lane.
Walking time: 2 hours.
30-minute visit: Wander through the woods off the A625, or head onto the moor to admire the heathland.

Get away from it all at Blacka Moor, a spectacular heathland in the Eastern Peak District Moors. The largest and most spectacular of Sheffield & Rotherham Wildlife Trust's nature reserves, the big skies and wonderful

wildlife will take your breath away.

Woodland, home to willow warblers and blackcaps, gives way to the sweeping open moor, which beams with the purples and pinks of different heathers in late summer. Bilberry grows here too, attracting bilberry bumblebees: a declining species found almost exclusively on moorland. Keep your eyes (and ears!) peeled for cuckoos in spring and look out for wheatears and pied flycatchers before they head back to Africa in autumn. Stonechats and majestic red deer are year-round residents and certainly not shy, though the reserve's common lizards are much more secretive.

If you like combining your wildlife walks with a slice of history, look out for the remains of Iron Age and medieval settlements scattered across the landscape.

SHEFFIELD AND ROTHERHAM

GRENO WOODS

Grenoside, S35 7DS; **OS Map** SK 328954; **Map Ref** P21

Access/conditions: Many footpaths and bridleways, and three downhill mountain bike trails. Limited access for wheelchair users and those with restricted mobility. The Trans-Pennine Trail running from Greno Gate to Sandy Lane is wheelchair accessible.

How to get there: Buses from Sheffield to Grenoside or along the A61, where there is a stop across from the reserve. By car, leave Sheffield on Penistone Road (A61) until it becomes Halifax Road, then turn left onto Foxhill Road. Continue to Main Street then onto Woodhead Road for around a mile, where the Forestry Commission car park will be on your left.

Walking time: Allow a whole morning or afternoon to lose yourself in this magical wood.

30-minute visit: Explore the Enchanted Forest Toddler Trail.

Greno Woods is an ancient woodland with something to charm every visitor. A network of footpaths and bridleways offer both long and short walks, while the nearby Trans-Pennine Trail reveals even more opportunity for adventure.

There is no shortage of ways to keep children entertained, including a den-building area, Toddler Trail and geocaching opportunities.

In spring, revel in woodland flowers including bluebells, honeysuckle and common cow-wheat: a Greno speciality with a fascinating lifecycle. Its seeds are coated in an oily liquid coveted by hairy wood ants, which spread the seeds across the woodland as they carry them away to their nests.

As summer approaches, the woods burst into birdsong as chiffchaffs, willow warblers and blackcaps arrive from overseas to join the robins, chaffinches and wrens. Summer also brings a change in plant life, with blackberries and bilberries replacing the spring blooms, and a butterfly boom that fills the sunny rides with commas, peacocks and red admirals. You may also see shy roe deer in quieter areas of the wood.

Autumn reveals a profusion of fungi and is a great time to see jays darting back and forth on nut-caching trips. In winter, crossbills compete for pine nuts with squabbling flocks of coal tits.

CHESHIRE

About the Trust

Cheshire Wildlife Trust works to protect wildlife and wild places across Cheshire, Halton, South Manchester, Warrington and Wirral. As part of its mission to safeguard our fragile natural heritage, the Cheshire Wildlife Trust manages 45 nature reserves, which are home to rare species and threatened habitats, and inspires people to take action for wildlife at a local level.

Cheshire Wildlife Trust
01948 820728
cheshirewildlifetrust.org.uk

Swettenham Valley

Holmes Chapel, CW12 2LF
OS Map SJ 799671;
Map Ref O15

One of Cheshire's hidden gems. Sympathetically grazed meadows brim with betony, devil's-bit scabious, common spotted-orchids and yellow rattle, while the mosaic of ancient woodland, ponds, scrub and species-rich grassland nurtures thriving populations of 14 species of butterfly.

Gowy Meadows

Ellesmere Port, CH2 4JH
OS Map SJ 435740;
Map Ref O12

An impressive 152 bird species have been recorded here, including reed and sedge warblers and whitethroats in summer, and wigeon and teal in winter. Great white egrets, marsh harriers, lapwings and skylarks are regular visitors. Watch banded demoiselles skip over the water from late May.

Eastwood Nature Reserve

Stalybridge, SK15 2QX
OS Map SJ 970980;
Map Ref O9

A hidden gem of a woodland. Pathways, boardwalks, bridges and steps lead you around a peaceful retreat blanketed by bluebells in spring. Treecreepers, nuthatches and woodpeckers busy themselves in the trees, while summer is the best time to spot warblers. The tumbling brook at the heart of the reserve welcomes dippers and occasional kingfishers in winter.

Red Rocks Marsh

Hoylake, CH47 1HN
OS Map SJ 206880;
Map Ref O11

Marsh orchids, birds-foot trefoil, sticky stork's-bill and fairy flax add splashes of colour to these striking sand dunes. Natterjack toads breed in the salty pools, filling the night air with rasping croaks. Spring and autumn offer the best chance of spotting migratory birds like redstarts, ring ouzels and maybe even a rarity like a bee-eater or shrike.

Trentabank Reservoir

Macclesfield, SK11 0NS
OS Map SJ 962713;
Map Ref O14

Best known for its heronry (around 20 breeding pairs). Also a fabulous place to see ravens and birds of prey. Stately red deer are shy residents of the forest and common crossbills are regularly seen feeding in the treetops. Goldeneyes and goosanders visit in winter.

HATCHMERE NATURE RESERVE
Frodsham, WA6 6NY; **OS Map** SJ 553718; **Map Ref** O13

Access/conditions: Footpaths around the reserve. The mere can be viewed from Delamere Road (by The Carriers Inn) and the remainder of the reserve is accessed via a footpath off Ashton Road in the village, just as you enter the forest.
How to get there: From J12 of M56 take A557 exit to Frodsham/Runcorn Airport/Widnes. Take A56/Sutton Causeway for one mile before turning left onto B5394/Fluin Lane. Turn left after half a mile, continue onto Vicarage Lane and Kingsley Road, then turn right onto Delamere Road.
Walking time: 2 hours.
30-minute visit: See what you can spot on the mere from the vantage point on Delamere Road.

Hatchmere Nature Reserve is a window into the past, as its lakes and peatlands were formed by glaciers at the end of the last ice age. The reserve is also home to Cheshire's first pair of beaver – a pair of 'ecosystem engineers'

released after 400 years of local extinction. These incredible mammals create diverse wetlands through their canal digging, damming and tree coppicing, while these wetlands, in turn, bring enormous benefits to other

wildlife. The walk around Hatchmere touches the edge of the beaver's enclosure, so you can see their home, footprints and gnawed branches. If you're around at dusk you may even catch a glimpse of them on their nightly outings.

As well as a mere where great crested grebes perform an elaborate spring courtship ritual, the nature reserve includes the surrounding fens, wet woodland and wet heath. Up to 13 species of dragonfly and damselfly have been recorded here, including the rare hairy dragonfly and the black darter. To the west of the mere the Trust has cleared large areas of birch to enhance the wet mossland vegetation, and you'll now find thriving communities of heather, bilberry, cotton-grass and sphagnum moss.

BICKLEY HALL FARM

Bickley, SY14 8EF; **OS Map** SJ 525479; **Map Ref** O16

Opening hours: Parking and toilets open 10am–3pm, Monday–Friday.

Access/conditions: Nature trail leading off Sandstone Trail walking route is accessible all year round.

How to get there: Reserve can be found off A41 and A49. Turn onto Bickley Lane then turn right (from A41) or left (from A49) onto a minor road leading to the reserve car park.

Walking time: Exploring the circular trail takes around 2 hours, but you can extend your adventure along the Sandstone Trail.

30-minute visit: From the car park, walk to the closest hay meadow (where the circular trail meets the Sandstone Trail) and back again.

A 210-acre (86ha) organic working farm where species-rich hay meadows, thriving pastures, buzzing wildflower margins, bird seed plots and hedgerows nurture a wildlife refuge humming with life. Fields of spring sown cereals are left to go to stubble in winter, providing vital food for hundreds of hungry finches including bramblings and lesser redpolls. The colder months also see redwings and fieldfares arrive in the hedgerows, lapwings and snipe forage on the floodplain and scrapes, and you may even see a green sandpiper or merlin drop by occasionally. The mosaic of wet meadows is managed specifically for wintering and

breeding birds, so there is plenty of life during the spring months too, when your walk could be accompanied by yellowhammers, skylarks and little owls.

Bickley Hall Farm is also great for invertebrates. Hundreds of butterflies flutter around the wildflowers at the height of summer, including small coppers, common blues, meadow browns, small whites and speckled woods. Four-spotted chaser and brown hawker dragonflies, and emerald and red-eyed damselflies fill the air with irridescence in spring and summer, breeding in ponds that also provide a safe haven for great crested newts.

ISLE OF MAN

About the Trust

Manx Wildlife Trust was founded in 1973 and is now the leading charity safeguarding wildlife and wild places in the Isle of Man. With the help of passionate staff, volunteers and members, Manx Wildlife Trust is creating a Nature Recovery Network of connected green space, championing nature-based solutions and connecting people with the nature on their doorstep.

**Manx Wildlife Trust
01624 844432
mwt.im**

Onchan Wetlands
Onchan
OS Map SC 400782;
Map Ref Q15

A peaceful retreat just two minutes' walk from Onchan shopping centre. A boardwalk and surfaced paths guide you through a miniature wonderland of cuckooflowers, red campion, yellow irises, grey wagtails and robins.

Earystane
Colby
OS Map SC 235715;
Map Ref Q17

Stroll through a wonderfully wild woodland and grassland. Butterflies feed on knapweed nectar in the small wildflower area before the early autumn cut. A wheelchair-accessible path leads to the bird hide where you may spot a raven or chough.

Cooildarry
Off the A4
OS Map SC 314901;
Map Ref Q14

A tranquil woodland with waterfalls and a scenic riverside walk. A thick canopy of elm, ash, alder, sycamore and beech keeps the wood moist, encouraging countless mosses, ferns and, in autumn, fungi. Spring bursts into life with the flowering of primroses, wood anemones, wood sorrel, lesser celandines and bluebells.

Dalby Mountain
Dalby
OS Map SC 233767;
Map Ref Q16

A wonderfully wild heather moorland. Summer is a riot of colour with blooming purple heather and bright yellow gorse. Sphagnum mosses and bog asphodel brighten up

the bog, while hen harriers cast an air of majesty when they soar overhead.

Glen Dhoo
Ballaugh
OS Map SC 351907;
Map Ref Q13

A remote refuge from daily life, with as much history as wildlife. A 'tholtan', or 'old house', is the sole reminder of the small farming community that lived here until the late 19th century. Wildlife highlights include heath spotted-orchids, dark green fritillaries, stonechats, peregrine falcons and hen harriers.

Ballachurry
Church Road
OS Map SC 210695;
Map Ref Q18

Manx Wildlife Trust has transformed Ballachurry from

arable farmland to a thriving nature reserve of woodland, grassland and wildlife-rich ponds. The reserve really comes to life in spring, with sedge warblers, willow warblers and chiffchaffs filling the air with multi-layered song. Summer is the time for insect-spotting, with hairy dragonflies and variable damselflies taking to the air.

Cronk y Bing
Lhen Bridge
OS Map NX 381017;
Map Ref Q11

Sand dunes decorated with pyramidal orchids, sea bindweed, restharrow, common stork's-bill, harebells and sheep's-bit. Oystercatchers and ringed plovers feed along the shoreline, while in autumn, the reserve becomes a birder's paradise with divers, grebes, skuas and diving gannets seen offshore.

CLOSE SARTFIELD

Ballaugh; **OS Map** SC 358955; **Map Ref** Q12

Access/conditions: Level, wheelchair-accessible paths and boardwalks.
How to get there: From the TT course (A3), turn onto B9 between Ballaugh village and Sulby Glen. Take the third right (Windmill Road) and follow this for nearly a mile. Reserve entrance and car park about 25m along a track on the right.
Walking time: Circular walk through meadows and curragh (open June–August) takes around 1 hour.
30-minute visit: Follow the path through Close Mean and down to the hide.

A wonderful mix of meadows and wet woodland ('curragh' in Manx Gaelic) where big skies, beautiful wildflowers and fantastic birds help you get away from it all. The meadows are cut in August, when most of the plants have flowered and set seed. Once the grass has grown back, Manx Wildlife Trust's four-legged conservation team – a flock of sheep – are brought onto the reserve to graze. Though this kind of traditional management was once the norm in the UK, the advent of industrialised farming saw it largely die out – and the majority of our wildflower meadows with it. At Close Sartfield, however, keeping wildlife-friendly management alive means the reserve erupts with a riot of colour and scent in spring and summer. The six wildflower meadows bloom with tens of thousands of orchids from mid-May to late June. But they're by no means the only stars – a supporting cast of cuckooflowers, yellow rattle, lousewort, purple loosestrife, meadowsweet and devil's-bit scabious fill the grassland with pinks, purples, creams and yellows. Delicate yet hardy flowers including marsh cinquefoil and lesser spearwort grow in the peaty areas alongside the magnificently bushy royal fern.

This incredible plant life and the soft, wet ground is perfect for a range of insects, and in summer there is a constant buzz of activity. These in turn attract blackcaps, warblers and tits, which pick them off during their foraging trips. The eerie call of curlews can often be heard and you may even see a hen harrier.

WALES

Some of the UK's most incredible wildlife can be found in this beautiful country, much of which remains undisturbed by humans, allowing the opportunity for some unforgettable encounters.

In Brecknock, home to the Brecon Beacons National Park, you'll find everything from majestic old oak woods to exposed rock faces and magical wildflower meadows. Meanwhile, on the Pembrokeshire coast, anemones, barnacles and gobies thrive in rockpools, and seals bask on nearby rocks. Rugged mountain ranges carve their way between the high and low areas of the country, buoyed by limestone grassland, heathland, woods and river valleys. Each area has its own speciality: orchids grow in the limestone grassland and upland birds, such as stonechats and merlins, live in the high heathland. About half of the UK's red kites live in Wales, with the Brecon Beacons one of the best places to see them.

An after-dark walk around many lowland areas can reveal glow-worms, especially in June or July when their abdominal illuminations twinkle from hedgerows, woodland, heaths and sand dunes. These are also the best months to see puffins, particularly at Skomer Island, off the coast of Pembrokeshire. It is a little like the Galapagos of Wales, where the water separating it from the mainland means that no predators have made their way across. Ground-nesting birds flourish here and on neighbouring Skokholm, including around 350,000 breeding pairs of Manx shearwaters.

The floral diversity of Wales is second to none. The bogs and wetlands of Ceredigion bloom with cross-leaved heath, cotton-grass, white beak-sedge, meadowsweet and bog asphodel, while the mountains are rich with pretty alpine species like the delicate Snowdon lily. Wales' damp climate and surviving ancient meadows also make it globally important for waxcap fungi. Species like violet, parrot and witch's hat waxcaps paint the grassland with rainbow swatches.

Thanks to the five Welsh Wildlife Trusts, this phenomenal natural heritage is protected on some of the UK's best nature reserves. Some are large, some very small; some can cope with large numbers of visitors while others are more fragile, but one thing is for sure: they are all very special.

NOT TO BE MISSED

● **Gilfach, Radnorshire**
Meadows filled with ancient grassland species including dyer's greenweed, moonwort, adder's-tongue fern, mountain pansy, heath dog-violet and eyebright.

● **Glaslyn, Montgomeryshire**
Montgomeryshire Wildlife Trust's largest reserve and its wildest. A true mountain experience with breathtaking views over the Dyfi valley. If you're lucky you may spot a pair of hen harriers 'sky dancing'.

● **Pentwyn Farm, Gwent**
A time capsule of traditionally managed hay meadows where more than 10,000 common spotted orchids bloom in spring.

● **Skomer Island, West Wales**
After one trip to Skomer, you'll be hooked for life, and no wonder, with 316,000 pairs of Manx shearwaters breeding alongside 22,000 puffins!

● **Spinnies Aberogwen, West Wales**
A calming coastal retreat, where rafts of eider ducks bob on the swell and waders flock to the tidal mudflats.

Opposite: Pembrokeshire Coast National Park, West Wales

NORTH WALES

Bryn Pydew

Conwy, LL31 9JT
OS Map SH 818798;
Map Ref V4

Limestone pavement, orchid-rich grassland and ash and yew woodland. More than 20 species of butterfly and 500 species of moth have been recorded: brown argus, common blue and chalk carpet among them. You may see the green glimmering of glow-worms on warm midsummer nights. Be careful on steep sections of path and rocky outcrops, which can be wet and slippery.

Caeau Tan y Bwlch

Clynnog Fawr, LL54 5DL
OS Map SH 430488;
Map Ref V10

A traditional wildflower meadow at its best in late June and early July when greater butterfly-orchids carpet the fields. Their subtle beauty is enhanced by surrounding eyebright, bird's-foot trefoil and black knapweed. Willow and grasshopper warblers nest in the wet grassland and willow carr. There are no formal paths and some fields can be boggy.

Cemlyn

Cemaes, LL67 0EA
OS Map SH 337932;
Map Ref V1

A wildlife haven with a spectacular seabird colony at its heart. Sea kale, sea campion and yellow horned-poppies grow on the shingle ridge. Waders and wildfowl can be seen around the lagoon year-round, while from May–July, Sandwich, common and Arctic terns nest on the islands within. Signs and friendly wardens will help you get the best views of the bustling colony.

Cors Bodgynydd

Betws-y-Coed, LL27 0YZ
OS Map SH 767597;
Map Ref V7

A remote upland retreat coated with brightly coloured mats of sphagnum moss. Scarce species such as the small chocolate-tip moth, lesser horseshoe bat, and the insect-eating lesser bladderwort have been recorded. Nightjars nest in summer, when keeled skimmer and emperor dragonflies take to the air. Please keep to the footpath.

Rhiwledyn

Llandudno, LL30 3AY
OS Map SH 813821;
Map Ref V3

The wildlife of land and sea meets at Rhiwledyn, overlooking Llandudno and the Irish Sea. Small birds breed in the prickly gorse; bloody crane's-bill, wild thyme and pyramidal orchids bloom in the grassland and, as you climb higher, the air fills with the sound of the cackling fulmars that nest on the cliffs below.

ABERDUNA

Gwernymynydd, CH7 5LD; **OS Map** SJ 205617; **Map Ref** V6

Access/conditions: Paths can be steep and unsuitable for wheelchairs and pushchairs.
How to get there: Three miles south-west of Mold. Parking sometimes available at the Wildlife Trust office; if not, park in Maeshafn and use the map to find one of the reserve entrances.
Walking time: 1 hour.
30-minute visit: Start from the village green and head north through the grassland, following the path until you come to some steps. Drop down and follow the path until you reach an information panel. Turn left and follow the path back through the woodland to the village green.

Aberduna is a striking reserve offering stunning views across the Alyn valley to Moel Famau and the Clwydian Range. The woodland, grassland and small ponds are underlaid by limestone, which encourages a wonderful range of plants to flourish. You could spot everything from early purple orchids and autumn gentian to rock-roses, moonwort and fragrant orchids. Enchanter's nightshade, herb-paris and wood sorrel brighten up the woodland and dog-violets grow in the dappled shade of the coppiced areas, providing food for the caterpillars of small pearl-bordered fritillaries. Common lizards bask on the warm exposed limestone in summer and whitethroats and blackcaps dart in and out of the scrub, which shelters them and their young. The onset of autumn brings a sea of colour in the changing leaves, burgeoning berries and wonderful fungi that emerge from the grassland, dead wood and leaf litter.

GORS MAEN LLWYD

Nantglyn, LL16 5RN; **OS Map** SH 975580; **Map Ref** V8

Access/conditions: Reserve is exposed and isolated and paths are uneven in places. Keep to paths to avoid disturbance to ground-nesting birds and reptiles.
How to get there: Seven miles from Denbigh on north shore of Llyn Brenig. Take A543 from Denbigh to Pentrefoelas, turn left onto road signposted to Llyn Brenig. After a mile, turn left again, go over the cattle grid and turn right into the car park around 500m later.
Walking time: 1 hour.

30-minute visit: Park in the top car park and walk onto the heath for great views.

Bursting with wildlife, this spectacular upland heather moorland feels truly wild. In spring, as the sun rises over the Clwydian Range to the east, the distinctive, peaty moorland aroma fills the air along with the calls of curlews, skylarks and cuckoos heralding the new day.

Sphagnum mosses, cotton-grass and bogbean fill the

blanket bog, while cranberry, mountain pansies, tormentil and harebells thrive in the drier areas, adding pinpricks of vibrant colour. Keep your eyes peeled for birds including wheatears, stonechats and hen harriers as well as our smallest bird of prey, the merlin. In winter, great crested grebes and wildfowl can be seen gathering on Llyn Brenig, while 15 species of mammal have been recorded on the reserve – look out for their tracks and signs.

MARFORD QUARRY

Marford, LL12 8TG; **OS Map** SJ 357563; **Map Ref** V9

Access/conditions: Steep with gravelly slopes. Disabled parking and a wheelchair/pushchair-accessible path available via RADAR key access.

How to get there: Take B5445 to Marford (between Rossett and Gresford). Turn into Springfield Lane, 50m north of Trevor Arms Hotel. Reserve entrance around 400m on the left, immediately before a railway bridge.
Walking time: Numerous trails include a 0.4-mile circular walk.
30-minute visit: Take the circular walk around the site.

With more than 1,000 recorded species, Marford Quarry is a wildlife oasis and one of the best places in Wales for invertebrates. Though quarried for many years, the reserve has been reclaimed by nature. The areas of open sand are brilliant for

burrowing bees and wasps, while a glut of ants attracts hungry green woodpeckers, which slurp them up with their long tongues. As well as seeing them, you may hear them making their cackling calls, called *yaffling*. Ruby-tailed wasps are one of the real highlights, with their vivid blue-green bodies and ruby-red tails glistening in the sunshine.

A wonderful array of plants adds yet more colour in spring and summer. The vivid colours of wild liquorice, pyramidal orchids and bee orchids accompany the reserve's leafy greens, while the flashes of colour from 35 butterfly species are sure to catch your eye.

CORS GOCH

Llanbedrgoch, LL78 8JZ; **OS Map** SH 504816; **Map Ref** V2

Access/conditions: Some steep, uneven ground. Narrow boardwalks can be slippery after rain.
How to get there: Follow A5025 from Pentraeth for 1.5 miles, then turn left towards Llanbedrgoch. You'll see a signpost for the reserve about a mile beyond Llanbedrgoch. Park in the layby on the left (space for two or three cars), then follow the track from the

layby to the reserve.
Walking time: Mix of public and permissive paths giving a network of five miles. Boardwalk trail takes 1 hour at an easy pace, but allow longer for a real taste of wildness.
30-minute visit: Head to the heathland to enjoy tremendous views over the whole reserve before dropping down to the edge of

the wetland and walking back along the foot of the slope.

Cors Goch has a rich local history. For centuries it was used for cattle grazing, reed cutting and stone quarrying – today, it is one of Wales' most diverse and colourful nature reserves. Limestone and sandstone meet on the higher ground, nurturing a colourful array of plants.

Heather, adder's-tongue ferns, dog-violets and marsh gentian thrive alongside an amazing range of limestone-loving orchids. Lower down, the reserve's wetlands have their own unique plant communities such as insect-eating common butterwort and the beautiful marsh helleborine. It's here that you'll find the best of the birds, with breeding grasshopper warblers, sedge warblers and reed buntings creating a wonderful riot of song. Dragonflies and damselflies can be seen from the boardwalk – flashes of colour darting above the wet ground beneath. Broad hedgerows and a rich woodland offer shelter and food for a wide range of birds and mammals, including the hungry flocks of

redwings and fieldfares that arrive to spend the winter. They also act as vital corridors linking the nature reserve to the surrounding landscape.

Be sure to give yourself a few hours to explore Cors Goch in its entirety and appreciate its deep sense of belonging in the landscape.

GWAITH POWDWR

Penrhyndeudraeth, LL48 6LY; **OS Map** SH 621389; **Map Ref** V11

Access/conditions: Mostly accessible tracks (contact the North Wales Wildlife Trust to arrange disabled access in advance). Upland tracks are rough, steep and have steps.
How to get there: Take the road out of Penrhyndeudraeth towards Pont Briwet (the bridge over the River Dwyryd to Harlech). Take the first road into Cooke's Industrial Estate, following it for around 80m to reserve gates. Park here (SH 616388) or further down the road towards Pont Briwet (SH 618384).
Walking time: 2.5 hours.
30-minute visit: Park at Pont Briwet, where there is a small picnic area, then head into the reserve and follow the track uphill. If you're quick you can reach the Pendulum Shed to learn about the

reserve's explosive past and still return in time, having enjoyed the splendid views to the mountain and across the Dwyryd estuary.

A fantastic post-industrial nature reserve with an

explosive history – quite literally! More than 17 million grenades were produced at Gwaith Powdwr during WWII – since then, it's nature that has exploded.

The woodland offers a safe home to nesting redstarts,

pied flycatchers and tree pipits, and on summer days the grassy glades are great places to spot butterflies and wildflowers. The heathland that covers the higher ground hides secretive nightjars and basking reptiles; in fact, four of the six UK reptile species are seen here, including slow worms and adders. The reserve's industrial past has provided perfect habitats for its most significant residents, lesser horseshoe bats, who make their homes in the old buildings and tunnels. They are one of the UK's smallest bat species, about the same size as a plum when their wings are wrapped around them at roost.

Gwaith Powdwr takes on a whole new atmosphere when the sun goes down, with nightjars *churring*, woodcock roding and glow-worms shining on summer nights.

SPINNIES ABEROGWEN

Bangor, LL57 3YH; **OS Map** SH 613720; **Map Ref** V5

Access/conditions: Please stay on the well-marked paths. Most paths (and two hides) are wheelchair accessible.
How to get there: Leave A55 at J12. Heading towards Bangor/Tal-y-Bont, look for brown nature reserve sign. Follow it down a minor road for one mile to reach the coastal car park (SH 615723). Walk back towards either reserve entrance.

Walking time: 1.5 hours.
30-minute visit: Visit the estuary hide (furthest from the entrance) to look over the lagoon and shoreline. The other hides are an even shorter walk from the car park.

With three bird hides and calming coastal views, Spinnies Aberogwen is a refreshing retreat that will help you feel completely at peace. Lagoons surrounded by reeds offer vital food and shelter for wildfowl, waders and smaller birds, particularly during the spring and autumn migrations. The reserve is next to the River Ogwen estuary and tidal mudflats of Traeth Lafan, and the ebb and flow of the tides attracts some amazing species including, on rare occasions, ospreys. One hour or so either side of high tide is the best time to watch the action, as birds like redshanks, greenshanks, whimbrels and little egrets fill up on nutritious invertebrates snatched from the mud. Peer out to sea in winter and you could spot rafts of eider ducks and red-breasted mergansers bobbing on the swell.

There is just as much to see as you walk from hide to hide. Broad-leaved helleborine – a locally rare orchid – hart's-tongue fern and male fern grow in the shadier spots, while in winter, the bright red discs of scarlet elfcup fungi emerge beneath the trees. For much of the year, kingfishers are a familiar and well-loved sight as they perch around the reserve and dive into the water.

MONTGOMERYSHIRE

About the Trust

Montgomeryshire Wildlife Trust has been protecting wildlife and wild places since 1982, and educating, influencing and empowering people to live and work in harmony with nature. It manages 18 of Montgomeryshire's best wildlife sites and works with other landowners to protect many more. The charity's mission is to rebuild biodiversity and engage people with their environment.

Montgomeryshire Wildlife Trust
01938 555654
montwt.co.uk

Coed Pendugwm

Powys, SY22 5JF
OS Map SJ 103143;
Map Ref V14

A 400-year-old wild wood nurtured by majestic sessile oaks. Though just eight acres (3.2ha) in size, this enchanting reserve is home to a vitally important range of plants and animals including elusive dormice. Spring is the best time to visit, when pied flycatchers raise the next generation above carpets of bluebells, primroses, wood anemones and violets.

Dyfnant Meadows

Llangadfan, SY10 0NL
OS Map SH 999156;
Map Ref V13

A hidden gem within the Dyfnant Forest, this is an area of old hill pasture, rich with tormentil, heath bedstraw, lousewort and, in the wetter

areas, devil's-bit scabious and common butterwort. The fields are bounded by ancient hedgerows and a wooded dingle, which drips with mosses, ferns and lichens.

Llyn Mawr

Caersws, SY17 5NE
OS Map SO 009971;
Map Ref V19

This upland lake provides the perfect conditions for aquatic plants such as bogbean, as well as a safe area for tufted ducks and goldeneyer to rest and feed. Bog asphodel, marsh violets and sundews grow profusely in the surrounding wetland, attracting wall brown butterflies and golden-ringed dragonflies.

Pwll Penarth

Newtown, SY16 3BA
OS Map SO 137927;
Map Ref V23

Once part of the neighbouring sewage works, this nature

reserve now boasts 98 species of bird, five reptiles and amphibians and 275 species of insect, including 14 different dragonflies and damselflies. The extensive reedbeds provide perfect nesting spots for birds like reed buntings and Cetti's warblers, and kingfishers and otters visit regularly.

Severn Farm Pond

Welshpool, SY21 7DF
OS Map SJ 229069;
Map Ref V15

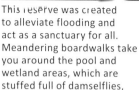

This reserve was created to alleviate flooding and act as a sanctuary for all. Meandering boardwalks take you around the pool and wetland areas, which are stuffed full of damselflies, dragonflies, frogs, newts and toads. A wildlife garden provides inspiration for your own projects.

Dolydd Hafren

Welshpool, SY21 8NN
OS Map SJ 201000;
Map Ref V17

This great diversity of habitats on a natural floodplain provides for a wealth of wildlife, from the rare plant mudwort, to brown hares. Curlews, hobbies, kingfishers, little egrets and yellowhammers are just a handful of the birds that feed, breed and visit here. Look out for starling murmurations in winter.

Red House

Near Abermule, SY15 6NB
OS Map SO 170968;
Map Ref V18

A mosaic of wet meadows, reed swamp, pools and wet woodland make this a fantastic place to spot everything from birds to plants to insects. Keep your eyes peeled for snipe and otters and see if you can spot the elusive white-letter hairstreak butterfly in summer.

CORS DYFI

Machynlleth, SY20 8SR; **OS Map** SN 703984; **Map Ref** V16

Opening hours: Visitor centre and café open 10am–4pm, Wednesday–Sunday.
Access/conditions: Boardwalks take you across the bog. The reserve is fully accessible for wheelchairs with the exception of the elevated bird hide.
How to get there: The reserve is 3.5 miles south-west of Machynlleth on the A487 Aberystwyth Road and is situated next to the Morben Isaf Caravan Park.
Walking time: The boardwalk takes you across the bog, up to the 360 Observatory. Allow plenty of time to enjoy the wildlife, the views, and to digest all of the information and refreshments!
30-minute visit: Grab a *paned* (Welsh for 'cuppa') and enjoy the wildlife from the comfort of the visitor centre.

This mixture of bog, swamp, wet woodland and scrub is small but perfectly formed, and only a railway track away from the Dyfi Estuary. The main attractions are the breeding ospreys, which live here from April–September, and a newly introduced family of three beavers, which are helping to transform the habitat in their enclosure.

The heady days of spring and summer are the best time to spot common lizards basking on the boardwalk; grasshopper, reed and sedge warblers singing in the reedbed; and, if you're lucky, maybe even an otter or dormouse! The air fills with the jewel tones of four-spotted chaser, common darter and black darter dragonflies as well as common blue, blue-tailed and azure damselflies. More than 500 species of moth have been recorded on-site, including the rare rosy marsh moth, a bog specialist that feeds on wonderfully aromatic bog myrtle.

LLANYMYNECH ROCKS

Llanymynech, SY22 6HD; **OS Map** SJ 262216; **Map Ref** V12

🅿 ➡

Access/conditions: Very uneven, hilly terrain.
How to get there: Bus stop by the Cross Guns pub. By car, head south along A483 from Oswestry. Around 1.5 miles after Llynclys crossroads, turn right onto Underhill Lane, 150m south of the Cross Guns pub. There is a car park here.
Walking time: 2 hours.
30-minute visit: Follow the track from the car park to the first open quarry area, where you can search for flowers and butterflies in the grassland or scan the cliffs for nesting birds.

A spectacular limestone outcrop straddling the border between England and Wales. From the early 19th century until the end of WWI, the site was a busy limestone quarry; since then, peace has returned, and nature has crept in to steal Llanymynech Rocks back for herself.

This human-made treasure is spectacular at any time of the year, but the spring and summer months are the most colourful and full of life. Cowslips and early purple orchids provide a colourful backdrop for pearl-bordered fritillary, dingy skipper and grizzled skipper butterflies, while jackdaws and peregrine falcons raise their families on the old quarry faces. As temperatures rise, common lizards bask on the rocks and a great diversity of flowers abound, with carpets of common rock-rose and common spotted-orchids. By August, look out for the large orange butterflies – dark green and silver-washed fritillaries – and listen out for the cackling *yaffle* of green woodpeckers. What ever the season, a clear day rewards you with outstanding views across England and Wales.

WILDLIFE FACT: COMMON LIZARD

These sun-worshipping lizards are widespread throughout England and Wales and are the only reptile native to Ireland. They're also called 'viviparous' lizards, owing to the way they give birth. 'Viviparous' means 'to bear live young', and common lizards bear up to 10 live babies when giving birth in July. In winter, they hibernate under rocks and logs.

GLASLYN

Machynlleth, SY20 8RE; **OS Map** SN 826941; **Map Ref** V20

Access/conditions: Path can be wet, muddy and uneven. Limited parking in layby by the gate; Montgomeryshire Wildlife Trust members can access the reserve car park with a code obtained from the office before visiting.
How to get there: Glaslyn is clearly signposted from the minor mountain road between the B4518 near Staylittle and the A489 at Machynlleth.
Walking time: Around 2 hours (allow another hour from the layby).

Glaslyn is Montgomeryshire Wildlife Trust's biggest nature reserve: an integral part of the Cambrian Mountains. Visiting here is a true mountain experience, with a sense of wilderness and isolation in the lake, bogs, heathland and steep ravine. The walk culminates in a breathtaking view of the Dyfi valley and green patchwork of Welsh lowlands below, with plenty of wildlife to accompany you along the way.

During winter, the exposed upland lake occasionally attracts diving ducks, including goldeneyes. In spring, male red grouse can be seen displaying and setting up territories while meadow pipits, skylarks and wheatears are also busy preparing for the breeding season. If you're lucky you may spot a pair of hen harriers 'sky dancing', or a spectacular male emperor moth fluttering over the vegetation as he follows a female's pheromone trail. It's worth looking over the ravine, where ring ouzels and peregrine falcons are often seen.

The bogs and wet heath are at their best in summer, when carnivorous sundews and butterwort grow alongside tufts of cotton-grass and bright yellow sprigs of bog asphodel. Glaslyn is also the most southerly location for cloudberry in the UK.

In autumn, the moor blooms with a sea of purple heather, which carpets the mountain in some years. The more secretive spring quillwort (a prehistoric underwater fern) reveals its presence when its leaves wash up on the lakeshore.

ROUNDTON HILL

Churchstoke, SY15 6EL; **OS Map** SO 293946; **Map Ref** V21

Access/conditions: The waymarked route to the top of the hill is long and demanding with some very steep sections. **How to get there:** Take A489 to Churchstoke and follow brown nature reserve signs up the lanes to Old Churchstoke and the entrance. Cross the ford to reach the car park. **Walking time:** 1–2 hours. **30-minute visit:** If you only have a little time, follow the path along the stream, through the oak woodland and past the bat caves.

This large, craggy hill may look imposing, but it affords spectacular views and nurtures a magical community of plants and animals with a much more subtle beauty.

The stream and oak woodland at the base of Roundton Hill are a fantastic introduction to this unforgettable nature reserve. Old mines offer perfect winter hideaways for roosting lesser horseshoe bats, while in spring, the wood sings with redstarts, willow warblers and pied flycatchers freshly arrived from Africa. As you climb ever higher, listen out for yellowhammers and whitethroats – birds that are sadly becoming rarer and rarer. This is also a great time to keep a sharp eye out for the shy and retiring 'spring ephemerals': tiny ground-hugging plants that thrive on areas of thin, dry soil.

As spring melts into summer, butterflies emerge to enjoy the nectar of knotted clover, carline thistle, heath bedstraw and bird's-foot trefoil. See if you can spot common blues, dark green fritillaries, graylings and small coppers. Rock stonecrop, a plant that conserves water in its fleshy leaves, grows on crags below the summit of the hill alongside limestone-loving plants including wild thyme and lady's bedstraw. The craggy rocks provide ideal nesting areas for peregrine falcons. Wheatears and meadow pipits breed in the scree and gorse, while the dry-stone walls provide the perfect hideaway for common lizards.

DOLFORWYN WOODS

Abermule, SY15 6JG; **OS Map** SO 158957; **Map Ref** V20

Access/conditions: Paths criss-cross the reserve. Some are narrow, steep and uneven; others are gently sloping forestry tracks.

How to get there: Turn off A483 between Newtown and Welshpool, north of Abermule, signed for Dolforwyn Castle. Follow the road for around a quarter of a mile, bearing left in front of Dolforwyn Hotel but not taking the left turn to the castle. Turn right up the track into the car park.

Walking time: 1 hour.

30-minute visit: Follow the track from the car park, then take the first right, heading uphill. At the crossroads, turn right again and follow the bridleway back down, along the sunken lane to the road, by the hotel. Return to the car park along the road.

There has been woodland on this hillside for centuries, but sadly, much was cut down to make way for plantation. Lucky for Dolforwyn, however, this plantation took the form of a great mix of tree species so that, with the remaining pockets of unplanted ancient woodland, the nature reserve still bursts with life.

Today, Dolforwyn Woods is filled with flowers and a rich medley of birdsong. This is especially true during spring, when bluebells carpet the woodland floor and pied flycatchers and wood warblers arrive from their wintering grounds. It's worth looking out for the scarce plant herb-paris, which grows here in good numbers. A decent population of hazel dormice calls the wood home, but they're elusive, and rarely emerge during daylight hours.

Summer means butterflies, with woodland specialists like speckled woods and silver-washed fritillaries basking in patches of sunshine. Green woodpeckers dart between the trees, hunting for anthills on the forest floor below, and when autumn arrives you have a much better chance of spotting the jewel-blue flash of a jay's wing as they busy themselves collecting acorns. The woods are at their most alluring in autumn; ablaze with fiery red, orange and yellow leaves punctuated by the many shades of bountiful fungi, from fly agarics to amethyst deceivers. As the leaves faint from the trees and there is less cover for birds, watch for treecreepers and nuthatches scaling the towering tree trunks.

RADNORSHIRE

About the Trust

Managing 18 nature reserves in the county, Radnorshire Wildlife Trust protects local wildlife, rebuilds biodiversity and engages people with nature. The charity believes that everyone deserves to live in a healthy, wildlife-rich natural world and works hard to ensure that everyone can experience the joy of wildlife in their daily lives.

Radnorshire Wildlife Trust
01597 823298
rwtwales.org

Abercamlo Bog
Near Crossgates, LD1 6RG
OS Map SO 073650;
Map Ref U7

Wet heath surrounded by birch woodland, scrub and tussocky grassland with three small basin mires where sphagnum mosses, round-leaved sundew and bogbean thrive. The scrub supports long-tailed tits, blackcaps and garden warblers and there is a lovely display of butterflies in summer.

Cefn Cenarth
St Harmon, LD6 5LR
OS Map SN 964759;
Map Ref U3

Cefn Cenarth means 'Ridge of Lichens', and more than 100 species of lichen and around 40 mosses can be found here. A great mix of birds live among the sessile oak canopy: chiffchaffs, treecreepers, mistle thrushes, pied flycatchers,

blackbirds, jays and redstarts.

Cwm Byddog
Clyro, HR3 5SL
OS Map SO 215447;
Map Ref U11

A woodland dingle decorated with ancient trees. Visit in spring to see pretty carpets of bluebells, yellow archangel, cuckoo-pint, wood anemones and wood sorrel. Summer brings yellowhammers, blackcaps and garden warblers to the scrub. Rare hazel dormice live alongside yellow-necked mice and common shrews.

Cnwch Bank
Beacon Hill
OS Map SO 179746;
Map Ref U2

Heather moorland and bilberry with a small gorge formed by the River Lugg. Breeding birds include meadow pipits, stonechats, merlins, red grouse, linnets, peregrine

falcons and ravens. Enjoy stunning views from the top of this wild upland common.

Mynydd Ffoesidoes
Bleddfa, LD1 5TN
OS Map SO 190649;
Map Ref U6

A lofty, isolated wild place dimpled with bog pools. The lack of paths and the deep springy heather make for challenging terrain, but visitors are rewarded with hen harriers, short-eared owls, merlins and peregrine falcons as well as more than 40 species of beetle. Day-flying northern eggar and emperor moths are insect highlights, on the wing in May and July.

Pentrosfa Mire
Llandrindod Wells, LD1 5NT
OS Map SO 062597;
Map Ref U9

A reminder of the wild expanse of wetland, heath and

woodland of days past. The mire is an important winter roost for snipe, jack snipe and pied wagtails. Keeled skimmer dragonflies and azure damselflies dance above the water in summer, and smooth newts hide among the sedges. Northern marsh orchids and bogbean are floral highlights.

Burfa Bog
Presteigne, LD8 2SH
OS Map SO 275613;
Map Ref U8

Ringlet, dark green fritillary and orange-tip butterflies dine on devil's-bit scabious and black knapweed. Warblers thrive in the coppiced alder

and marsh tits shelter in the denser trees. Marsh and heath spotted-orchids grow in the wet fen meadow and fantastic waxcap fungi appear in autumn. This reserve is suitable for assistance dogs only, to protect the ground-nesting birds.

GILFACH

St Harmon, LD6 5LF; **OS Map** SN 962718; **Map Ref** U5

Opening hours: The Byre at the Old Farmyard is open daily during daylight hours.
Access/conditions: Visitor centre and hides suitable for wheelchair access. Short Easy Access Trail for the less mobile from the Old Farmyard. Access via kissing gates throughout most of the reserve.
How to get there: Just off A470, two miles north of Rhayader and seven miles south of Llangurig. Follow the brown nature reserve signs.

Visitor centre is one mile across the reserve.
Walking time: Nature Trail (three-mile circuit) takes around 2 hours. Oakwood Trail (one-mile circuit) takes around 45 minutes. Allow extra time to stop at the visitor centre and Otter Hide.
30-minute visit: Follow the Nature Trail (yellow signs from both the visitor centre and A470 car park) to the waterfall on the River Marteg.

For centuries Gilfach was a working hill farm. Now, it's a spectacular nature reserve tucked away in the Marteg Valley, where traditional grazing still conserves its wildlife richness. The meadows nurture ancient grassland plants, including dyer's greenweed, moonwort, adder's-tongue fern, mountain pansy, parsley fern, heath dog-violet and eyebright. Bell heather, common heather and gorse bring a blaze of

colour to the hillside in late summer, and this plentiful plant life attracts throngs of insects. Keep your eyes peeled for bilberry bumblebees – upland specialists that are sadly declining across the UK – and butterflies and moths including small pearl-bordered fritillaries, green hairstreaks and fox moths.

Gilfach is famous for birds, with 55 species breeding on-site and many more popping in to feed and roost. Redpolls, yellowhammers, whinchats, linnets, red kites, spotted flycatchers and cuckoos all spend time here, while other visitors include curlews, goshawks and merlins.

The River Marteg runs through Gilfach and adds some real magic to walks here. Kingfishers hunt along its length in a blaze of blue, pied flycatchers and dippers perch on the rocks, and in autumn you may spot leaping salmon. Keep your eyes peeled for the shimmering passage of beautiful demoiselle and emerald damselflies.

TYLCAU HILL (FLOSS BRAND)

Llanbister, LD1 6UN; **OS Map** SO 134765; **Map Ref** U1

Access/conditions: The ground is uneven with some steep inclines.

How to get there: From A483 at Llanbister, take B4356 Llanbister to Llangunllo road. Drive over the common and after two miles take a sharp left signposted Llanbadarn Fynydd. Continue for just over a mile, turn right at the red phone box, going around the cattle grid and driving to the end of the tarmac lane. The reserve car park is on the right.

Walking time: The 1.25-mile circular waymarked trail around the reserve takes 45 minutes to explore. The 5.5-mile circular walk on the hills around Tylcau takes 4–5 hours.

30-minute visit: Explore the recently planted orchard and scrapes near the brook.

There is always something to see at Tylcau Hill, where flower-rich farmland, traditional rhos pasture and dingle woodlands nestle on a natural hillside. Mountain pansies bloom on the higher slopes and patches of adder's-tongue ferns grow in the meadows, affirming their ancient roots. Small pearl-bordered fritillaries love the wetter fields, and you can spot them swooping close to the ground as they search for thistles and bugles to drink from. In late spring, green hairstreak butterflies perch on hawthorn twigs and birdwatching opportunities kick up a notch. Cuckoos call and curlews utter their undulating cries as they fly overhead. The old hedgerows, ditches and patches of scrub offer a haven for important breeding birds like yellowhammers, pied flycatchers, meadow and tree pipits, redstarts and linnets.

The little Camddŵr brook running through this nature reserve is a haven for wildlife too. Bullheads lurk under stones, waiting for passing invertebrate prey, and otter spraints have been found on the banks – every indication that this is a wonderfully clean run of water. Look out for frogs and toads sheltering in the damp grass as you stroll around – you may even spot a common lizard scurrying through the drier undergrowth.

SOUTH AND WEST WALES

About the Trust

The Wildlife Trust of South and West Wales cares for some of the most precious wild places across Brecknock, Carmarthenshire, Ceredigion, East and West Glamorgan, and Pembrokeshire. From picturesque islands and rugged mountains to ancient woodland and the heritage-rich ex-coal-mining valleys, the Trust safeguards 109 diverse nature reserves and their special wildlife.

The Wildlife Trust of South and West Wales
01656 724100
welshwildlife.org

Ffrwd Farm Mire

Pembrey, SA16 0YB
OS Map SN 418021;
Map Ref U27

Embark on a journey of wildlife discovery through relict sand dunes, rough pasture, species-rich fen, reedbeds and open water where you'll find marsh-marigolds, bogbean and the near-threatened marsh pea. Watch hairy dragonflies and listen to Cetti's warblers, sedge warblers and water rails. Winter brings snipe, teal and, occasionally, bitterns and marsh harriers.

Gelli-Hir Wood

Swansea, SA4 3PR
OS Map SS 562924;
Map Ref U28

A picturesque wood nestled in a deep glacial drift. Wander beneath oaks, birches and willows; ash, sweet chestnuts, sycamores and beeches; alders, hazels and hollies. This wonderfully rich mix of trees is perfect for breeding birds of prey like sparrowhawks, buzzards and tawny owls. Blue-tailed damselflies skim over the ponds and silver-washed fritillaries dance along the rides. There is wheelchair access to the central ride.

Pengelli Forest

Felindre Farchog, SA41 3PY
OS Map SN 123396;
Map Ref U14

The largest block of ancient oak woodland in west Wales and the only known location for the Midland hawthorn in Pembrokeshire. Delicate common cow-wheat and beautiful bilberry grow alongside wood anemones, violets and water avens. Redstarts, wood warblers and chiffchaffs add an inspiring chorus in spring, woodcock visit in winter and dormice thrive here.

Cae Bryntywarch

Trecastle, LD3 8YD
OS Map SN 853267;
Map Ref U17

This beautiful wildflower meadow has always been traditionally grazed by cattle and ponies. It's what is known in Wales as 'rhos pasture', an increasingly rare habitat. Spring brings pretty pink common spotted- and heath spotted-orchids followed by brilliant yellow bog asphodel and dyer's greenweed. Summer blooms with delicate devil's-bit scabious. Skylarks nest in the rough grass and, in some years, cuckoo calls ring out across the reserve. Watch for buzzards and red kites soaring overhead.

Drostre Wood
Llanywern, LD3 0TW
OS Map SO 095305;
Map Ref U16

A woodland escape where speckled wood butterflies chase each other through sunny glades blossoming with yellow archangel, herb-robert, wood sorrel and bluebells. Dead wood offers sanctuary for lesser stag beetles, great spotted woodpeckers and treecreepers. Badgers rootle their way through the undergrowth at night. Visit in autumn for a fantastic fungi display, including striking purple amethyst deceivers.

Glasbury Cutting
Glasbury, HR3 5NS
OS Map SO 185394;
Map Ref U12

A peaceful stroll along a disused railway cutting brimming with ferns, primroses, cowslips and green-winged orchids. Green woodpeckers *yaffle* from the trees and pipistrelle bats dart up and down the cutting on night-time feeding trips. Look out for hazelnuts nibbled by the secretive hazel dormice, who hide away during daylight hours.

LAVERNOCK POINT
Lavernock, CF64 5UL; **OS Map** ST 181681; **Map Ref** U34

Access/conditions: Public footpaths and permissive paths. There are several stiles, and kissing gate access 100m beyond the gate. Some clifftop paths are prone to erosion.
How to get there: Five miles south of Cardiff and four miles east of Barry. Bus from Cardiff, Penarth and Barry passes close by. By car, access is from B4267 via Fort Road, signposted Lavernock Point.
Walking time: 1.5 hours.
30-minute visit: Head through the meadow and south to the coast to get the best of the views.

Lavernock Point is a beautiful patch of limestone grassland alive with meadow plants and butterflies. The Oak Copse north of Fort Road is home to the elusive purple hairstreak butterfly, while meadow browns, ringlets, gatekeepers and commas can be seen fluttering around flowers right across the reserve. The spectacular floral displays change with the seasons: cowslips and early purple orchids in spring then common centaury, yellow-wort, dyer's greenweed and devil's-bit scabious in summer. Spring also heralds the return of migrant birds that breed in the scrubby areas, including whitethroats, lesser whitethroats and chiffchaffs.

When they leave in autumn they're succeeded by a new set of overseas visitors: fieldfares and redwings hungry for juicy berries.

Don't leave without taking in the stunning views across the Channel.

OLD WARREN HILL

Llanfarian, SY23 4LY; **OS Map** SN 612786; **Map Ref** U4

Access/conditions: A circular footpath leads around the wood and is steep in places.
How to get there: Reserve is three miles south-east of Aberystwyth. Aberystwyth circular town bus service stops in Penparcau, from where the reserve is just over a mile's walk. By car, take the minor road signposted Nanteos from B4340 to Trawsgoed. Park in the dedicated layby near the entrance.
Walking time: 1.5 hours.
30-minute visit: A short walk up the stream gulley to the west of the reserve will reveal spectacular fallen trees and the best of the bluebells.

A beautiful mixed woodland merging human history with natural history. An Iron Age hill fort lies at the summit, with a large badger sett concealed within its ramparts. Atmospheric old oaks with gnarled branches grow alongside beeches, sycamores and birches; heaven for great spotted woodpeckers, nuthatches and treecreepers, who add their calls to the summer chorus of wrens, robins, blackbirds and other common songsters. Pied flycatchers and redstarts breed here in spring, so keep your eyes peeled, but don't be discouraged if you don't manage to spot one – there is so much else to see, including spectacular carpets of bluebells in April and May. Come autumn, woodland fungi take centre stage and the wood blazes with colour. As the days grow colder and the trees lose their leaves, look up through the canopy to see buzzards and ravens drifting overhead.

PARC SLIP

Tondu, CF32 0EH; **OS Map** SS 882843; **Map Ref** U32

Opening hours: Visitor centre open 10am–4pm, Wednesday–Sunday. Closed Mondays and Tuesdays and over the Christmas period.
Access/conditions: Accessible paths for wheelchairs, walking sticks and those with sight problems. Visitor centre and café are fully accessible, with accessible toilets.
How to get there: Bus from Bridgend bus station stops outside the Fountain Inn at the bottom of Fountain Road, and there is a train station at Tondu. By car, the reserve is signed from J36 of M4.

A 4km stretch of the Sustrans National Cycle Route 4 passes through the reserve.

Walking time: The full circuit takes around 1 hour at an easy pace, but you could easily spend a whole morning or afternoon exploring and relaxing in the café.

30-minute visit: Watch the wildlife on the scrapes near the visitor centre.

Parc Slip is testament to the fact that, given the opportunity, nature can recolonise an area once dominated by heavy industry. Once an opencast coal mine, this quiet escape is now a thriving mix of wildlife-rich woodland, grassland and wetland. Some of Wales' rarest wildlife lives here: great crested newts breed in the ponds and lakes, elusive harvest mice hide in the meadows and lapwings display over the Northern Wetlands area. In spring,

sand martins fill the sky over the ragged-robin-coated wetlands and brown hares begin their boxing matches. The grassland comes alive with thousands of southern marsh orchids in summer, as well as bee orchids and buttercups. On sunny days, small blue and dingy skipper butterflies busy themselves around the flowers while scarce blue-tailed damselflies dance above the shallow pools. But insects aren't the only sun-worshippers – you could also spot basking grass snakes!

If you can tear yourself away from the wildlife, pop into the visitor centre to relax with a cup of tea overlooking the wildflower meadows.

COED DYRYSIOG

Soar, LD3 9LS; **OS Map** SN 980310; **Map Ref** U15

Access/conditions: Open-access reserve with no formal footpaths. Keep to the circular, waymarked, unsurfaced trail. Can be wet all year round.

How to get there: Reserve joins minor road running north-west towards Soar from Aberyscir. If travelling from Aberyscir, the reserve is on the left opposite Llyn-Llwyd Farm.

Walking time: 1.5 hours.

30-minute visit: Via northern entrance, follow the path until you can see the Nant Bran river below. Return the same way.

The perfect place for a peaceful walk with just the

sound of the Nant Bran below you and the woodland birds above. In early spring this ancient woodland is speckled white with wood sorrel and wood anemones, as well as the occasional pink spikes of early purple orchids. Bluebells cast a purple hue across the reserve in late spring before singing chiffchaffs and pied

flycatchers mark the start of summer. Look out for delicate moschatel, also known as 'town hall clock' because its flowers are arranged like the four faces of a clock tower.

Coed Dyrysiog is a safe refuge for bats. Daubenton's and noctule bats roost in cavities in the trees while whiskered bats use bat

boxes put up by the Trust as summer maternity roosts. Woodpeckers flourish, with both great and lesser spotted woodpeckers recorded hammering into the trees. Woodcock hunker down in the damper parts of the wood, flawlessly camouflaged against the leaf litter and vegetation.

DARREN FAWR

Merthyr Tydfil, CF48 2NT; **OS Map** SO 022102; **Map Ref** U19

Access/conditions: Open-access reserve with steep and hazardous terrain. Don't venture onto the cliffs and scree slopes. Park at Merthyr Tydfil golf club.
How to get there: From A470 travelling south to Merthyr Tydfil, turn left (Vaynor Road) towards Cefn Coed and Pontsticill. Take first left (Cloth Hall Lane) and follow it to Merthyr Golf Course car park. Park here, then the reserve is a mile north-north-east on foot.
Walking time: 2 hours.

Scree slopes with aromatic flowers, sheer cliffs peppered with the rarest tree species in Britain (Ley's whitebeam), ravens soaring over limestone pavement, and panoramic views – Darren Fawr is one of the Trust's most spectacular nature reserves.

Spring sees the gradual greening of this upland wilderness, with splashes of colour from bird's-foot trefoil and the common blue butterflies it tempts in. Get down low to admire the salad burnet, wild thyme, rock-

rose and limestone bedstraw growing out of the crevices in the limestone, where you may also spot common lizards basking in the sunshine. It's an idyllic scene, changed only by the electric excitement of seeing a hunting peregrine darting along the cliff edge. In autumn, ravens display up high, while in winter a delicate dusting of snow marks out the high peaks of the Brecon Beacons mountain range. Pause for a moment at the top of the reserve to really take in the view.

SKOMER ISLAND

Pembrokeshire, SA62 3BJ; **OS Map** SM 725095; **Map Ref** U26

Opening hours: Boat to the island runs from Martin's Haven between Good Friday/ 1 April–30 September. Sailings depart Tuesday–Sunday on a first come, first served basis, 10am–12pm. Crossing is weather dependent – call 01646 636800 for updates. There is a landing fee and boat fee: both £20, and free for under ones. Fees are £15 during August and September.

Access/conditions: Narrow, sloping access to landing jetty to board the boat. Easy walking on the reserve with 87 steep steps from the landing stage.

How to get there: Take the Dale Princess ferry from Martin's Haven. The 'Puffin Shuttle' bus serves Martin's Haven, but the timetable varies throughout the year. Call Richards Brothers (01239 613756) for more info.

Walking time: Day trips last around 4 hours.

30-minute visit: If you don't manage to get a place on the ferry, pop into Lockley Lodge on the mainland for live cameras showing the bird colonies, seal beaches and Manx shearwater chicks in their burrows.

After one trip to Skomer you'll be hooked for life and will soon learn that one visit is never enough. Together with neighbouring Skokholm Island, Skomer hosts the largest known breeding population of Manx shearwaters – over half the world's population! Around 316,000 pairs take up residence alongside 22,000 puffins to create one of the UK's most incredible seabird spectacles. Then there are the carpets of bluebells and sea campion, which cast an unforgettable heady scent across the island in early summer.

Your island adventure begins before you've even reached dry land. Hundreds of puffins whirl around the boat as you draw closer to shore, the air filling with the sounds of the barking, yawning seals that recline on rocks in the sheltered bays. The cliffs echo with a cacophony of thousands of bickering, chattering seabirds, offering a taste of the encounters that await at the top of the cliffs. In peak season kittiwakes, razorbills, fulmars, guillemots and choughs all crowd onto the craggy rocks to raise their chicks. April and May are the best months to witness their breeding displays and to see short-eared owls hunting throughout the day. Watch puffins returning to the island

with beaks full of sand eels through June and July, when you could also spot dolphins and harbour porpoises swimming off-shore. August and September are the best

months for an overnight stay, when you can stay up late to hear thousands of noisy Manxies returning to their burrows after a day spent at sea.

OVERTON MERE

Port Eynon, SA3 1NQ; **OS Map** SS 460850; **Map Ref** U33

Access/conditions: Access the reserve by taking the first field gate on the left on the track out of Overton village, or by the coastal footpath and stile from Port Eynon Point. No wheelchair access. **How to get there:** Buses from Swansea Quadrant bus station stop at Overton village. By car, the reserve is 500m south of Overton. Pay and display parking at Port Enyon. **Walking time:** Around 1 hour.

Sitting on the stunning South Gower coast, Overton Mere offers breathtaking views out to sea and overlooks a tranquil bay that gives the reserve its name. With hawthorn and blackthorn scrub, gorse and heath,

open limestone scree and unimproved limestone grassland, Overton Mere encapsulates the best of the South Gower cliffs in one wonderful wild place.

Lime-loving flowers including common rock-rose, milkwort, eyebright and wild thyme flourish in the grassland. Grayling butterflies bask on the scree slopes, but

look closely – their incredible camouflage helps them blend in perfectly. Linnets, meadow pipits and stonechats search the scrub for food, while oystercatchers and other shore birds scamper across the Mere at low tide.

Overton Mere is an insect lover's paradise, with bloody-nosed and green tiger beetles regularly spotted on the path in summer. The rare silky wave moth hides in the gorse, and a fantastic range of solitary bees and wasps nest in tunnels dug into the soft sediments of the wave-cut platform.

TEIFI MARSHES

Cardigan, SA43 2TB; **OS Map** SN 187430; **Map Ref** U13

Opening hours: Visitor centre open 10am–4pm, Wednesday–Sunday. Closed over Christmas (check the Trust website for updates).
Access/conditions: Four themed nature trails: some with easy access and some more challenging. Parking is free for Trust members and residents living in SA43 and SA37 postcodes.
How to get there: Buses from Cardigan stop in Cilgerran village. The reserve is signposted Welsh Wildlife Centre from A487 at Cardigan.
Walking time: It'll take at least an afternoon to explore the trails, relax in the hides and pop into the visitor centre, where you can hire binoculars from the shop and enjoy panoramic views from the Glasshouse Café.
30-minute visit: Walk along the Badger Trail, which takes in the wildflower meadow and views of the river, reedbed and marsh.

Teifi Marshes is one of the most glorious wetland refuges in Wales. Whether you're strolling along the trails or enjoying a peaceful family picnic, it's always a good idea to keep one eye on the wildlife!

Otters play in the river and kingfishers are regularly spotted from the bird hides.

In winter, the evening sky fills with a glorious starling murmuration. Winter is also a great time to watch teal, wigeon and other wildfowl busying themselves about the pools and marsh, or to spot a peregrine falcon eager to plunder this living larder. Remember to keep your ears pricked as well as your eyes sharp – this is the time of year you're most likely to hear the squeal of a water rail ringing out from the reeds.

Spring brings boundless new life. A walk along the woodland trails will etch a blanket of bluebells, red campion, wood anemones, lesser celandines and primroses onto your memory. The trees sing with nesting nuthatches and pied flycatchers, whose pretty chorus is rivalled only by the urgent calls of the reed and sedge warblers that nest in the reedbed. As summer dawns, insects reach their peak. Marvel at the aerial acrobatics of emperor, broad-bodied chaser and southern hawker dragonflies; just three of 16 species recorded here. Butterflies – including brown and purple hairstreaks – dance through the air almost everywhere.

VICARAGE MEADOWS

Abergwesyn, LD5 4TP; **OS Map** SN 850526; **Map Ref** U10

Access/conditions: Open-access reserve. A small section of boardwalk crosses a stream. Paths can be very wet all year round.
How to get there: From A483 at Llanwrtyd Wells, take minor road north-west through Llanwrtyd and Cwm Irfon towards Abergwesyn. Park considerably on the roadside.
Walking time: Exploring the whole reserve takes up to 1 hour. You could extend your walk onto Nant Irfon National Nature Reserve, opposite.
30-minute visit: Go straight through the first field and into the second field to admire the colourful display of wildflowers.

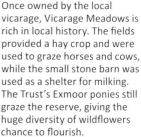

Once owned by the local vicarage, Vicarage Meadows is rich in local history. The fields provided a hay crop and were used to graze horses and cows, while the small stone barn was used as a shelter for milking. The Trust's Exmoor ponies still graze the reserve, giving the huge diversity of wildflowers chance to flourish.

The western meadow is a sheet of bluebells in spring then a carpet of orchids in summer, including fragrant orchids and greater butterfly-orchids. The floral display only brightens as the days grow longer and warmer, with betony, great burnet and dyer's greenweed adding yet more colour. The striking yellow spikes of bog asphodel grow in the damper areas. Small pearl-bordered fritillaries feed from the fragrant flower heads, while skylarks sing above. You may even catch sight of a startled common lizard scurrying away from your feet. In autumn, the surrounding trees put on a beautiful golden display, and a brisk winter walk reveals the remote solitude of this lovely valley.

GWENT

About the Trust

With 33 nature reserves, two learning centres, 9,000 members and 250 volunteers, Gwent Wildlife Trust is the leading conservation charity working for a wilder Gwent. From the lower Wye to the Rhymney river valley to the Gwent Levels, the Trust safeguards dormice, orchids and fritillary butterflies, meadows, ancient woods and precious fenland across the county.

Gwent Wildlife Trust
01600 740600
gwentwildlife.org

Branches Fork Meadows

Wainfelin, NP4 6QA
OS Map SO 269015;
Map Ref U25

Three magical grasslands joined by woodland. Longhorn beetles flit among brambles in the marshy grassland populated by purple moor-grass. In the central grassland, bilberry, heath bedstraw and devil's-bit scabious draw large skipper, small heath and meadow brown butterflies. A wooden bridge leads into the final grassland, where you'll find pink patches of lousewort and the golden blooms of tormentil and greater bird's-foot trefoil.

Brockwells Meadows

Caldicot, NP26 5AH
OS Map ST 470896;
Map Ref U29

One of the best areas of limestone grassland in Gwent, with more than 70 plant species recorded in the undulating fields. The flowers are at their best in late spring and summer, when the deep purple of green-winged orchids, bright yellow-wort and delicate white spirals of autumn lady's-tresses vie for attention. You may spot two rare insects: the large scabious bee and hornet robberfly.

Dixton Embankment

Dixton, NP25 3SY
OS Map SO 527149;
Map Ref U18

Sandwiched between the River Wye and the A40, this little gem of a grassland is a vital refuge for nature. Mammals forage, birds sing and reptiles bask in the woodland and scrub. In spring and summer, the grassland is peppered with anthills and ablaze with pink clovers, bee orchids and pyramidal orchids. Abundant flowers attract marbled white butterflies, white-legged damselflies and buff-tailed bumblebees.

Priory Wood

Bettws Newydd, NP15 1JN
OS Map SO 353058;
Map Ref U20

A wonderful mix of oak, ash, birch, beech and yew trees. Priory Wood is renowned for its wild cherry trees, whose snow-white blossoms contrast with coppery-red trunks in spring, when you can also see wood sorrel, bluebells and wild garlic coating the woodland floor. The dead wood left in the wood is vital for invertebrates, while noctule bats roost in the deep crevices of the old trees. You may even spot a hawfinch foraging for tree seeds.

CROES ROBERT WOOD

Croes Robert, NP25 4PL; **OS Map** SO 475059; **Map Ref** U24

Access/conditions: The reserve is on a hillside with steep slopes and muddy paths.
How to get there: Bus from Monmouth to Chepstow stops at the village of Trellech, then a 40-minute walk. By car, go south along B4293 to Trellech. As you enter the village, turn right (signposted Cwmcarvan). Turn right again after 1.25 miles, also signposted Cwmcarvan. Follow the lane downhill until you see a small unpaved layby on the right. Park here.
Walking time: 2 hours.
30-minute visit: Walk along the top path from the car park into the woods. Admire the display of woodland flowers in spring.

A fairy-tale woodland, where bluebells carpet the ground in spring and the birdsong never stops in early summer. Lesser celandines, wood anemones and early purple orchids put on a colourful show, but don't discount the subtle beauty of the opposite-leaved golden saxifrage that grows around the trickling streams. As the weather warms, the sunny glades fill with flowers and insects before autumn replaces flowers with fungi.

Rare hazel dormice seek refuge in the tree canopy, while secretive badgers, brown hares and fallow deer slip, unseen, through the vegetation below. Goshawks rule the wood, darting after prey like heat-seeking missiles.

This is a great place to see sustainable conservation in action. Through coppicing, the Gwent Wildlife Trust creates a varied age and structure of trees, which supports a diverse community of plants and animals. Some of the coppiced wood is left as dead wood while the rest is sold locally as firewood or charcoal.

NEW GROVE MEADOWS

Lloysey, NP25 4PH; **OS Map** SO 501066; **Map Ref** U23

Access/conditions: Uneven, unpaved footpath around the edge of the fields. Access via gates into the southernmost field.
How to get there: Drive south on B4293 and, about 1.5 miles from Monmouth, take left fork signposted Trellech and Chepstow. Continue on B4293, following signs for Trellech, then take a right turn signposted Wet Meadow. There is a forestry car park a short distance down the track.
Walking time: 1–2 hours.
30-minute visit: Stroll along the path in the first field before heading back to the forestry car park.

The stunning colour and diversity of the wildflowers in these traditional hay meadows steals the show in spring and summer, before giving centre stage to autumn fungi. In fact, the range of flowers is so varied that the reserve was chosen as Monmouthshire's 'Coronation Meadow' in 2013.

Walking here is like stepping into the past, to a time before the intensification of agriculture robbed us of so many of our wildflower meadows. A late-summer hay cut, followed by grazing through autumn and winter encourages a dazzling cast of flowers to bloom. Cowslips, common knapweed and five species of orchid – including spectacular displays of green-winged and common spotted-orchids – fill the grassland with yellows, pinks and purples. The mature hedgerows offer food and shelter for many species of insect, bird and mammal, including hazel dormice. The weird and wonderful autumn fungi include butter waxcaps, snowy waxcaps and vermillion waxcaps.

GREAT TRASTON MEADOWS

Pye Corner, NP18 2BX; **OS Map** ST 346843; **Map Ref** U31

Access/conditions: Flat but uneven in places. Can be wet and muddy.
How to get there: Exit M4 at J24 and, at the roundabout, take the exit signposted City Centre (A48). Stay on this road for around 2.5 miles until the fifth roundabout. Here, take first exit onto Nash Road.

Turn right at T-junction and follow the road as it bends right. The turning to the reserve is on the right.
Walking time: The circular walk takes around 30 minutes. For a longer stroll, head onto the Wales Coastal Path, which passes through the reserve.

A summer visit to this wildflower wonderland will take your breath away. Vibrant pink vetches and bright yellow buttercups are joined by more than 5,000 southern marsh orchids in June and July. The riot of colour and scent attracts hundreds of butterflies, bees and other insects desperate to dine on the nectar and pollen. Keep your eyes peeled for marbled white butterflies and the UK's rarest bumblebee: the shrill carder. It's a small grey-green bee with a single black band across its thorax, two dark bands on its abdomen and a pale orange tip to its tail. Dragonflies and damselflies dart after prey and soak up the sunshine along the waterways, while the sky is speckled with swifts and swallows feasting on the insect bounty.

Though all grows quiet in autumn and winter, don't write off a visit to this reserve. As the plants and grasses die back it's easier to see some of the meadows' more elusive residents like cheeky otters and perfectly camouflaged snipe.

MAGOR MARSH

Whitewall, NP26 3DD; **OS Map** ST 428866; **Map Ref** U30

Access/conditions: The reserve is flat, with a wheelchair-accessible path and boardwalk as far as the bird hide (400m from the car park). Surfaced trail around the reserve. Steps and boggy, uneven ground in parts.
How to get there: Bus runs

from Newport to Magor-Withy Walk bus stop, then walk 10–15 minutes via Redwick Road. By car, exit M4 at J23A and take first left signposted Magor/Caldicot on B4245. At the roundabout, take third exit to Magor and once there, take the right turn

signposted Magor Square. Follow the road around to the right and past the ruins of the Priory. Cross a narrow railway bridge, turn left immediately and follow the road for about 400m.
Walking time: 1 hour.
30-minute visit: Follow the

signs to the bird hide for good views over the pond.

Magor Marsh is the last remaining piece of fenland on the Gwent Levels. It's hard to believe that wetlands like this once covered much of Britain. They're now one of our most threatened habitats, and it was the threat of losing Magor Marsh in the 1960s that brought local naturalists together to form Gwent Wildlife Trust. With the addition of Barecroft and Bridewell Common to the reserve, the Trust now protects even more of this special place.

Meadows, marsh, reedbed and woodland come together to nurture a thriving population of plants and animals. The marsh comes alive with birdsong in spring as Cetti's warblers flit between the reeds, and scrub and cuckoos announce the changing of the seasons. In summer there is an explosion of colour as wildflowers carpet the meadows and the air fills with insects feeding on the nectar-rich flowers. As the pace of life slows, autumn is the best time to see kingfishers darting along the waterways. In winter, the pond becomes the centre of attention and you can watch flocks of dabbling teal and shovelers from the bird hide. You may even get lucky and see an otter!

PENTWYN FARM

Pentwyn, NP25 4SE; **OS Map** SO 523094; **Map Ref** U22

Access/conditions: The gently sloping grassland is uneven in places. Footpaths lead around the field edges and there are several kissing gates.
How to get there: In Penallt, follow signs for The Bush Inn pub, turning off at the war memorial. Where the road forks, keep on the straight

track leading past the large industrial barn and follow this to the end. Parking available above and below the medieval stone barn.
Walking time: A full circuit of the reserve takes around 40 minutes, but you can extend this to include Wyeswood Common.

30-minute visit: From the car park, follow the unsurfaced green lane up to the medieval barn and admire the hay meadows.

Walking through these magnificent hay meadows is like stepping back in time to glimpse the countryside

of Britain's past. Intensive farming has eradicated much of the UK's hay meadows, but the traditional farming methods championed here – steering well clear of fertilisers and chemicals – have encouraged an incredible diversity of wildflowers and grasses to thrive.

Spring begins with cowslips and early purple orchids and ends spectacularly with thousands of green-winged orchids joining more than 10,000 common spotted-orchids. Late spring is also when a multi-coloured carpet of common knapweed, ox-eye daisies, yellow rattle and eyebright bursts into life; a

veritable buffet for the medley of butterflies and bumblebees that fill the air around you.

The meadows themselves aren't the only rare habitat at Pentwyn Farm – ancient hedgerows offer vital refuge for wildlife. Hazel dormice shelter among the twigs, while redwings and fieldfares feast on their fruits and berries.

SILENT VALLEY

Ebbw Vale, NP23 7RX; **OS Map** SO 187062; **Map Ref** U21

P ➡

Access/conditions: Reserve entrance along a rough track. Footpaths are steep and narrow in places, and slippery when wet. There are sections of boardwalk and steep steps.
How to get there: From Ebbw Vale, take A4046 south towards Newport. At the start of Cwm bypass, turn left and continue down the hill. Pass a pub and, after the first block of terraced houses, follow the brown nature reserve sign and turn left into Cendl Terrace. Car park at the top of the street. From Newport, follow signs for Festival Park Shopping Centre until you reach the roundabout. Drive past Cwm on the bypass until a signpost to Cwm; turn right here and follow the directions above.
Walking time: 2.5 hours.
30-minute visit: A short walk through the wood to the glade takes in a peaceful portion of the reserve.

Silent Valley has always been important to the local community, providing an escape from a bleak industrial landscape. A towering beech woodland brimming with birds gives way to heath and flower-

rich grassland on the steeper slopes of the Ebbw Valley.

Spring is the best time to stroll through the woodland, when the beech leaves unfurl and flowers like wood sorrel and lesser celandines coat the ground with pinpricks of white and yellow. Birds tune up for the breeding season across the reserve and are joined in their chorus by croaking common frogs, which spawn in the small pools. Bluebells cover the upper slopes as far as the eye can see, nodding gently in the breeze.

Summer means butterflies, with graylings, small pearl-bordered fritillaries and small heaths twirling among the flowers. You may also spot common lizards basking in the warmth of the sun, flattening their bodies to make the most of the heat. Come autumn, the beeches put on a fiery display of yellow and red, and fungi of all shapes and sizes erupt in the woodland. Winter is harsh, but it's a great time to watch ravens roosting before launching their acrobatic courtship flights in January.

The Scottish landscape is ever-changing. With every turn in the road, shift in the weather and point of the compass, the breathtaking scenery transforms before your eyes. Eager explorers will find rolling hills in the Southern Uplands, mountain splendour in the Highlands, iconic islands in the windswept north and mystical sea lochs to the west. This dramatic meeting of land and sea plays host to more than 90,000 different species, from the bottlenose dolphins of the Moray Firth to the capercaillie of the Central Highlands. Thousands of puffins nest high on grassy headlands and hardy hares and ptarmigan eke out a living on the high mountains, donning snow-white winter coats to camouflage themselves among the snow.

The coast and offshore islands attract thousands of different birds. The Isle of Eigg, in the Inner Hebrides, welcomes red-throated divers, while Montrose Basin, in Angus, is the retreat of choice for pink-footed geese and eider ducks. Further south, the Falls of Clyde, near Lanark, is a peaceful place to watch kingfishers and is also a playground for badgers.

The most iconic mammal in Scotland is undoubtedly the red squirrel. Though incredibly rare in the UK, Scotland is a stronghold, with Dumfries and Galloway, Argyll, Loch Lomond and the Trossachs, and the Cairngorms National Park being some of the best places for sharp-eyed wildlife lovers to see them.

Red squirrels aren't the only Scottish mammal that can be hard to spot. Pine martens are nocturnal and secretive, and were once persecuted almost to extinction. Thankfully, they are now expanding their range through the country and are even found on the Isle of Skye.

Scotland's coast is just as spectacular as its mountainous interior. In summer, the Orkney Islands and craggy west coast are brilliant places to watch sleepy seals lazing on the rocks in the sunshine. Bottlenose dolphins can be seen all around the coastline, as well as harbour porpoises and minke whales.

With such a diverse range of landscapes and habitats on offer, there are endless places to explore in Scotland and once you've had a taste, you'll find yourself going back for more.

Opposite: Quinag, Sutherland

NOT TO BE MISSED

• Falls of Clyde, Lanarkshire
One of Scotland's most popular nature spots thanks to its badger watch events and wildlife-rich river path.

• Handa Island, Sutherland
A Torridonian sandstone island where nearly 100,000 seabirds breed each summer. Enjoy watching guillemots, razorbills, great skuas and puffins.

• Red Moss of Balerno, Lothian
A raised bog right in the City of Edinburgh and a wonderful place to spot reptiles, dragonflies and carnivorous plants.

• Loch of the Lowes, Perth and Kinross
Loch of the Lowes is famous for its breeding ospreys, and their eyrie sits just 150m from the nature reserve's viewing hide.

• Montrose Basin, Angus
Visited by more than 90,000 pink-footed geese in the winter months. Eider ducks breed in summer and ospreys fish in the estuary.

SCOTLAND

About the Trust

For more than 50 years the Scottish Wildlife Trust has worked with its members, partners and supporters in pursuit of its vision of healthy, resilient ecosystems across Scotland's land and seas. Through campaigning, partnerships and education, it inspires people to take positive action for wildlife. The Trust cares for around 120 wildlife reserves across Scotland, including some of the country's islands.

Scottish Wildlife Trust
01313 127765
scottishwildlifetrust.org.uk

Carlingnose Point

North Queensferry, KY11 1EU
OS Map NT 135809;
Map Ref S6

This lovely species-rich grassland supports rare plants including dropwort and field gentian. Dense stands of gorse offer safe nesting places for finches and warblers, and you may spot fulmars circling the quarry cliffs. Lesser whitethroats visit in summer.

Carstramon Wood

Gatehouse of Fleet, DG7 2BL
OS Map NX 592605;
Map Ref S13

An ancient oak wood with fantastic veteran beech trees. The lush conditions nurture ferns and lichens, and breathtaking bluebells in spring. Summer birds include pied flycatchers, redstarts and wood warblers. There's a good chance of seeing red squirrels, and if you're very lucky, a pine marten.

Dumbarnie Links

Leven, KY8 6BJ
OS Map NO 441022;
Map Ref S5

Rare dune grassland with cowslips, meadow crane's-bill, greater knapweed and that favourite of bees: viper's-bugloss. Bird highlights include skylarks, stonechats, meadow pipits and an array of shore and seabirds. Common blue, small copper and meadow brown butterflies splash the Links with colour.

Hill of White Hamars

Stromness, KW16 3PA
OS Map ND 322888;
Map Ref T1

Rugged cliffs, looming sea stacks and spectacular coastal views on Orkney. In spring, spot the endangered Scottish primrose alongside white campion and heath spotted-orchids. In summer, the cliffs brim with nesting guillemots, shags, fulmars and gulls.

Loch of Lintrathen

Kirriemuir, DD8 5JQ
OS Map NO 278550;
Map Ref S2

A beautiful inland loch. Ospreys, common terns, yellowhammers and spotted flycatchers are summer highlights. Winter favourites include tufted ducks, shovelers, pink-footed geese and snipe. Exciting mammals live here too: otters, red squirrels and even beavers. The east shore hide is wheelchair accessible.

Red Moss of Balerno

Balerno, EH14 7JT
OS Map NT 164636;
Map Ref S9

A raised bog right in the City of Edinburgh, nestled on the edge of the Pentland Hills. Heather, sundews, ragged robin and sphagnum mosses blanket the reserve through summer and autumn. Dragonflies dart around the damp peatland and common lizards bask on the boardwalk, which is wheelchair accessible.

Seaton Cliffs

Arbroath, DD11 5SD
OS Map NO 667416;
Map Ref S4

These spectacular red sandstone cliffs are home to thrift, sea campion, marsh-orchids and six vetches. The beautiful and varied wildflowers attract more than 300 species of invertebrate, including small blue butterflies and garden tiger moths. Birds such as fulmars, tree sparrows, skylarks and shags can all be seen. Dolphins jump and dive offshore.

Knowetop Lochs

Corsock, DG7 3ED
OS Map NX 707788;
Map Ref S12

Knowetop Lochs might be small, but this wildlife reserve is bursting with life. Two small lochs, birch woodland, reed-swamp, dry heath and bogs create a rich mosaic home for otters, adders, Scotch argus butterflies, barn owls, water voles and pipistrelle bats. Black darter and golden-ringed dragonflies hunt alongside emerald and azure damselflies.

Gight Wood

Ellon, AB41 7HY
OS Map NJ 823393;
Map Ref T4

One of the last remnants of ancient woodland in Aberdeenshire. Wander among hazel, oak and rowan trees, in the paw prints of badgers, brown hares, foxes and red squirrels. Bluebells blossom in spring and are succeeded by countless other wildflowers in summer.

WILDLIFE FACT: RED SQUIRREL

A rare sight in the UK's woodlands, it's hard to believe there used to be around 3.5 million red squirrels in Britain. The introduction of grey squirrels from North America brought with it the squirrel-pox virus, which doesn't harm the grey squirrels that carry it but has worked with habitat loss to devastate red squirrel populations. The best time to spot red squirrels is in autumn, when they are busy searching for food to see them through winter.

AYR GORGE WOODLANDS

Mauchline, KA5 5NN; **OS Map** NS 457249; **Map Ref** S11

Access/conditions: There is a network of footpaths on the west side of the river. These are steep in places.
How to get there: From the centre of Ayr, take A719 north-east for about three miles to the junction with the A77. Continue straight over the roundabout onto B743 Mauchline Road and continue to Failford. The main entrance is at the west end of Failford village.
Walking time: Walking the circuit nearest to the village takes about 1 hour. Continuing around the southern half of the reserve will add an additional hour.

30-minute visit: Immerse yourself in the woods. Stop and stand awhile – you'll be amazed by the amount of wildlife you can see and hear.

An impressively steep ravine covered with oaks, ash trees and some very old, majestic beeches. It is one of the most important ancient woodlands in Ayrshire for plants, fungi, bats and invertebrates, with rare spiders and beetles taking refuge. In spring, the canopy comes alive with birdsong, with spotted flycatchers and great spotted woodpeckers among the species worth looking out for. The summer months are a great time to appreciate woodland plants like foxgloves, enchanter's nightshade and glossy green ferns. While mammals can be less active in autumn and winter, the disappearing foliage means you have a much better chance of spotting a roe deer or otter. Then there's the spectacular scenery, painted red, yellow and orange in autumn as the leaves start turning.

According to local legend, it was in these woods that Robert Burns and Highland Mary met to arrange leaving Scotland for the West Indies.

ISLE OF EIGG

Eigg, PH41 4QD (Mallaig port); **OS Map** NM 474875; **Map Ref** T5

Opening hours: A number of non-Wildlife Trust-owned refreshment options are available on the island. Check the Isle of Eigg website for full details and opening hours.
Access/conditions: Eigg is accessible by ferry from Mallaig and Arisaig. Some paths can be steep and slippery. Tides affect activities.
How to get there: There is a Caledonian MacBrayne ferry (foot passengers only) from Mallaig – take the A82 north from Fort William for about 1.25 miles then turn left onto the A830 to Mallaig. A private ferry runs on most days in summer (check timetable at arisaig. co.uk) from Arisaig, about nine miles from Mallaig. Both ferry crossings take 1 hour.
Walking time: Eigg has five walking routes, each 1–4 hours in duration.

An exceptional wildlife refuge where unimproved farmland and native woodland meets moorland and raised bogs. In spring, the hazel woodland transforms with a rolling carpet of bluebells, wild garlic, wood anemones,

wood sorrel and primroses. The summer months herald a whole new range of plant life, with honeysuckle and enchanter's nightshade taking over. Above the trees, golden

eagles, buzzards and ravens patrol their high kingdoms. Back on solid ground, cuckoos, whinchats, whitethroats, willow warblers and twite all fill the air with heart-swelling song. The busy activity of 18 species of butterfly and many dragonflies and damselflies fills the air, while out on the sea, minke whales are regularly seen en route to the island between July and September. As the days shorten and the temperature cools, keep a sharp eye out for great northern divers and jack snipe, as well as passing redwings, fieldfares, snow buntings and bramblings.

JUPITER URBAN WILDLIFE CENTRE

Grangemouth, FK3 8LH; **OS Map** NS 920810; **Map Ref** S7

Opening hours: Open all year, Monday to Friday, 9.30am–4.30pm.

Access/conditions: Disabled access including disabled toilets. Paths are wheelchair-friendly.

How to get there: North of A9 between J5 and J6. From Beancross Road turn north onto Newlands Road, then left to Newhouse Road and left onto Wood Street. The reserve is on your right.

Walking time: You can spend anything from 30 minutes to a whole day exploring Jupiter.

30-minute visit: Whizz around the nature trail, or pick up some information on the bugs and beasts of Jupiter from the centre to enjoy a self-led adventure.

In the middle of industrial Grangemouth, Jupiter is a fantastic example of how wasteland can be transformed into an urban green space that provides a rich haven for wildlife. This unique urban oasis is also a hub for volunteers, school groups, community groups and all who visit. One of the main draws is the wildlife garden, which offers a wealth of ideas for how you, too, could transform your outdoor space for wildlife.

Two large ponds are a window into an alien world, where creatures like water scorpions await eager pond-dippers. Two low hillocks, formed using excavations from the ponds, bloom with gorgeous wildflowers through spring and summer. Spring is also the best time to see and hear a variety of woodland birds in full song. Sunny August days bring the most impressive array of dragonflies to the reserve, while September and October are fantastic for fungi including candlesnuff fungus.

HANDA ISLAND

Scourie, IV27 4SS; **OS Map** NC 138480; **Map Ref** T2

Access/conditions: Challenging terrain. Weather conditions can change quickly and the ferry crossing can be very wet – take warm, waterproof clothing, even in midsummer.

How to get there: Pedestrian ferry service runs from Tarbet on the mainland from April–August, 9.30am–4.45pm. Last ferry to Handa leaves at 2pm. No service on Sundays. Tarbet is signposted from A894, about three miles north of Scourie and three miles south of Laxford Bridge. Check ferry website for updates (handa-ferry.com).

Walking time: The path around the reserve takes 2–3 hours, but stopping to admire the views and gatherings of seabirds is essential. You can easily spend the day here.

A trip to Handa is a journey of discovery. The Torridonian sandstone cliffs rising from the Atlantic don't just provide stunning ocean panoramas, but safe breeding areas for nearly 100,000 seabirds each summer. Internationally important numbers of guillemots, razorbills and kittiwakes raise their families at these lofty heights. April–July is the best time to see

the gathering at its most spectacular, with May–June being particularly good times to watch puffins around the Great Stack. Look out for their 'beaking' displays, where they tap their colourful beaks together to reaffirm their lifelong bond.

Handa's grassy clifftops spring into life with colourful wildflowers after winter. Bluebells, primroses and heath spotted-orchids come first, followed by lousewort and pretty pink carpets of heather. Butterflies fill the grassland on sunny spring and summer

days, sometimes accompanied by a stunning and increasingly rare day-flying moth: the garden tiger. Otters, too, take refuge on Handa, and Boulder Bay is the best place to try and see one.

FALLS OF CLYDE

New Lanark, ML11 9DB; **OS Map** NS 881423; **Map Ref** S10

Opening hours: Unmanned visitor centre open daily from 10am–4pm.
Access/conditions: Surfaced footpaths, including the top section of the Clyde Walkway. Stick to the paths as the gorge edges can be unstable. Visitor centre is wheelchair accessible.
How to get there: The reserve lies around one mile south of Lanark and is reached

through the historic village of New Lanark (signposted from all major routes). From New Lanark car park, walk down into the village, through the iron gates and down the steps to the right of New Lanark Visitor Centre. Turn left and follow the road to the Falls of Clyde Visitor Centre.
Walking time: 4 hours.
30-minute visit: Dundaff Linn, the smallest of the

waterfalls, is on the riverside path (dippers, kingfishers and otters can be seen here), and the 25m Corra Linn waterfall is a brisk walk away.

Enjoy an enchanting waymarked walk in an inspiring landscape with three dramatic waterfalls and abundant wildlife. So enchanting are the Falls of Clyde that this wild place

even inspired the works of Wordsworth and Turner.

The river-edge trail is an excellent place to see flowers like red campion, water avens and marsh-marigolds; a beautiful backdrop to dipper and kingfisher sightings. In autumn, the woodland glows with a mosaic of colour, and a dizzying array of mushrooms and slime moulds emerge to delight visitors of all ages. Winter is the best time to try and catch sight of an otter on the river.

Spotted flycatchers, bullfinches and yellow-hammers are just three of the bird species spotted on the reserve during the spring and summer months, but they're not the only winged visitors. Five species of bat live at Falls of Clyde, and summer evening strolls are often accompanied by the flashes of fluttering common pipistrelles or, over the river, Daubenton's bats. Evenings also see badgers come out to play; joining a badger watching event is an unforgettable experience.

CUMBERNAULD GLEN

Cumbernauld, G67 3DY; **OS Map** NS 777763; **Map Ref** S8

Access/conditions: Most paths are tarmacked and suitable for wheelchairs, though there are some steep sections. Please don't walk on the Mountain Bike Trail (Glen Mile).
How to get there: Exit M80 at J6 for A8011 and follow signs for Cumbernauld Theatre. There is a car park opposite the theatre, with the reserve a short walk away.
Walking time: 2–3 hours.
30-minute visit: Stroll along the riverside path and back.

This ancient oak woodland is a haven for wildlife and people alike, offering a peaceful retreat for walkers, cyclists and horse riders. Kingfishers dart along the river in spellbinding flashes of blue, and in spring and summer the whole wood sings with a wonderful range of birdsong. Cumbernauld Glen is a great place to see and hear wood warblers, which spend the warmer months here each year. You may even spot crossbills feeding in the pine trees.

Early spring sees pockets of snowdrops appearing among the trees. As the season warms, they're succeeded by azure carpets of fragrant bluebells and the white stars of wood anemones. There is a lovely meadow at Cumbernauld Glen, bursting with flowers that attract butterflies, including the rare small pearl-bordered fritillary. In autumn, the woodland blazes with seasonal colour.

LOCH FLEET

Golspie, KW10 6TD; **OS Map** NH 794965; **Map Ref** T3

Access/conditions: Many woodland and coastal walks, as well as four car parks.
How to get there: Situated east of the A9 between Dornoch and Golspie. As you enter Golspie, turn right onto the golf course road to Littleferry. There are two car parks at Littleferry and two smaller car parks before this.
Walking time: Various walks from 1–2 hours long, particularly in the pinewoods, through Ferry Links and along the beach, which includes a 1.8-mile stretch at Coul Links.
30-minute visit: Common seals

and birds can be observed from the road along the south shore. Take a quick stroll to the seaward opening of the estuary for excellent views.

This large tidal basin has rolling sand dunes, expansive mudflats, picturesque coastal heath and peaceful pinewoods for you to explore. The pine woodland is a wonderful place to lose yourself among crested tits, pine martens and Scottish crossbills, as well as more common but no less special species like treecreepers, sparrowhawks and great spotted woodpeckers. You may even spot the unusual plant one-flowered wintergreen, also known as St Olaf's Candlestick. Countless other flowers and plants await in the sand dunes and heathland, with the most breathtaking displays from May–July.

The estuary is a hive of activity, especially in the summer months when Arctic terns, common terns and ospreys hunt for fish, and eider ducks dine on mussels. In winter, incredible numbers of wigeon graze the eel-grass growing on the tidal flats and long-tailed ducks and common scoters seek shelter from the harsh weather. You may even catch sight of a peregrine falcon or hen harrier spooking the crowds of wildfowl. Low tide is the best time to watch seals hauled out on sandbanks both within the estuary and along the coast.

LOCH OF THE LOWES

Dunkeld, PH8 0ES; **OS Map** NO 041435; **Map Ref** S3

Opening hours: 1 March–31 October: 10.30am–5pm daily; 1 November–28 February: 10.30am–4pm, Friday–Sunday. Entrance to the visitor centre is £4 for non-Wildlife Trust members and £3 for concessions.
Access/conditions: Visitor centre and hide are wheelchair accessible.
How to get there: The reserve is 17 miles from Perth and two miles from Dunkeld, off the A923 Dunkeld to Blairgowrie road (signposted from A9). There are trains and buses to Dunkeld, and the 2-mile Fungarth Walk links Dunkeld to the reserve.

Walking time: Around 4 hours.

30-minute visit: Head into the visitor centre to learn about the history of the site and the conservation of ospreys. You'll also have time to sit in the hide and view the wildlife.

The perfect opportunity for wildlife watching all year-round, with plenty to inspire families and keep younger nature lovers entertained. Pop into the Children's Hide to discover interactive displays and explore the children's trail in the woods.

Spring brings the exciting return of migrant swallows and sand martins, and the woodland erupts with birdsong. Keep your eyes peeled for nuthatches, treecreepers, bramblings, and redstarts in their fancy plumage, and watch cheeky red squirrels from the Observation Window. The stars of the show, however, are the ospreys, which breed here every year from April–August. They nest just 150m from the Observation Hide, offering breathtaking views. And when the ospreys fly back to Africa? Huge gatherings of wildfowl and wading birds take over: goldeneyes, wigeon, teal and whooper swans bob about on the loch.

MONTROSE BASIN

Rossie Braes, DD10 9TA; **OS Map** NO 700564; **Map Ref** S1

Opening hours: Mid-February–31 October: 10.30am–5pm daily; 1 November–mid-February: 10.30am–4pm, Friday–Monday. Entrance to the visitor centre is £4.50 for non-Wildlife Trust members and £4 for concessions.

Access/conditions: Visitor centre is wheelchair accessible.

How to get there: The reserve is one mile outside Montrose on the Arbroath Road. Take a train to Montrose then a bus (every hour). Bus stop is 500m from the visitor centre.

Walking time: A number of walks take in the reserve. Pick up a walks guide from the visitor centre.

30-minute visit: Go to the visitor centre or take a leisurely stroll along the river from Old Montrose Pier.

Its resident population of swans gave Montrose Basin its old, more poetic name: the 'Sea of Swans'. But these beautiful birds aren't the only star attraction. An enclosed, 1,850-acre (750ha) estuary of the South Esk river, the basin is home to more than 80,000 geese alone through both the spring and autumn migrations. Winter brings up to 90,000 pink-footed geese on their 1,500km journeys from Greenland and Iceland, as well as thousands of wigeon, which can be seen from the aptly named Wigeon Hide on the western side of the reserve. Keep your eyes peeled for redshanks, knot and oystercatchers too. Common terns arrive in April, raising their young alongside an internationally important population of breeding eider ducks. Between May and September you may witness the spectacle of ospreys fishing in the estuary, accompanied by a backing track of staccato sedge warbler song. Don't miss a visit to the four-star visitor centre where you can relax, enjoy breathtaking views across the water and get close to the birds through high-powered telescopes.

NORTHERN IRELAND

Northern Ireland is proof that size doesn't matter. This small country is a stunning mish-mash of landscapes, habitats and geology that, together, create unforgettable wildlife-watching opportunities.

The dramatic landscape of County Antrim might be one of the most popular wild places in the country, but don't let that put you off. The Giant's Causeway, where some 40,000 interlocking basalt columns rise out of the wild North Atlantic sea, will take your breath away. But the natural wonders don't begin and end with these volcanic pillars – this whole stretch of coast is set against a backdrop of rugged cliffs and atmospheric glens, where you could spot rare choughs and red squirrels.

Looming invitingly in the south of County Down are the impressive Mourne Mountains, which were a key inspiration for the land of Narnia in C. S. Lewis's *The Lion, The Witch and The Wardrobe*. Peregrine falcons, ring ouzels and green hairstreak butterflies hide among the crags and folds.

Travel further west and inland to enter County Armagh, where you'll find Lough Neagh, the largest lake in the UK. Dragonflies and butterflies whirl around your head in summer, while in winter, thousands of whooper swans, pochards, tufted ducks, scaup and goldeneyes amass. Further west again takes you into County Fermanagh with its wonderful wetland habitats surrounding Lower and Upper Lough Erne. This is a great place to watch wading birds including curlews, redshanks, lapwings and snipe. If you're lucky, you could spot a secretive pine marten scampering through the forests of Fermanagh.

Hop north and you'll reach County Tyrone and County Derry-Londonderry, where the landscape flows into the sparse highlands and lush river valleys of the Sperrin Mountains. You'll be spoilt for choice when it comes to exploring here, with internationally important blanket bog and plenty of wildlife to look out for: foxes, pine martens, red squirrels and sparrowhawks.

A visit to Northern Ireland is truly unique, its rolling hills and jagged coastline making for some of the most exciting wildlife walks in the UK.

NOT TO BE MISSED

Bog Meadows, County Antrim
A wildlife haven in the heart of Belfast. A mosaic of reedbeds, meadows, ponds and hedgerows nurtures butterflies, warblers and kingfishers.

Slievenacloy, County Antrim
A lush wilderness in the Belfast Hills, home to rare orchids, butterflies, waxcaps, and birds including skylarks and cuckoos.

Milford Cutting, County Armagh
A wonderful woodland home to the biggest population of Irish whitebeam trees in Northern Ireland, as well as marsh helleborines.

Straidkilly, County Antrim
A little slice of heaven in woods brimming with bluebells, blackcaps and sparrowhawks. Keep your eyes peeled for red squirrels.

Opposite: Slievenacloy, Belfast

ULSTER

Edenderry

Belfast, BT8 8LD
OS Map J 318683;
Map Ref W7

Small and secluded, this woodland nature reserve nestles along the banks of the River Lagan and offers an escape just four miles south of Belfast city centre. Beech, Spanish chestnut and yew trees offer sanctuary to wonderful wildflowers, beautiful birds and interesting insects. Look out for song thrushes, jays, treecreepers and goldcrests.

Balloo Woodland

Bangor, BT19 7QZ
OS Map J 795508;
Map Ref W3

A stroll through this small but long-established woodland offers a pleasant retreat from the hustle and bustle of Bangor. In spring, carpets of wood anemones, bluebells and wild garlic offer a feast for the senses, along with the sounds of songbirds such as blackcaps and chiffchaffs. Look out for butterflies on sunny summer days – from common blues and peacocks to ringlets and the scarce holly blue, which was formerly restricted to County Down. In winter, the reserve is a great place to watch goldcrests and gregarious flocks of long-tailed tits roving through the trees.

Moyola Waterfoot

Magherafelt, BT45 6LQ
OS Map H 963894;
Map Ref W2

A short but sweet woodland walk along the final stretch of the Moyola River. The half-mile trail also offers access to the shore of Lough Neagh. As you stroll along the river you may spot grey wagtails on the rocks and kingfishers flashing vividly above the water. In winter, wildfowl including whooper swans, goldeneyes and great crested grebes can be seen off the river mouth from the bird hide. Summer brings sedge warblers to the reedbeds, and in winter, small flocks of long-tailed tits, goldfinches and redpolls forage along the riverside path.

Milford Cutting

County Armagh
OS Map H 859427;
Map Ref W8

A wonderful woodland and species-rich grassland with medium terrain and a 500m-long walking trail. A summer visit is essential to see common twayblades, fragrant orchids, common spotted-orchids and rare marsh helleborines painting the reserve with shades of green, pink and purple. The wealth of wildflowers attracts a wide array of butterflies – up to 18 species to date – including small coppers, peacocks and ringlets. Then there are the birds: willow warblers, chiffchaffs and blackcaps bursting into song during spring. The long corridor is the perfect hunting ground for buzzards and sparrowhawks, and you may see a kingfisher speeding along the nearby river. Hidden within the woodland are several rare Irish whitebeam trees – the largest colony of this species in Northern Ireland.

STRAIDKILLY

Carnlough, BT44 0LQ; **OS Map** D 302165; **Map Ref** W1

Access/conditions: 1.2-mile circular trail but no formal paths. Medium terrain with steep inclines.
How to get there: Take the Coast Road (A2) to Straidkilly Road then continue straight for almost a mile. The reserve will be on your left.
Walking time: 1 hour.
30-minute visit: Take a brisk walk around the trail.

This secluded hazel woodland, interspersed with wildlife-rich grassland cuttings, is a little slice of heaven. A spring visit reveals just why the wood is so well known for its plant life. The ground is awash with bluebells and lesser celandines alongside more unusual species like wood vetch, stone bramble and the parasitic toothwort, which craftily takes its nutrients from tree roots. So, too, do two of Straidkilly's rare plant species: yellow bird's-nest and bird's-nest orchid. There are birds aplenty, with summer being the best time to experience their operatics and busy activity. Keep an eye out for blackcaps, willow warblers and bullfinches in the tree branches, and buzzards and sparrowhawks overhead.

Despite being one of Ulster Wildlife's smaller nature reserves, Straidkilly is a wonderful refuge for mammals. Red squirrels, badgers and pygmy shrews live in the wood, while the picnic area – with its panoramic views across the Irish Sea – is a great vantage point to watch harbour porpoises. On your way back down, look out for the fiery flashes of silver-washed fritillary butterflies in the sunny glades.

BALLOO WETLAND

Bangor, BT19 7PG; **OS Map** J 792505; **Map Ref** W4

Access/conditions: A 500m trail on easy terrain suitable for wheelchairs.

How to get there: Take A8 towards Belfast (A2). At Sandyknowes Roundabout, take third exit onto M2 and continue straight onto M3. Continue onto A2 for 9.8 miles, turn right onto Rathgael Road and, at Rathgael Roundabout, take second exit onto Balloo Road.

Walking time: A full circuit should take no longer than 30 minutes. To extend your visit, rest a while in the picnic area.

Formed in 2008 as an area of wet wasteland, Ulster Wildlife has transformed Balloo Wetlands into a thriving natural wetland where ponds, reedbeds and wet woodland offer solace to a wonderful variety of wild creatures. Frogs and newts breed in spring while dragonflies create an impressive aerial spectacle as they hunt over the ponds. Four-spotted chasers and common darters are just two of the species that fill the air with dazzling flashes of colour. Otters

also visit the nature reserve, but they're much more elusive.

Little grebes and moorhens can be seen on the pond all year round and it isn't unusual to spot little egrets hunting for fish. Small numbers of wildfowl move in during winter, including mallards and teal.

Summer is the best time to take in the beauty of the wildflower meadow around the pond, when the diverse mix of flowers and insects is at its peak.

SLIEVENACLOY

Lisburn, BT28 3TE; **OS Map** J 245712; **Map Ref** W6

Access/conditions: Formal road network and off-road paths with medium terrain. Some steep slopes and stiles.

How to get there: From Belfast take the Colin Glen

Road (A501) heading towards Lisburn. Turn right just before the petrol station onto the Ballycolin Road. After half a mile, take a left onto Flowbog Road, where you can park.

Walking time: 3–4 hours.

30-minute visit: Walk up the hill to Hill House and head left for a panoramic view of the reserve, the earthen ring and the cattle.

A lush wilderness offering breathtaking views across five of the six counties of Northern Ireland. Slievenacloy is one of Ulster Wildlife's largest nature reserves and undoubtedly one of its most beautiful; a treasure trove through every season and a great place to spot Ireland's only reptile, the common lizard.

Spring begins with primroses, cuckooflowers and early purple orchids painting the grassland with splashes of colour. Good summers bring thousands of common spotted and butterfly-orchids, plus rarer varieties like lesser butterfly, small white and frog orchids. It goes without saying that insects thrive here too. Look out for beautiful grassland butterflies such as orange-tips, small coppers, common blues and dark green fritillaries. Rare moths include the spectacular narrow-bordered bee hawk-moth. On summer days, scan the fields, fence posts and hedgerows for skylarks, stonechats and linnets. Listen out for cuckoos and grasshopper warblers – both scarce in Northern Ireland. Autumn brings a multitude of brightly coloured waxcap fungi to the grassland, with the most striking being the vibrant pink ballerina waxcap. Though bleak and windswept, even winter is a brilliant time to visit, with snipe and fieldfares some of the top birds to spot.

BOG MEADOWS

Belfast, BT12 6EU; **OS Map** J 312726; **Map Ref** W5

Access/conditions: Easy paths suitable for wheelchairs and pushchairs.
How to get there: From Belfast city centre take the bus and get off opposite Falls Park. Pedestrian access available from Falls Road, St Katherine's Road and Milltown Cemetery. By car, exit at J1 of the M1 onto Donegall Road, then follow the signs. There is parking on site.
Walking time: 1 hour.
30-minute visit: From the car park, go down the path between the playing fields and the stream. Cross the footbridge and turn right. Continue until you reach another footbridge with turrets. Don't cross; instead follow the footpath around

to the left and then take the first left. This will lead you to a pond where you can watch the ducks and enjoy views over the reserve. To return, follow the path, turning right at the junction, then left over the first footbridge to return to the car park.

Situated in west Belfast, beside the M1 motorway, this mosaic of species-rich meadows, reedbeds, ponds and hedgerows is an oasis for wildlife and people in the city. Fourteen species of butterfly have been recorded here, with orange-tips, speckled woods, meadow browns and small tortoiseshells fluttering over the wildflower meadows in summer. Stand at the edge of the reedbed to be astounded by the scratchy symphony of sedge and reed warblers, and watch summer-visiting sand martins, swallows and swifts swooping low over the pond as they hoover up insects. Look skywards to watch for peregrine falcons and buzzards hunting overhead – you may even spot a kingfisher whizzing across the M1 from the Blackstaff River to collect sticklebacks.

In autumn, the berry-laden hedgerows and trees host feeding flocks of fieldfares and redwings visiting all the way from Scandinavia.

GLOSSARY

Biodiversity The amazing variety of life on Earth, encompassing the number of species of plants and animals, the genetic diversity within them and the different ecosystems they are a part of.

Carr A wet woodland, for example alder carr, willow carr.

Coppice stool The established root system and stump of a tree that is left after it has been coppiced.

Coppiced/Coppicing Woodland management technique of repeatedly felling trees at the base (or stool) and allowing them to regrow, helping more light reach the woodland floor and providing a sustainable timber supply.

Coronation meadow A wildflower meadow created to celebrate the 60th anniversary of the Coronation. The Coronation Meadows Project was led by Plantlife, in partnership with The Wildlife Trusts and the Rare Breeds Survival Trust.

Culm grassland Unimproved wet pasture found in Devon and south-west Wales.

Improved grassland Grassland with a low diversity of species, which has been 'improved' using artificial fertilisers, ploughing and re-sowing to encourage aggressive grasses.

Lammas meadow Common meadows opened for communal grazing on Lammas Day.

Permissive path Path where landowner has given permission for it to be used.

Rhos pasture Rough, damp grassland in Wales that provides cover for wading birds.

Unimproved grassland Grassland that hasn't been artificially fertilised, ploughed or reseeded, so is rich in different species.

Valley mire Areas of waterlogged deep peat in valley bottoms.

COMMON ABBREVIATIONS

AONB Area of Outstanding Natural Beauty
CGS County Geological Site
NNR National Nature Reserve
SLINC Site of Local Importance for Nature Conservation
SSSI Site of Special Scientific Interest

PHOTO CREDITS

We're incredibly grateful to all the Wildlife Trusts who have sent through images of their reserves for use in this book. The following photographers have also kindly allowed the use of their images:

Adrian Wallington: 63; Agnes Kiemel: 130B; Alan Anderson: 258; Alastair Cook: 42T; Alexander Mustard/2020VISION: 10–11, 17B; Amy Lewis: 15T, 23B, 197, 244; Andrew Mason: 228; Andrew Walter: 184, 186; Andy Fairbairn: 62T; Andy Karran: 251; Andy Lear: 135; Andy Rouse/2020VISION: 2, 60, 237, 266B; Andy Slater: 160; Arnhel de Serra: 75B; Ashley White: 37; BareFoot Photographer: 48, 49; Bari Glew: 54; Barrie Wilkinson: 141, 144, 145; Barry Yates: 88; Beccy Wilmetts: 27T; Ben Hall/2020VISION: 7B, 124B, 219; Ben Watkins: 14, 15B, 16, 18; Bertie Gregory/2020VISION: 116; Bob Chapman: 55T; Bob Izzard: 98T; Brian Bleese: 41; Carl Everitt: 102; Charlotte Varela: 202, 206; Chris Cachia Zammit: 266T; Chris Gomersall/2020VISION: 122, 158, 222; Chris Senior: 215; Christopher Tomson: 214; Claire Huxley: 218; Colin Hayes: 157; Colin Williams: 93B; Dan van den Toorn: 199, 200B, 201; Daniel Bridge: 117; Daniel Greenwood: 75T; Danny Green/2020VISION: 175T, 204; Dave Chamberlain: 22; Dave Watts: 114; David Chapman: 17T; David Goldsmith: 176; David Lovelace: 166; David Nichols: 213; David Parkyn: 220B; David Tipling/2020VISION: 7C, 198T, 229B; Dawn Monrose: 174B; Don Lewis: 74; Duncan Hutt: 181B; Emily McParland: 119; Emyr Evans: 232; facebook. com/stevenleaphotography: 203; Frieda Rummenhohl: 67, 68, 69; Gary Mantle: 39B; George Bird: 124T; George Stoyle: 210B; Gill Smart: 260; Gina Gavigan: 243T; Graham Dennis: 57B; Graham Roberts: 130T; Guy Edwardes/2020VISION: 50, 167T, 226, 247, 248; H W Atkin: 84; Harriet Hickin: 136B; Henry Richards: 123; Hugh Gregory: 253, 274B; Ian Cameron-Reid: 52, 56; Ian Pratt: 58; instagram. com/fell_n_mountain: 205; James Adler: 210T; James Benwell: 161, 162; James Burland: 45; Jane Corey: 255; Jeff Bevan: 25, 26; Jim Voce: 129; Joe Cornish: 256; Joe Francis: 118; John Bridges: 246B; John Faulkner: 182; John Morrison: 185; Jon Hawkins – Surrey Hills Photography: 61, 78, 127, 241; Jonathan Clarke: 268; Josh Kubale: 70, 71T; Joshua Copping: 46; Julia Garner: 188, 190T; Julie Dickson: 64; Kasia Piekut: 59, 65; Kate Sugden: 177B; Kate Titford: 66; Katherine Beasley: 163; Katrina Martin: 265T; Kevin Palmer: 155, 159T; Kieron Huston: 240; Les Fitton: 187; Lewis Wetton: 262; Linda Thompson: 271; Lister Cumming: 263; Lizzie Wilberforce: 229T, 242; Lorna West: 47; Louise Hartgill: 38; Lowri Watkins: 249, 250, 252; Luke Massey/2020VISION: 170B; M Sisson: 149B; Marcus Wehrle: 79; Mark Foxwell: 265B; Mark Hamblin/2020VISION: 126, 149T, 175B, 189, 191, 224, 243B, 275; Matthew Roberts: 115B, 120, 207, 212, 234; Michael and Paula Webster: 136T; Mick Jones: 62B; Mike Alexander: 245, 246T; Mike Read: 57T; Mike Snelle: 211; Mornee Button: 34; Nabil Abbas: 216; Nanette Hepburn: 254; Nathan Millar: 32, 33T, 36; Neal Trafankowski: 106; Neil Fletcher: 93T; Neil Roberts: 142; Nick Upton/2020VISION: 35, 209B; Nicky Hoar: 42B; Nigel Symington: 89, 92; Paul Eaton: 27B; Paul Lane: 168, 169, 170T; Paul Lloyd: 167B; Paul Lyons: 209T; Paul McCormack: 29T, 31B; Paul Williams: 44; Penny Dixie: 76; Peter Cairns/2020VISION: 9C, 55B, 146, 259; Peter Simpson: 105; Rachel Bradshaw: 220T, 221; Rachel Palmer: 239; Ray Lewis: 83, 85B, 86, 87; Richard Osbourne: 103, 104, 107, 108, 109; Richard Walliker: 230; Rob Jordan/2020VISION: 227B; Robert Enderby: 96, 100, 139, 143; Robert Mackin: 132; Roger Llewellyn: 156T; Ronald Surgenor: 273; Ross Hoddinott/2020VISION: 9T, 81, 133, 174T, 190B; Ruth Taylor: 140; Sabba Choudry: 77; Sam Roberts: 90; Simon Bateman-Brown: 85T; Simon Williams: 20, 23T, 24T; Sophie Baker: 98B, 99; Sophie Cowling: 164; Sophie Webster: 183; Stephen Barlow: 148; Stephen Davis: 39T; Steve Ashton: 198B, 200T; Steve Aylward: 110, 111, 112, 113; Steve Gardner: 267; Steve Kenny – Birds Eye Studios: 71B; Steve Smith: 72; Sue Steward, New Leaf Images: 177T; Tammy Stretton: 231, 233T, 235, 236; Terry Whittaker/2020VISION: 73, 91, 94, 151T; Tim Curley: 31T; Tim Hill: 178; Toby Roxburgh/2020VISION: 12; Tom Marshall: 7T, 9B; Tricia Sayle: 223; UK Wild Otter Trust: 24B; Vaughn Matthews: 21, 128, 233B; Vicky Nall: 227T; Wendy Carter: 171, 172; www. tonyclarke.co.uk: 134; Zsuzsanna Bird: 33B.

MAPS

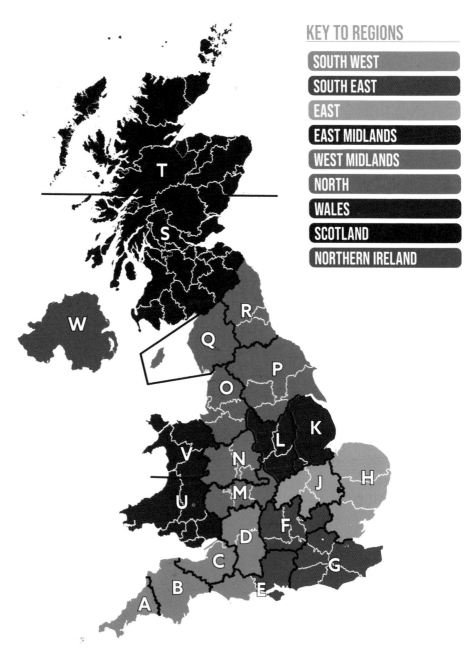

KEY TO REGIONS

SOUTH WEST
SOUTH EAST
EAST
EAST MIDLANDS
WEST MIDLANDS
NORTH
WALES
SCOTLAND
NORTHERN IRELAND

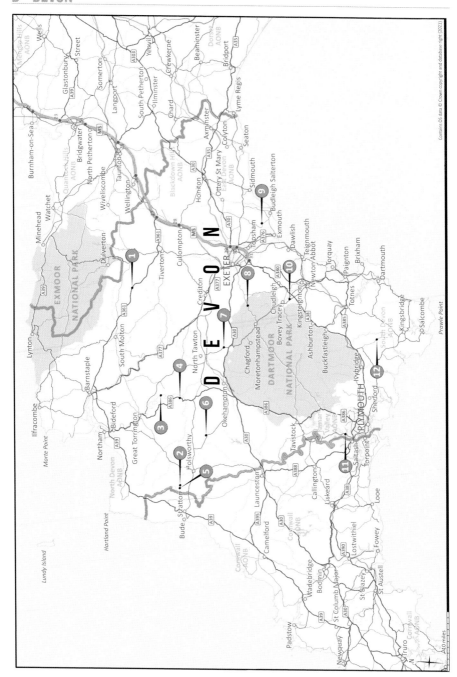

Contains OS data © Crown copyright and database right (2021)

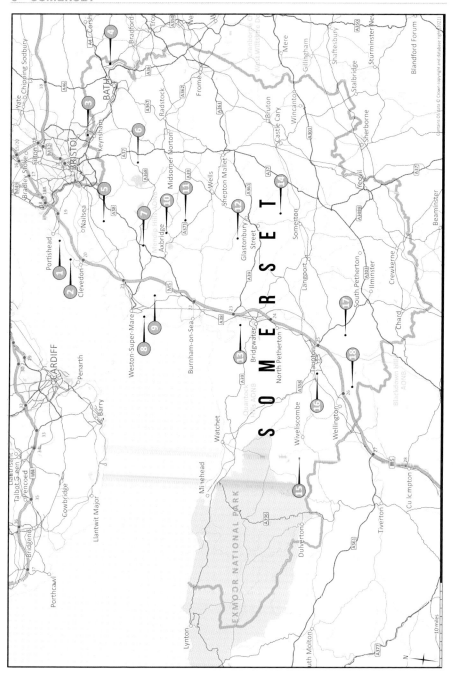

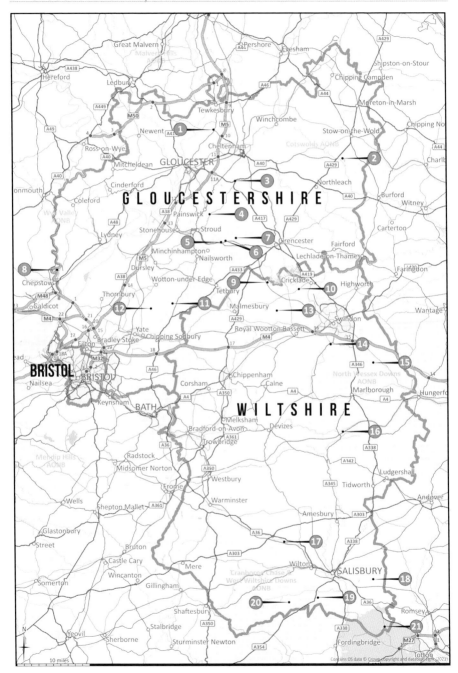

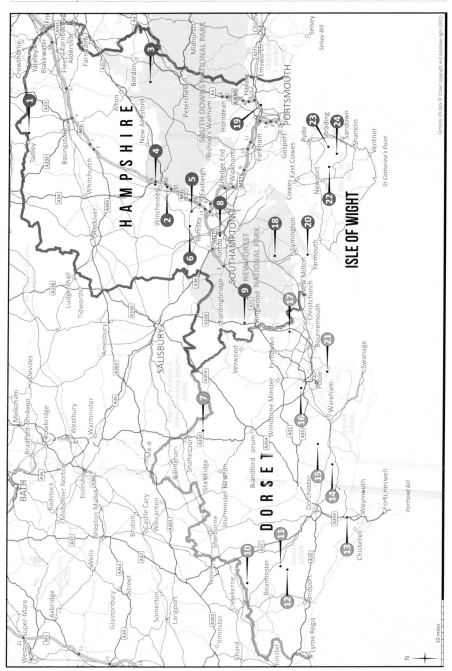

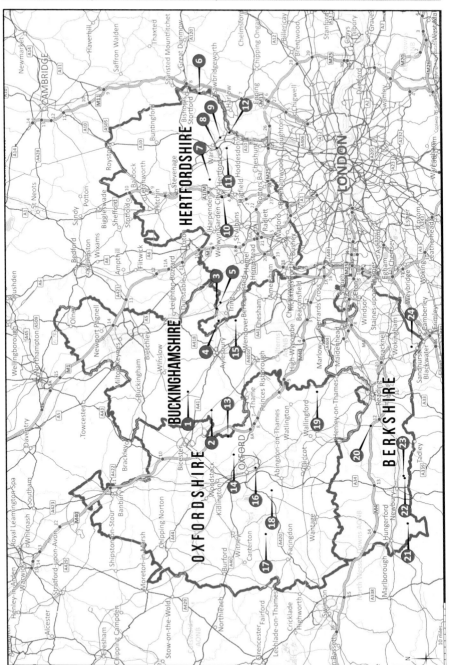

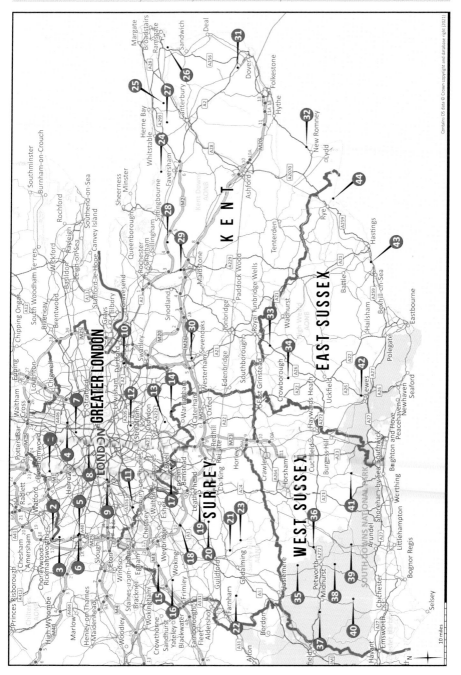

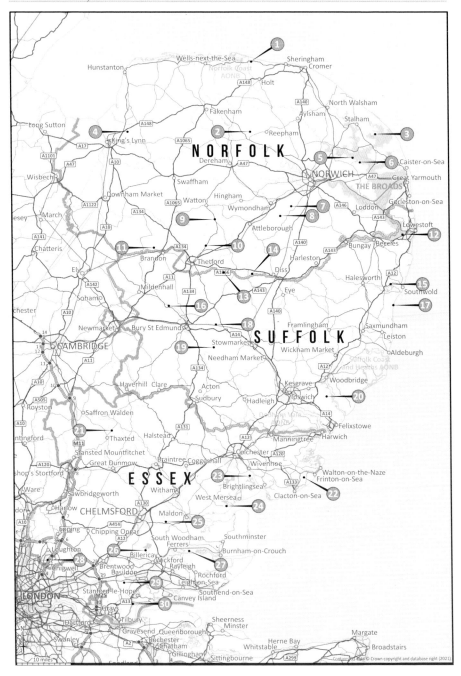

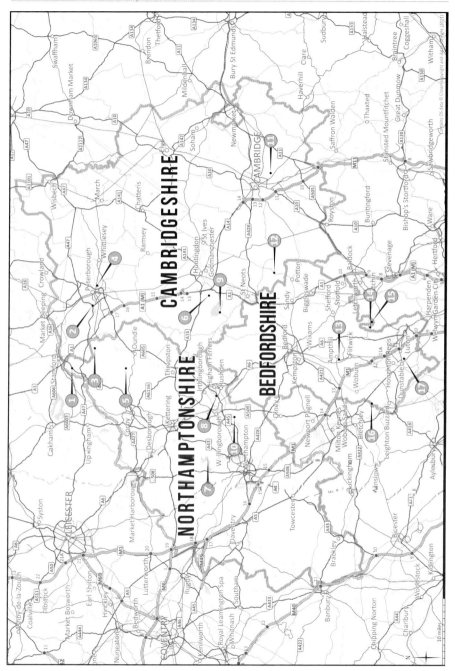

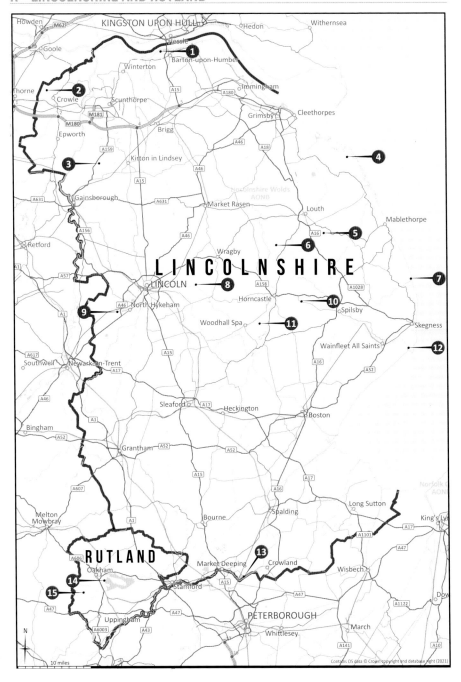

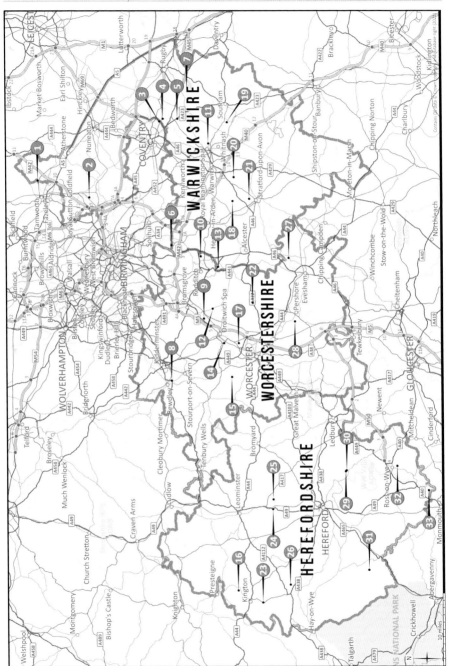

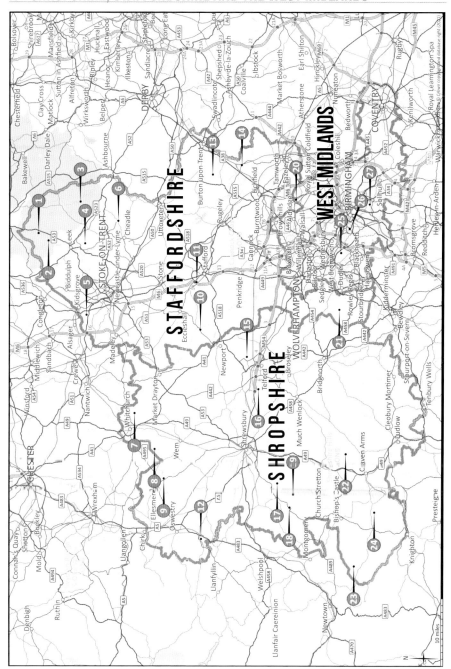

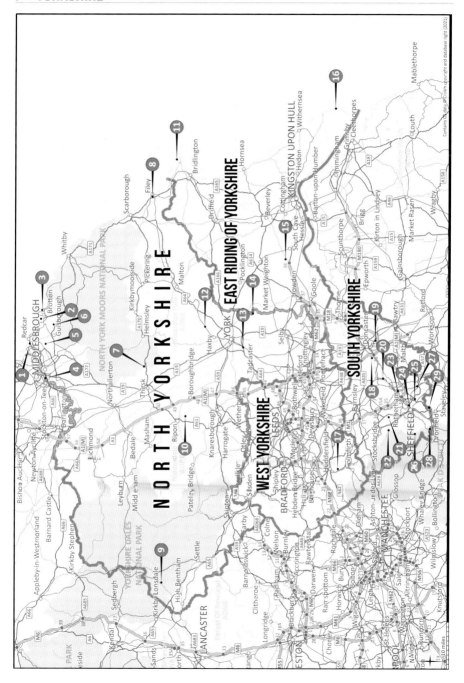

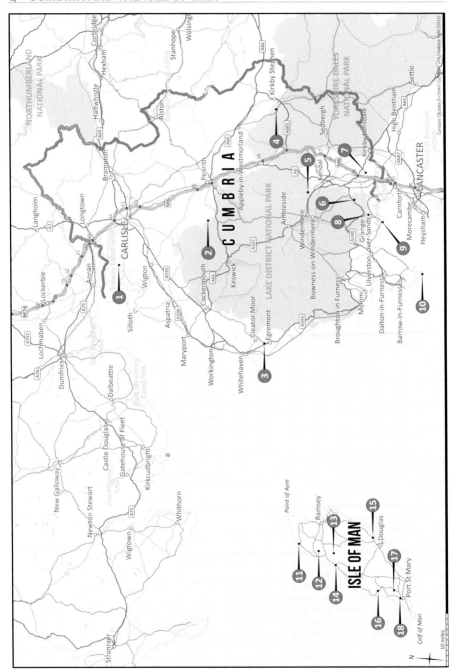

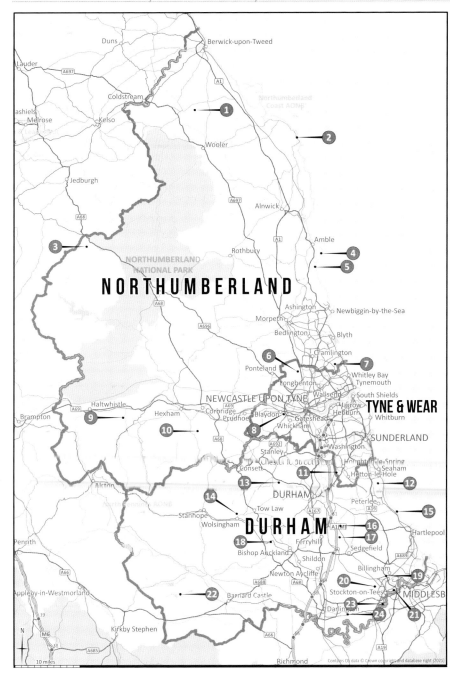

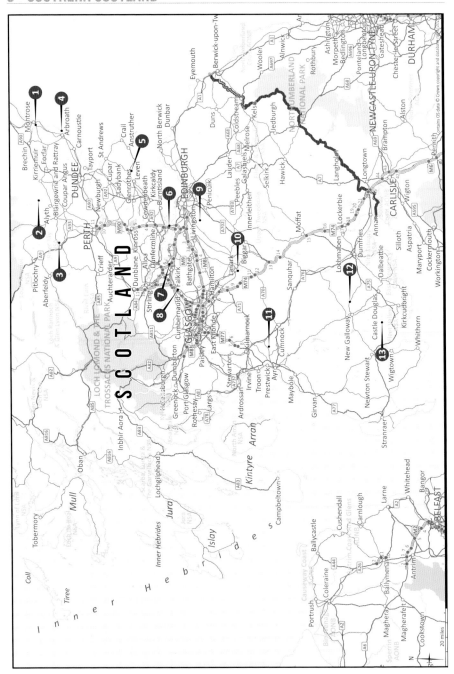

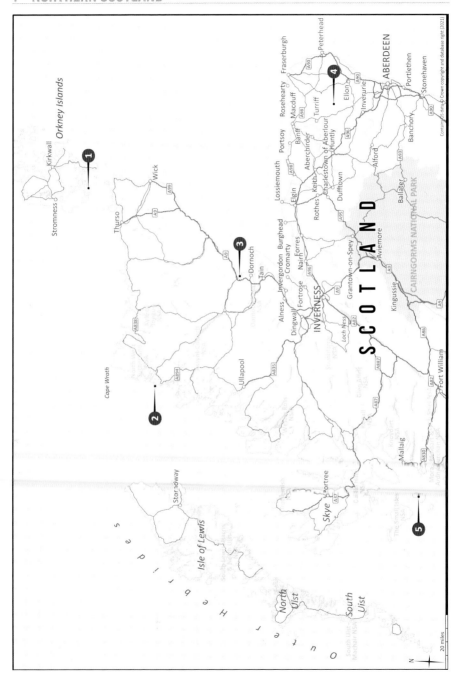

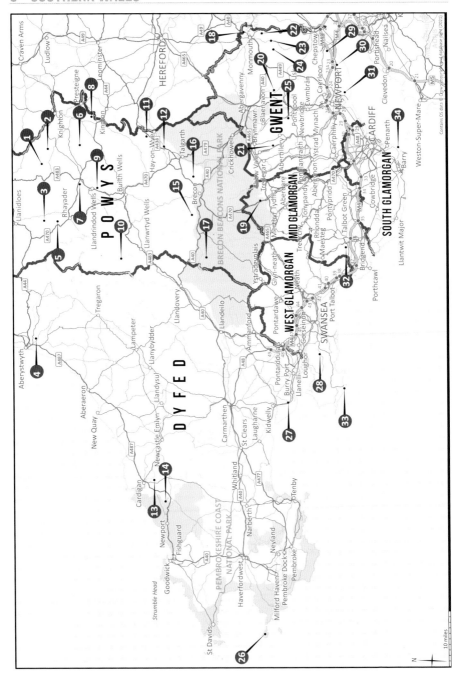

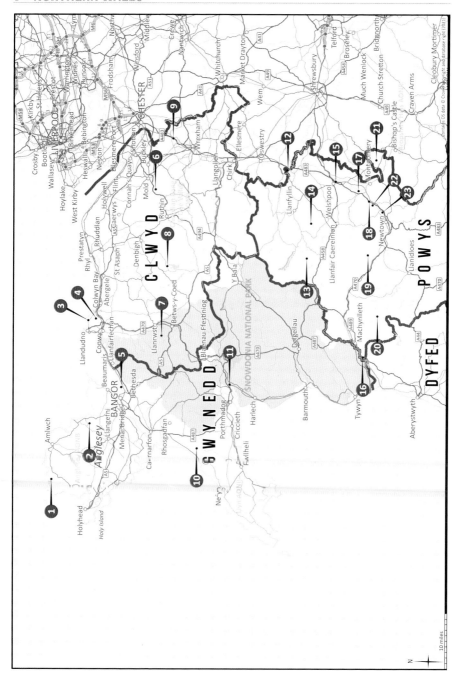

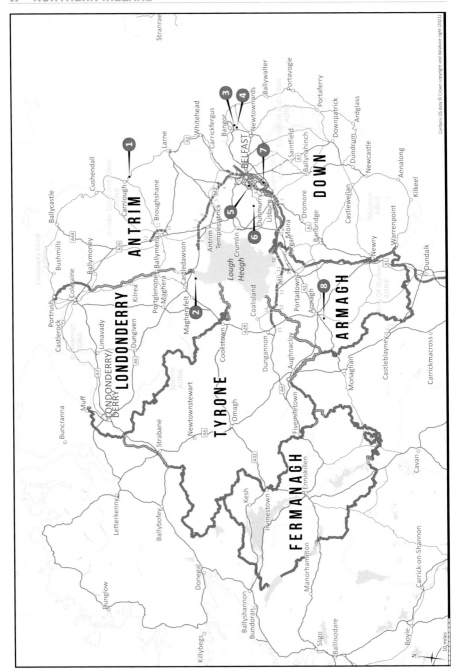

INDEX